ALSO BY ERNEST L. ABEL

Ancient Views on the Origins of Life

The Roots
of Anti-Semitism

Ernest L. Abel

Rutherford ● *Madison* ● *Teaneck*
Fairleigh Dickinson University Press
London: Associated University Presses

© 1975 by Associated University Presses, Inc.

Associated University Presses, Inc.
Cranbury, New Jersey 08512

Associated University Presses
108 New Bond Street
London W1Y OQX, England

Library of Congress Cataloging in Publication Data

Abel, Ernest L   1943-
   The roots of anti-Semitism.
Bibliography: p.
   1. Anti-Semitism—History. 2. Christianity and Anti-
Semitism I. Title.
DS145.A4   909'.04'924   73-8286
ISBN 0-8386-1406-X

PRINTED IN THE UNITED STATES OF AMERICA

To my parents,
Rose and Jack Abel

Contents

Preface

The roots of anti-Semitism reach far beyond Nazi Germany, the Middle Ages, or the emergence of the Christian Church to the time when the Jews first came into personal contact with the Greek-speaking peoples of the world. It was during this formidable era that the two cultures clashed in what can only be regarded as cultural shock. For their part, the Greeks were not adverse to having Jews among them as long as these Jews were willing to accept the responsibilities that went with living in a Greek *polis*. For the orthodox Jew, however, observance of these duties was simply not possible, for an integral part of the Greek style of life was the recognition of foreign deities. But it was not only the Jew's refusal to participate in civic duties that irritated the Greek. It was also the contempt with which the Jew reacted to the Greek concept of religion. Furthermore, to preserve their identity, most Jews who lived in the Diaspora refused to have much to do with the Greeks socially, an attitude that earned them the accusation of "misanthropy."

But by far the most important aspect of their behavior that generated hatred of the Jews in the ancient world was their allegiance to the heads of government. The Greeks, for instance, jealously guarded their freedoms and they were ever watchful of rulers who tried to curtail their independence in municipal affairs. In the ensuing struggles between rulers and subjects, the Jews more often than not chose to support the former, thus alienating themselves from the people among whom they lived.

When the Roman empire came into power, the special favors that had been accorded the Jews under the Greek kings remained intact for the most part, although the various privileges previously enjoyed by the Greek populace were ab-

9

rogated. Greek reaction soon expressed itself in literary resentment directed not against the Romans, but against the Jews. Had the economic situation of these times been stable, these feelings would probably have been confined to pen and papyrus. But the economy also took a turn for the worse due to Rome's exploitation of the subject populace. When meeting the obligations to their own families became a problem, the frustration felt by these people was expressed in aggression. They could not turn against the Romans, however, for these overlords were too powerful. So instead they channeled their hostility against the Jews who were weak and vulnerable.

But such attacks were still sporadic and disorganized. There was no general anti-Semitic movement in the world until the Church came into power. Turning to the Greco-Roman world after it was anathematized by the Synagogue, the Church opened its doors to all those who chose to enter. It was thus that the anti-Semitism of the pre-Christian world influenced the Church.

In the fifth century A.D., the Church, which had once been persecuted, now became the persecutor. All forms of heresy were outlawed, and although Judaism was allowed its existence, all the former privileges accorded to the Jews were rescinded. The hope was that the Jews would eventually come to the Church if obstacles were placed in the way of their practicing their religion and everything was done to achieve this end. For example, laws were passed which prohibited Synagogues from being repaired, the idea being that if one fell to the ground, there would be one less place of worship. When these laws failed to gain their desired effect, the Jews were offered a final choice: Christianity or expulsion from their homes and countries.

The anti-Semitism of the Middle Ages and the modern era can thus be seen as the outgrowth of a process which has its roots in the ancient world. To understand how such a holocaust as that seen in the twentieth century could ever have come about, one must know at least some of the factors that contributed into making the Jew the scapegoat of society's ills.

The Roots of Anti-Semitism

1

Prolegomenon

The Origins of the Jews

The origins of the Hebrews as a nation is mostly conjecture. Outside of the Bible there is no mention of the patriarchs and the stories found in Genesis are most likely traditions that were passed along by word of mouth until they were finally written down in their present biblical format. How these traditions came into being is not known, but more than likely, the patriarchal movements, such as Abram's journey from Ur of the Chaldees to Palestine via Harran, were in some way associated with the extensive ethnic migrations taking place in Mesopotamia around 1700-1800 B.C.[1]

The only time that the term Hebrew is actually used to describe Abraham, however, is in Genesis 14.13. Indeed, the term itself rarely occurs in the Old Testament at all except in the story of Joseph and in passing reference to the ancient laws. In these cases, it is nearly always a foreigner speaking, or else an Israelite identifying himself to some non-Israelite.

Although there is a superficial similarity between the term Hebrew and Eber, one of the patriarchal ancestors (Gen.

1. T. J. Meek, *Hebrew Origins* (New York: Harper Brothers, 1936), p. 15.

10.21,25; 11.14-17), scholars have generally discounted the possibility that there is any relationship between the two names because of the cursory treatment afforded Eber in the Old Testament. An alternative, but problematical explanation is that the name Hebrew is related to the term *Habiru* or its variant, *apiru*.[2] These latter names are quite commonly encountered in the cuneiform documents of this period, but typically the reference to these people is not in the way of a distinct ethnic group but rather as a semi-nomadic segment of Near Eastern society. Some of these *Habiru* are described as living in peaceful coexistence with their neighbors whereas others are mentioned as mercenaries and brigands. The term thus seems to be a reference not to some ethnic unit but to a class of people.

On the other hand, the similarity between the Hebrews and *Habirus* is challenging, especially since Abraham is cast in a role perfectly fitting the life of the *Habiru* as it is presently known. His movements are very much those of the nomad and it is of no little significance that the one time that he is called a Hebrew is at a time that he truly acts like an *Habiru*, in other words, when he becomes bellicose. Moreover, although the *Habiru* were not of a common ethnic background, an examination of the names of these people indicates that the majority of them were of Semitic origin, as were those of the Hebrews. It is for these reasons that many scholars hold to the opinion that while not all *Habirus* were Hebrews, all Hebrews were *Habirus* at one time.

The early Hebrew/*Habiru* migrations did not take place as concerted efforts designed to conquer Palestine. Rather, they were slow nomadic wanderings that gradually resulted in an infiltration of that country. Meek[3] places the biblical account of Abraham's migration around 1750 B.C., making it contemporary with the western movement of the Hurrians. Relations between the Hebrews and the Hurrians appear, in fact, to have

2. For a discussion of the *Habiru*, see J. Bottéro, *Le Problème des Habiru* (Paris: Imprimé Nationale, 1954), and M. Greenberg, *The Hab/piru* (New Haven: American Oriental Society, 1955).
3. Meek, p. 15.

been rather close at one time and a number of Hebrew customs as described in the Bible can be directly traced to Hurrian influence. Among some of the identical practices of both cultures, the most outstanding concerns the possession of the household gods, called *teraphim*. According to Hurrian belief, the *teraphim* brought prosperity and protection to the tribe and actual possession of them ensured leadership. This is why Laban was so upset when he found that Jacob had stolen his *teraphim*, since it meant that leadership had passed from himself and his sons to the Hebrew.

The major event of these times, however, was the Hyksos invasion of Egypt, in which the Hebrew/*Habirus* may have played a considerable part as allies of the invaders. It is during this period of Hyksos domination in Egypt that the story of Joseph should probably be placed. With the resurgence of Egyptian nationalism, however, the fortunes of the Hebrews/ *Habirus* quickly fell and they were forced to flee Egypt or else suffer the displeasure of the new Egyptian rulers. But Egypt could only muster power temporarily and at its ebb additional groups of Hebrews/*Habirus* began to reinfiltrate Egyptian holdings, some of them settling in the Wadi Tumilat (the land of Goshen). When the pendulum of power swayed once more in favor of the native Egyptians, these people were likely forced into servitude and it is concerning their descendants that the biblical story of the Exodus was probably written.[4]

On the basis of the Exodus narrative, one might accuse the Egyptians of being the first people in history to persecute the Jews. But this accusation is untenable, for during the period described by the narrative, there were neither Jews nor Hebrews in existence. The people leaving Egypt were neither monotheists nor worshippers of Yahweh, who was unknown to

4. The exodus did not involve the vast number of peoples suggested by the biblical narrative but rather concerned those who had come out of Egypt and had joined the Hebrew confederacy. Later, their history was incorporated into the Hebrew tradition and was made to extend to all the Hebrew tribes.

them at this time.[5] The oppression of the *Habirus,* the confrontation before Pharaoh, the exodus, and the sojourn in the desert, although plausible, must all be critically examined in light of present archeological discoveries and modern biblical exegesis if one is to arrive at a proper understanding of the Exodus narrative.

For many years, four separate sources have been identified in the present text of the Bible, and each of these sources can be placed in a definite era.[6] Moreover, each source presents a biased view that reflects not the period of interest, but the period in which the author himself lived. These writers did not chronicle history, they interpreted it, and sometimes they even created it! Such historians tended to be highly influenced by the ideas and feelings of their particular ages and for the most part their purpose was mainly the glorification of their god. Oppression and deliverance were emphasized since they served to advance his omnipotence. The Hebrews *(Habiru)* were not the only minority group in Egypt, but we read only of their oppression in the Bible because this is the only minority group of interest to the writers.

The Egyptians, for their part, likely viewed the various alien groups as a valuable economic asset and accordingly conscripted them into the slave labor force.[7] [8] This was not an unusual practice in the Near East and it may have been stoically accepted by those so treated. However, the time must have come when the slaves felt that they were powerful enough to demand their freedom and they made their intentions known to the king. But the Pharaoh would not readily consent

5. Attempts to trace monotheistic Yahwehism to the monotheistic doctrine of Akhenaton, the Egyptian iconoclast, should likewise be dismissed since Akhenaton's influence was too short lived to have created such an impact.
6. See C.A. Simpson, "The Growth of the Hexateuch," *Interpreter's Bible,* vol. I. p. 185-200.
7. See M. Noth, *The History of Israel,* (London: Adam and Charles Black, 1960), p. 113.
8. The biblical historian ascribes their enslavement to their potential political and cultural threat (Ex. 1:10). But when slavery only made them more fertile so that their numbers reached alarming proportions, an extermination policy was adopted (Ex. 1:22).

to a cutback in the labor force, especially when he was actively involved in an internal construction policy. Instead, he
increased their burdens and increased the police force that
supervised the constructions. Yet despite his refusal, the slaves
left the country.

The story of the plagues and the futile negotiations are
ahistorical[9] and are most likely due to the invention of a fanciful imagination. The most probable explanation of the event is
that when it occurred, the country was in a state of internal
disorder with the authorities occupied elsewhere. Thus, when
the slaves began their exodus, they were met with minimal opposition.

Although the theme of Israelite religion as it is presented in
the Old Testament is that of a continuity between the religion
of the patriarchs and the religion of Moses and his followers,
even a cursory examination of the traditions shows that this
theological outlook is more imaginary than fact. If there is any
real continuity between the two, the distinct patriarchal religion
must somehow have evolved into what was eventually to become Mosaic religion, during the exodus in the desert.

The Hebrew confederacy, in fact, did come into being during the period prior to the invasion of southern Palestine. It
was at this time that the refugees from Egypt were joined by
other tribes who had traditions of their own but who agreed to
be bound by the laws and customs that had become centered
about the worship of the newly adopted god, Yahweh.
Nevertheless, each of these tribes retained its own individuality
and after the conquest of Palestine by these people, there were
two distinct and separate Hebrew cultures in Palestine—Israel
in the north and Judah/Levi in the south. Unification eventually came under the direction of Saul, but this was temporary

---

9. Noth, p. 115, n.1, arguing *ex silentio* says that the exodus caused such little concern to the Egyptians that the Pharaoh was not even present to stop them. Had he
actually been present, Noth feels certain that it would have been recorded.
Moreover, the disaster that befell the Egyptian chariots could not have been so
insignificant as to preclude notice of the catastrophe as seems to be the case
judging from the silence.

and only occurred through the necessity of maintaining a united front in the face of common enemies rather than through mutual acculturation.

The outstanding event arising from the entire Exodus episode is thus not the departure from Egypt, but the formation of a new religious and polical organization that embraced the worship of one god above all others. This was the new confederacy's guiding principle. However, this does not mean that the confederacy practiced monotheism. Rather, it marked the recognition that there were many gods, but that there was one who was more powerful than any of the others. It was not until the time of David that monotheism took root. Once the state cult was secure, this concept further evolved such that Yahweh was regarded not only as a nationalistic entity, but as the god of all the world. This viewpoint was largely the work of the prophets, those fanatics whose overwhelming passion was to bring God to his people. But the prophets also taught that Yahweh was a jealous god—a god that would not recognize any other divinity—a god who denied tolerance to any rival divinities.

The concept was extremely radical. Other religions had provisions for the acceptance of other deities and in fact, a general practice of conquering nations was to admit vanquished gods into the pantheon of conquerors. But the Jews[10] never yielded nor made any attempts that hinted at a compromise of their monotheism once Yahweh was adopted.

Were it not for the intolerant attitude of the Jewish religion and the practices and culture dependent on it, there would have been little in Judaism to cause resentment toward the Jews who lived in various parts of the world. At the same time, however, had it not been for this very attitude, there probably would not be any Jews today. The other paradox is that the only thing that saved monotheistic Judaism was polytheistic paganism. Nonmonotheistic religions seem to have one mag-

---

10. The term "Jews" derives from the name given to the people living in Judah.

nanimous quality that Judaism, Christianity, Islam, etc. do not—an allowance for freedom of belief.

The exodus from Egypt was followed by the conquest of southern Palestine, thus creating two Hebrew[11] cultures in the country: Israel in the north and Judah/Levi in the south. Under the direction of King Saul, these cultures united, not through acculturation, but rather through the necessity of maintaining a united front in the face of common enemies.

This period of common cause produced two important figures—David and his son, Solomon. Under David, Jerusalem became the religious capital of the confederacy and so profound was the impression that he created on his people, that future salvation via the Messiah was anticipated only through his descendants.

Although Solomon was revered for extending the political importance of the nation far beyond all expectations, his most memorable achievement was the construction of a Temple that soon emerged as the national shrine and the unifying force behind Judaism.

But despite the impressive splendor of Solomon's kingdom, the empire was internally spent and in 933 B.C. it split back into two factions. Israel, the northern kingdom, was three times as large as Judah to the south and contained the majority of the Hebrew population since it was comprised of ten tribes, while Judah contained only two—Judah and Benjamin. But it was Judah and not Israel that survived the longest after the schism. This was due both to the fact that Israel had more enemies (since it provided the greater potential threat), and because internally it was more disunited than Judah, owing to its larger number of tribes. Judah, by comparison, presented a strongly united front since the kingdom was consolidated by its loyalty to Jerusalem, the religious center, and to its kings, who were direct descendants of David.

11. The term *"Habiru"* will no longer be used.

In 722 B.C. the new Mesopotamian war machine, the Assyrian army led by Sargon II, captured Samaria, the northern capital of Israel, and the inhabitants were deported in accord with Assyrian foreign policy. Thus, the legend of the ten lost tribes of Israel was born. Judah, on the other hand, continued to exist in quasi-independence until 597 B.C., when the next warlord, Nebuchadnezzar, the Chaldean, captured Jerusalem and took thousands of the inhabitants into captivity. After an abortive revolt by the remaining inhabitants, Jerusalem was destroyed, the Temple was burnt, and most of the remaining inhabitants were carried off into captivity.

Although the deported tribes of Israel had become "lost" by this time, the people of Judah were not to suffer the same fate since the unifying spirit of the law, the Torah, and the memory of the Temple still kept them remindful of their past. In Babylon, where the majority of deported captives were settled, large closely knit communities were created, held together by a new central institution, the synagogue, which developed its own organization and ritual and like the Temple, it too came to occupy a central part of the religious life.

The Babylonian deportation marked the beginning of the Diaspora—the dispersion of the Jews into the world. This was an event that actually served to guarantee the existence of Judaism, however, for with the emigration of the Jews to distant parts of the world, the fate of Judaism in one country had little bearing on its survival or continuation in another. The synagogue likewise assured Judaism's survival, since it became the social and educative center and place of worship for Jews not living in Palestine.

When the Chaldean dynasty fell to the Persians, this set the stage for the next development in Judaism. Cyrus, the new conqueror, innovated a new policy for dealing with conquered subjects. Instead of trying to frighten them into submission, he attempted to win their support through consideration. With respect to the Jews, one of the first steps he took was to allow those who so desired to return to Judea. However, political conditions in Judea were to be different from those which had previously existed. In place of a king, the High Priest of the Temple was to be the central figure in Judea. Consequently, after the captivity, Judea became a theocracy with the High Priest as religious and political head of state—a position that became hereditary.

Under the Persians, the Jews seem to have prospered and they could be found engaging in almost every possible activity, even to the extent of holding governmental office as illustrated by the accounts of *Ezra* and *Nehemiah*. Papyri dating back to the fifth century B.C. also indicate the presence of a Jewish military colony located at Elephantine (Yeb) at the first cataract of the Nile.[12]

The brief history of this small Jewish colony is rather indicative of the position adopted by the Jews living in the Diaspora many years later. When the Persians conquered Egypt (from the north) they found this small military outpost guarding Egypt's southern frontier. Most likely they had been allowed to settle on the island in the Nile by the Pharaoh in return for their promise to guard the access to the empire from the south. Following the conquest of Egypt, these Jews promised to provide the same service for the Persians. This switch in allegiance did not endear them to the native population, which saw anyone supporting the conquerors as traitors. When the Egyptians were once again able to assert their independence, the Jewish colony, because of its loyalty to the Persians, was overrun and destroyed.

Thus, the Elephantine colony illustrates the *modus vivendi* of the Jews in the Diaspora and the consequences of such behavior. Since they were always a noticeable minority, they had to rely on the protection of the king if they wanted safeguards in the practice of their strange customs. Hence, they always supported the government against the common people. Thus, when the Egyptians were defeated, they switched their loyalty

12. See A.E. Cowley, *Aramaic Papyri of the Fifth Century B.C.* (Oxford: Oxford Clarendon Press, 1923).

to the Persians, although the natives would naturally be against such a switch in allegiance. Once nationalism reasserted itself, those supporting the enemy were punished for their alleged misdeeds.

The brief description in the preceding pages is not meant to be a definitive presentation of Jewish history during the biblical period. Rather, its intention is to introduce the subject matter and to acquaint the reader with a few historical facts that may make exposition of the theme somewhat clearer.

Although free from any definitive anti-Semitic overtones, this period is still relevant to that subject since it was during this time that the attitudes regarding assimilation to other religions and peoples of the world were outlined and adopted. This came as a result of the prophetic influence in Israel and the early experiences of the Jews during the captivity.

The only anti-Semitic reference during this biblical period comes from the Book of Esther, which supposedly reflects conditions prevalent during the Persian period. According to that account, Haman, the grand vizier of Persia, was bent on exterminating all the Jews of the kingdom because of his hatred for the Jew Mordecai. But Esther, the Persian king's Jewish wife, intervened and secured an order for Haman to be executed (ironically) on the same gallows that Haman had originally prepared for Mordecai.

On the surface, the book seems to document an important historical event during the Persian period. However, modern biblical scholars confute most of the historical data and some even go so far as to suggest that the whole story is pure fiction. A great deal of evidence, in fact, can be cited to question the narrative's authenticity[13] so that this hypothesis must be granted serious consideration. Current interpretation of the book places its composition during the Maccabean crisis (ca. 165 B.C.) and assigns it to the sphere of allegory, written to give the Jews strength in their confrontation with the Syrian counterpart to Haman—Antiochus IV.

13. For details, see the Article, "Esther," *Interpreter's Bible*, vol. 3, p. 823-32.

2

The Jews in the Ptolemaic Empire

The General Political Situation in Palestine
after Alexander the Great

IN 334 B.C. the Persian empire was attacked by Alexander the Great and eleven years later it collapsed. Under Alexander, it might have been governed as an intact unit, but the conqueror's unexpected death immediately resulted in a partitioning of the empire by his rapacious generals as each sought to possess the largest and richest areas of Asia for himself. By 301 B.C., however, there were only two major claimants left: Ptolemy I, who retained possession of Egypt and Palestine, and Seleucus I, who controled the rest of the Asian Empire.

The fate of Palestine during these unsettled years is not unimaginable. Lying in a central position between the Syrian and Egyptian Empires, it was the crossroads for the various advancing and retreating armies. Up to the time of the Battle of Ipsus (301 B.C.), it changed possession five times. The Egyptian victory at Ipsus only secured it temporarily.[1] Ptolemy,

1. Ptolemy's desire to hold on to Palestine was not on account of its wealth but because of its strategic position. Lying as it did on the only possible route for an army bent on an invasion of Egypt, possession of Palestine was indispensable to Egyptian defense.

however, had no legal claim to any of Palestine, for the territory had been granted to Seleucus by international agreement[2] following the defeat of its former ruler Antigonus. Seleucus, however, never really forced his claim against Ptolemy because the latter had saved his life by giving him sanctuary in Egypt when his enemies had tried to kill him. But in the eyes of his Seleucid descendants, Palestine was rightfully theirs and Egyptian claims to the country were never recognized. Yet until the Seleucids could muster enough military strength, they could only dispute it verbally. Occasionally, they were able to retain possession of Palestine for some short periods, but from the time of the Battle of Ipsus to the Battle of Panion (199 B.C.), Palestine was an Egyptian province.

Palestine under the Ptolemies

In the extant literature there are two contradictory traditions relating Ptolemy I's conduct toward the Jews[3] and both of these are preserved by the Jewish historian, Josephus. The earliest account was written by the Greek historian Hecataeus of Abdera, who was a contemporary of the events he describes and who lived in Alexandria presumably at the time that he wrote his narrative. As far as Hecataeus knew, Ptolemy I was considered a moderate and well-liked ruler by the Jews since many of them had voluntarily come back with him to Egypt following one of his campaigns; among these emigrants was Hezekiah, the High Priest (C.Ap. 1.21).[4] It is not known whether Josephus had another source relating these events, but concerning such emigrations into Egypt, he states that "there were not a few other Jews who, of their own accord, went into

---

2. Polybius, *The Histories* (New York: G. P. Putnam's Sons, 1927), 5.68.
3. The *Letter of Aristeas* also refers to these events, but the fictional nature of that source renders it almost useless.
4. Most likely this event occurred in 312 B.C. since the political situation was most favorable toward such an occurrence at this time (cf. V. Tcherikower, *Hellenistic Civilization and the Jews* (Philadelphia: Jewish Publication Society, 1959), p. 57.

Egypt, as invited by the goodness of the soil, and by the liberality of Ptolemy" (Ant. 12.1.1).

The second tradition stems from Agatharchides, another Greek historian, but one who lived in the second century B.C. According to his account, Ptolemy tricked the Jews of Jerusalem into opening the gates of the city by claiming that he wished to worship their god, and once inside, he "made himself master of the city without difficulty and ruled it harshly" (Ant. 12.1.1). Following Jerusalem's capture, Ptolemy scoured the countryside assembling the inhabitants of Judea whom he brought back to Egypt as slaves. Although attempts have been made to place these two accounts in chronological order,[5] it would appear from a detailed examination of the sources, that Hecataeus' narrative is the more probable since Agatharchides had to rely on either Hecataeus or some other source which is no longer extant, while Hecataeus himself was a contemporary of the events.[6]

Historians know little of the hundred and some odd years that the Ptolemies ruled Palestine. We may tentatively assume that these were years of peace, but this assumption is based only on the fact that we have no information of any turmoil in the Near East during this period. Those documents which do relate to this era deal with the economic and bureaucratic organization of the Ptolemaic province and indicate that the ambition of the Ptolemies was to make Egypt and themselves as wealthy and as powerful as possible. In order to accomplish this end, it was necessary to extract as much from the country and its surrounding territories as could be removed. That Palestine was bled of its resources is fairly certain since it was part and parcel of the Ptolemaic reservoir. Every possible commodity was taxed and every tax had some bureaucratic official to oversee its collection. In turn, every tax collector had to make sure that not only did the king receive his due, but that he him-

5. Cf. Tcherikowever, p. 57.
6. See Abel, "Myth of Jewish Slavery in Ptolemaic Egypt," *Revue des études Juives* 127 (1968): 253-58 for an extended discussion of the slavery question.

self made some sort of profit. Some of the intracacies of this tax system have come to light in a collection of papyri emanating from an important government official named Zenon,[7] who supervised the economic rape of Palestine in 295 B.C. As a result of his correspondence, which numbers some thousand-odd pieces, historians have been able to piece together some of the social and economic details by which the Ptolemies ruled their empire.

For example, to safeguard possession of territories in Syria-Palestine, military garrisons *(cleruchies)* were established in various provinces, yet at the same time certain native sheikhs were allowed to maintain a fair degree of autonomy. One of the papyri in the Zenon collection[8] informs us that one particular sheikh, a Jew named Jeddous, refused to pay a debt he owed Ptolemy and when one of the bureaucrats came to collect in person, Jeddous attacked and drove him out of his village. Such boldness suggests that some of the districts of Palestine were not firmly under the control of the Ptolemies. Another powerful Jewish sheikh named Tobiah, was the head of one of the *cleruchies* in Transjordan[9] and his son eventually became the chief tax collector in Palestine.

According to Tcherikower,[10] the source of the sheikhs' power in Syria lay in the king's reliance on their support in the event that war would break out with the Seleucids. Alienating the sheikhs would have meant an important decrease in the number of native supporters; hence, the king was not as willing to enforce the same stringent practices there as he imposed in the Egyptian villages.

Although the Ptolemies did not forceably attempt to Hellenize the Jews, they did take an active part in the Hellenization of various cities located along the Phoenician coast. A

7. The article by Tcherikower in *Mizraim*, vol. IV-V (1937) discusses Palestine in light of these papyri, while the work by Tcherikower and A. Fuks, *Corpus Papyrorum Judaicarum*, vol. I, relates a few of the papyri directly concerned with the Jews.
8. *C.J.P.*, no. 6.
9. *Ibid.*, nos. 4 and 5.
10. *Hell. Civil.*, p. 66.

twofold purpose lay behind this plan, involving both economic and political considerations. Alexandria was a seaport; the most magnificent seaport of the ancient world. But for all its splendor, it would only be an isolated harbor should the important sea routes leading to it be blockaded by some foreign power. Moreover, the cities that dotted the coast of Asia Minor were important commercial centers in their own right, and access to these ports by Egyptian ships depended on freedom of movement along the coasts of Palestine and Phoenicia. Additionally, the cities of Palestine were potential allies if the Seleucids ever decided to invade Egypt. Hence, their strategic position, located on the only feasible route to Egypt, necessitated their friendship and alliance, and accordingly, the Ptolemies allowed these cities a fair degree of autonomy. In some cases the Ptolemies even encouraged the development of these cities by bringing in Greeks from other parts of the Hellenistic world and by granting these people the special privileges accorded to citizens of a Greek city-state. Thus, as a result of their political and economic interests, the Ptolemies indirectly introduced Hellenism to Palestine.

In Jerusalem, the leading advocates of Hellenization were the Tobiads, the descendants of the Transjordian sheikh, Tobiah. According to Josephus,[11] Tobiah's son, Joseph initially came to Jerusalem to try to persuade his uncle, the High Priest Onias II, not to precipitate an Egyptian invasion by refusing to pay the tribute demanded by Ptolemy.[12] When Onias refused

11. The story of the Tobiads as narrated by Josephus (Ant., 12.4) requires careful evaluation since it is evident that Josephus took little care in reading his sources. For various interpretations of the events of this period see Tcherikower, *Hell. Civil.*; S. Zeitlin, *The Tobias Family and the Hasmoneans. PAAJR 4*, (1933): 169-223; or S. Zeitlin, *Rise and Fall of the Judean State* (Philadelphia: Jewish Publication Society, 1962).
12. Ptolemy Philadelphus faced a difficult problem with the Jews. He had proclaimed himself the supreme deity to all his subjects and had demanded recognition as such. Priests had even been appointed for this purpose. But the Jewish theocracy was hereditary and could not be compromised. Realizing the antagonism he would create by violating the tradition, and yet unwilling to lose face, the king ordered the High Priest to pay a tax of 20 talents of silver to maintain his position and this was to be paid not from Temple funds, but from the High Priest's own resources (*Ant.*, 12.4.1).

to listen, Joseph turned to the people and successfully persuaded them to allow him to go to Ptolemy on their behalf in order to negotiate some settlement.[13] This turned out to be a very significant event in Judea's political life since it meant that the monopoly formerly held by the priestly class over both religion and government was now broken and Judea ceased to be a completely theocratic state.

As a result of his visit to Egypt, Joseph became the chief tax collector as well as head of the civil government in Judea.[14] Joseph, however, was not content with such small plums. With a daring proposal, he asked the king to be put in charge of the entire Syrian provinces promising to double the tax collection previously received by the king.[15] The king, of course, was delighted with any plan which would increase his revenues and agreed, thereby making Joseph the highest ranking Jewish official in the Ptolemaic Empire.

However, promising revenues and collecting them were not synonymous. Although the king might approve of Joseph's offer, the Greek citizens of Syria-Palestine were not as eager to comply with the plan and it was necessary for Joseph to have the aid of the Ptolemaic army to carry out his promise. When the citizens of Ascalon and Scythopolis flatly refused to pay, Joseph sent in the army, arrested the leaders of the city, and executed them.[16] After that, the king's tribute was paid in full.

The Tobiads cannot be underestimated for their importance in the events that followed in Palestine. In his position as tax collector, Joseph directly and indirectly reshaped the cultural milieu of Jerusalem. First, many Greek officials serving under him moved to Jerusalem to reduce traveling distances and these people brought the characteristics of their culture and temperament into contact with Judaism. Secondly, Joseph had wrested political control away from the priestly class and had

13. *Ant.*, 12.4.2.
14. *Ibid.*
15. *Ibid.*, 12.4.4.
16. *Ibid.*, 12.4.5.

placed it in the hands of the wealthy aristocratic families, whose economic interests insured the growth of Hellenism in Jerusalem. Joseph himself had had to relinquish his binding Jewish religious and cultural habits[17] for they tended to alienate him from important contacts in the Greek world and he did this to such an extent that he and his family became the leading figures in the attempt to Hellenize Jerusalem.

After Joseph's death, the political situation in Palestine remained rather uneventful but within his family two factions arose, one pro-Syrian and the other pro-Egyptian.[18] Eventually these two confronted one another in a war of survival, like that which occurred in 242 B.C. In that year, war[19] broke out between Egypt and Syria and the Jewish theocratic rulers switched their allegiance from the Ptolemies to the Seleucids since a close liason with the Jews of Babylonia promised more than an intimate relationship with the Jews of Egypt. For one thing, the Jews of Babylonia were an important source of contributions to the Temple. For another, they followed Jewish traditions more conscientiously than did the Egyptian Jews.

17. Josephus informs us that Joseph not only violated the Jewish dietary laws by eating at the king's table, he also was not adverse to the intimate company of the king's dancing girls (*Ant.,* 12.4.6). Such conduct in a Jew was unbelievable in those times. However, in evaluating Joseph's career, Josephus comments that by introducing Hellenistic pastimes into Jerusalem, Joseph brought the Jews from "poverty" and "meanness" to greater splendor (Ant., 12.4.10).

18. Hyrcanus, Joseph's youngest son, had a true Machiavellean character. Realizing that as the youngest he would not likely succeed his father as tax collector, he wormed his way into the good graces of the Egyptian king and won for himself the promise that he would attain his father's position at Joseph's death (*Ant.,* 12.4.7-10). But despite his great abilities, Hyrcanus was unable to discharge his duties since his brothers were able to keep him from entering Jerusalem. Finding no support from his father, whom he had alienated by his extravagance at the king's court (*Ant.,* 12.4.9), or from the inhabitants of the city, he had to withdraw. Eventually, however, he established his own estate in Transjordania where he was able to collect the king's tribute without interference.

Tcherikower *(Hell. Civil.,* p. 138) conjectured that Hyrcanus' brothers' attack on him was to draw the attention of the Syrian king Antiochus III to the fact that they no longer supported the Ptolemies. By this means they hoped to regain the importance and position taken from them by Hyrcanus, in the event that the Syrians should take over the country. Although the chronological time of these events is uncertain, it appears to have occurred after 209 B.C. since this is the date at which Hyrcanus left for Egypt to represent his father (Zeitlin, p. 66) and after 200 B.C. since at this time Antiochus III controlled Palestine.

19. The Laodicean War.

Furthermore, they also spoke Aramaic, which was much more understandable to the Judean Jews than was Greek, despite the growing Hellenization of the country. Finally, should the Seleucids be defeated, it would mean that ties with Babylonian Jewry would be encumbered. Therefore, the theocratic rulers decided to support the Seleucids openly.[20]

However, the early Syrian advances were soon stopped and the Egyptians regained control of their territories. Although he had been faced with a fifth column, Ptolemy did not seem particularly disturbed by the disloyalty of the Jews since he did not take any retaliatory measures against them.

In 219 B.C. war again broke out when Antiochus III invaded Palestine but the Battle of Raphia (217 B.C.) saw the complete defeat of the Syrians and they were forced to withdraw once again. This time, the king (Ptolemy IV Philopator) may have decided to punish the Jews for he is reported to have visited Jerusalem and to have tried to gain entrance to the Temple[21] (which was somehow prevented).

In 202 B.C., Antiochus III once more invaded Palestine and this time there was an influential pro-Syrian party in Jerusalem.[22] The Egyptian general Scopas, however, successfully drove the Syrians from the field. Then he turned on Jerusalem. After overcoming some minor resistance,[23] an Egyptian garrison was stationed in the city and some of the pro-Seleucid leaders were taken back to Egypt to pay the penalty of their disloyalty.

The last campaign against the Egyptians occurred in 199 B.C., where at the Battle of Panion, the Syrians finally won the upper hand. The victory ushered into Palestine a new era of

20. Despite Josephus' sequence, this is most likely the time when Onias II refused to continue payment of tribute to Ptolemy since he probably believed the Syrians were about to take over.
21. The only reference to Ptolemy's visit to Jerusalem is that preserved by the *Third Book of the Maccabees,* but the fictitious nature of the story of Ptolemy's paralyzing fit and his subsequent anti-Semitic retaliation has long been recognized as having little basis in fact (cf. Tcherikower's comment on this, in *Scripta Hierosolymitana* 3 (1961): p. 1-26; and E. W. Emmet's remarks in Vol. 1 of the *Apocrypha and Pseudepigrapha of the Old Testament,* ed. by R.H. Charles.
22. See note 18.
23. *Ant.,* 12.3.3.

Hellenism, one which eventually culminated in the Maccabean war. But in 199 B.C., the only major change in Palestine was the substitution of Egyptian soldiers and taxes by their Syrian counterparts.

At this point we must turn to the position of the Jews in Egypt proper, for it is in that country that we encounter the first evidences of anti-Semitism in the ancient world.

Jewish Settlement in Ptolemaic Egypt

The earliest evidence for the presence of Jews in Egypt are the Biblical references that have come down to us in the form of the Exodus story, but we have already mentioned the difficulties inherent in placing these events in their proper context. Certainly Jews had been living in Egypt under the ancient Pharaohs, and just as certain is the fact that they did not leave the country en masse when Moses departed. The earliest non-biblical reference to their presence in Egypt occurs in the Elephantine papyri,[24] which mention them at the time of the Persian conquest and leads us to believe that they were settled there long before the Persians entered the country. The evidence from these invaluable papyri, coupled with the statements in the book of Jeremiah,[25] indicates that Jews were in Egypt at the time of the Persians, and that they were not there as slaves. Rather, the evidence suggests that they were relied upon to guard the borders of Egypt against possible invasion and it was as soldiers that they were brought into the country.

Mention has already been made of the narratives of Hecataeus and Agatharchides[26] and the two different views that these historians give concerning the entrance of the Jews into Egypt under Ptolemy I. The only other reference that we possess of the Jews being slaves in Egypt during this period is that given in the *Letter of Aristeas*.[27] However, the sycophantic

24. See ch. 1.
25. Jer. 42-44.
26. See ch. 2.
27. M. Hadas, *Aristeas to Philocrates* gives the text and comments upon it.

nature of that work should lead to scepticism. The entire narrative is fantastic, especially the details of Ptolemy's munificence in personally paying the owners of Jewish slaves to release them. The Ptolemaic kings were in Egypt to acquire wealth, not to spend it enfranchising slaves.

However, the tendency of modern historians interested in this period, has still been to infer that because a great many slaves were brought into Egypt from Syria and Palestine, undoubtably many Jews were included in these processions.[28] There can be little doubt that some Jews probably came to Egypt as slaves, but to infer that they came in such large numbers that they were a significant element has never been demonstrated. Slavery itself was not an important institution in Egypt since native employment was as cheap an economic commodity as could be desired.[29] The native Egyptians certainly could not have supported slaves since they had difficulty in supporting themselves. The only inhabitants who could afford them were the Greeks who used some slaves in their households. However, the Ptolemaic government was opposed to slavery and heavy taxes were levied on the slave trade,[30] thereby discouraging their obtainment.

The more probable explanation is that the Jews voluntarily emigrated to Egypt as farmers, artisans, merchants, soldiers, etc. and found conditions in Egypt so agreeable that word went back to relatives in Palestine that the country was socially and economically worth settling.[31] Egypt also became the asylum for Jews seeking to escape the political and social revolution in Palestine that followed the Maccabean crisis.[32] The military particularly attracted large numbers of Jews because of the inducements that came with military service. These included

28. Cf. Zeitlen, p. 52.
29. M. Rostovtzeff, *Social and Economic History of the Hellenistic World* (Oxford: Oxford Clarendon Press, 1941), p. 370.
30. *Ibid.*
31. Not all Jews found conditions in Egypt prosperous. Two papyri relating to Jewish laborers indicate that they had to beg for assistance in order for them to meet every day needs (C.P.J., nos. 12,13.).
32. I *Mac.*, 15, 16 ff.

grants of large plots of land and the right to farm these out and to collect revenues from them. Some of these Jewish soldiers attained very high rank in the Egyptian army, such as Chelcias and Hannaniah, who were put in charge of the Egyptian forces during the time of Cleopatra I.[33] For the most part, Jewish soldiers were settled in *cleruchies* and in fortresses where they guarded the king's possessions and maintained peace in the country. The military also had other privileges, such as special quarters or new houses, but their most important privilege was exemption from compulsory government labor to which everyone else in Egypt was subject, with the exception of the priesthood. It is no wonder then that Jews voluntarily emigrated into Egypt from Palestine, given the inducements that the Ptolemies offered for military service.[34]

Ptolemaic Organization of Egypt.[35]

To understand the part played by the Jews in the economic, political, and social life of Egypt, some of the salient features of the government of Egypt during this period must be introduced.

Following the pattern established by Ptolemy I Soter, Egypt became the private estate of the king. As self-proclaimed successor to the Pharaohs, the king called for the loyalty of the native populace, but in the native mind there was little doubt that the Ptolemies were not in Egypt to help the lot of the Egyptians, who formed the main body of inhabitants and numbered in the many millions.

From the outset, the Egyptian was relegated to an inferior position. It is true that those Egyptians who had been wealthy and influential before the conquest continued to exercise aristocratic authority, and that the temples that were the centers of

---

33. *Ant.*, 13.13.1.
34. The native population was excluded from these positions and from most of the important government offices.
35. The following is based mainly on the description given by Rostovtzeff.

religious life were respected and left alone. But the common peasant and the less important Egyptian officials now became the country's main source of cheap economic labor. Few distinctions were made and almost every Egyptian was subject to compulsory duty whenever he was needed. This is not to say that the immigrants or the priesthood were exempt from this burden. The king in all fairness refused to excuse them while he burdened the natives. However, these former groups could escape the corvée if they could pay an exemption fee—the native populace did not have this privilege extended to them; nor could most of them afford it had the opportunity been given them.

The foundation of Egypt's economic empire was its agricultural resources. The land was the greatest source of wealth and in theory all the land belonged to the king; but in his magnanimity he granted portions, often sizable sections, to private individuals. We have already mentioned the military as recipients of sizable areas of territory and along with them we can include most government officials, many of whom also received sizable portions. The revenue accrued from the produce of this land, however, was supposed to pay their salaries.

The royal lands, that is those leased by the king to private individuals, were farmed by 'royal peasants'. These were Egyptian freemen who paid rent and taxes to the king for the privilege of growing food on his lands. These rents and taxes amounted to approximately one-half of the harvest.[36]

To insure that the king received his proper share, the harvests were closely supervised by government officials who maintained a constant vigilance on the king's behalf. Considering the taxes, rents, the king's share, and the fact that the peasants had to buy their grain from the king, these peasants would have been better off as slaves—at least then they would have been properly taken care of. Thus, it was in the wisdom of the founders of the Ptolemaic dynasty that more was to be gained

36. Rostovtzeff, p. 279.

by giving the native his freedom than by enslaving him. The Ptolemaic Empire was clearly built on exploitation and the entire structure supported and demanded such exploitation.

When the Ptolemies originally took over power in Egypt, they found themselves in control of a country which had no significant military organization to speak of.[37] It was readily apparent that if the country were to be held against predators, the military power would have to be built up. But the Ptolemies refused to allow the native inhabitants to participate in the protection of the country or in the machinery of the government and instead they encouraged large numbers of foreigners, especially Greeks, to settle in Egypt. In order to lure these mercenaries and settlers it was necessary to pay them well, and to guarantee them attractive privileges. As a result, the foreigners, who numbered in the thousands, were entrusted with the management of the native populace, which numbered in the millions.

The consequence, of course, was a government which was Greek both in form and language. Knowledge of Greek was thus mandatory, if only to be heard by some official, the importance of whom depended either on one's own status or the size of a bribe.

Greek cities also had to be built or else existing cities had to be expanded. As a result, Alexandria, Ptolemais, Naucratis, Memphis, and Thebes became the foremost cities of Egypt and the main sites of foreign settlement. Relationships between the Greeks and native Egyptians were nonexistent in these large cities, however, and the bureaucratic system that evolved saw to it that the Egyptian native was made aware of his inferiority. The Greeks did not understand the Egyptian language, but since Greek was the language of government, it became incumbent upon the native to learn Greek and not vice versa. Moreover, the Egyptian was faced with the fact that a Greek king and Greek gods ruled his country,[38] and all his toil and

37. Rostovtzeff, p. 262.
38. Despite the pervasiveness of Greek culture and religion, there was no attempt to

taxes went not toward his own king or deities, but to foreign gods and men who became richer as he became poorer. It would require no great effort to imagine the feelings that the Egyptians felt toward the Greeks or toward those who were in their service. Consequently, when we speak of the Jews, a group which played an integral part in the internal government and politics of Egypt, we may be quite certain that they were included in the bitterness and hatred directed against the rulers.

Foremost among the despised officials of the bureaucracy were the tax collectors.[39] Every year the king auctioned off the right to collect his various duties and taxes and although the actual monetary return from this position was not great, the office was eagerly sought. Interestingly, Jews often numbered among the government's tax collectors[40] even though the position brought with it hatred and a very small likelihood of actual monetary return. The only probable explanation for the presence of Jews in these offices was the status associated with a government position in the Ptolemaic Empire.[41] Jews could also be found in the thankless roles of policemen, probably for much the same reason.[2] Oddly enough, there is no evidence of any Jewish merchants in Egypt. This may have been a result of the discouragement of private enterprise by the Ptolemies, or it may simply be due to the fact that the papyri mentioning them are no longer extant.[43]

This quick survey of the economic and administrative system of Ptolemaic Egypt must lead one to the conclusion that the Ptolemaic kings were not concerned with the welfare of the Egyptian populace as a whole when they organized the country. But this thesis is not the subject of the present work. As far as

subjugate the Egyptian gods; they were simply not patronized to the extent that Greek gods were. Some cults, however, did manage to supersede the Greek, for example, Serapis, but this occurred during the Roman period.

39. The main function of the tax collector was to underwrite the taxes owed to the king. Whatever he collected over and above this, was his to keep.
40. For papyri referring to Jewish tax collectors, see *C.J.P.*, nos. 1, 48, 90, 100, 107, 110.
41. *Ibid.*, p. 19.
42. *Ibid.*, p. 18.
43. *Ibid.*, p. 10.

the Jews were concerned, there is no evidence that the kings discriminated against them politically and in fact, Jews were allowed to play an important part in Ptolemaic government. It is therefore no wonder that the number of Jews who came to Egypt was large. Although there were many Jews in the army and in the Fayum, by far the greatest population was centered in the cosmopolitan city-state of Alexandria of which they comprised one-fifth of the entire population. In this context it is noteworthy that Alexandria was the first center for the literate as well as physical demonstrations of anti-Semitism in the ancient world.

The Social Position of the Jews in Ptolemaic Egypt

Alexandria was not representative of the typical city in the ancient Greek world—it was not just a city, nor even a city-state; it was a state within Egypt. It was not even considered a part of Egypt; it was a country bordering Egypt! Situated between Lake Mareotis and the Mediterranean Sea, the city was bordered on the east by the Canopus Gate and by a similar gate on the west.[44] Alexandria was unique in many respects especially as regards its drainage system, whereby fresh water from the Nile poured into the city via a canal system that even carried it to the doorstep of some of the wealthy private homes. Such a system was unprecedented in the ancient world.

Alexandria itself was divided into five sections, each called by a different letter of the Greek alphabet. The Jews of the city were mainly settled in the Delta region which was located near the sea front. To the west of their sector stood the king's palace. The cynosure of the city was the gymnasium, the social center of all Greek cities. Only those possessing Greek citizenship were allowed to educate their children in the gym-

---

44. See E. R. Bevan, *History of Egypt under the Ptolemaic Dynasty* (London: Methuen Co., 1927), p. 91. W.W. Tarn, *Hellenistic Civilization* (Cleveland: Cleveland World Pub. Co., 1961), p. 183 gives a short bibliography of the city of Alexandria.

nasium, and at the same time, a gymnasium education was a prerequisite to obtaining citizenship.[45]

The city also contained the headquarters of the king's officialdom and the central storage areas for various foodstuffs. Tradesmen, shopkeepers, etc. were located along the main road and plied their wares much the same as in any cosmopolitan city, except on a much grander scale.

The cosmopolitan atmosphere, however, precluded the emergence of a closely knit city-state *(polis)* and instead Alexandria was the geographical locale for a number of Egypt's ethnic groups *(politeumata)*,[46] the most important of whom were the Greeks. When one refers to the citizens of Alexandria, one usually means the members of the Greek *politeuma* but there were others who also became citizens.[47]

45. The entire question of citizenship in Alexandria is one full of controversy and debate. Not all the Greeks living in Alexandria were included in the citizen body, even though they spoke and lived in the same manner as Greek citizens. If there were Greeks living in Alexandria who were not citizens, what could the status of the Jews in that city have been? This was one of the most hotly debated questions among Jewish scholars at the turn of the century, but at the present it is usually conceded that the Jews as a whole did not possess such citizenship. We will consider this question in more detail when we discuss the Roman occupation of Egypt.

46. Ethnic communities in Greek cities were designated either as *politeuma* or *katoikia*. The former consisted mainly of a group of people ethnically and religiously bound together, whereas the latter usually designated colonies of people of foreign ancestry domiciled in the city as soldiers (cf. Rostovtzeff, p.298). The Jewish community at Hierapolis was regarded as a *katoikia* whereas in Alexandria they constituted a *politeuma*.

The *politeuma* of the Jews or of any other ethnic group did not allow them any claim to citizenship in the city, that is political autonomy, but meant rather that they had a certain amount of freedom to self-govern themselves. This was particularly important for their religion.

In all cases the king's assent had to be obtained before any ethnic community could be founded. Tcherikower *(Hell. Civil,* p. 300) believed that such an act of permission along with the rights included in it were given to the community in a charter, but no such document has been uncovered as yet.

47. Tcherikower maintained that under the Ptolemies there were no special privileges associated with Alexandrian citizenship and so the Jews did not actively move to become citizens *(Hell. Civil.,* p. 41). The privileges accorded to Alexandrian citizens were exemption from the liturgy and the right to be beaten with blades instead of being scourged should one be found guilty of a crime. In addition, the citizens had their own law code.

These privileges could not have been an incentive to the Jew and were generally regarded lightly. However, what may have been of interest was the status that went with the title of citizen of Alexandria and this gymnasium, which was the prerequisite to citizenship.

Although the Jewish community in Alexandria contained numberous synagoges[48] that served as social and educational centers,[49] the Jews lost touch with their mother tongue and the Greek language eventually became their language of communication. Since the Jews could no longer understand Hebrew, it was necessary to translate the scriptures into the new language if prayer books were to have any meaning. The *Letter of Aristeas* was then composed to explain to the public how the Jewish scriptures came to be written in Greek. Even though we may dismiss the explanation as being fictional, we cannot dismiss the fact that during the Ptolemaic period the Jews of Egypt had become so Hellenized, they were no longer able to understand the language in which their sacred writings had been transmitted to them. This Greek translation also meant that Jewish law and history were now available to any Greek who chose to inspect the Jewish books, and no doubt a copy of the Septuagint was housed in the famous library of Alexandria.

In some cases biblical law was also superceded during the Hellenization process. For instance, we find the precept against lending money at interest being violated by some Jews[50] and when Jews were involved in legal disputes with other Jews, it was to a Greek, not a Jewish court, that they resorted.[51] A further example of the extent of Hellenization among some of the Jews is given in one of the Zenon papyri citing Tobiah's greeting to Apollonius as ''many thanks to the gods!''[52] an expression which would have been anathema to an orthodox Jew.

In summary, the Jews of Egypt enjoyed a semi-autonomous political life and complete religious freedom. Their social position was not inferior to that of any group, except perhaps the

---

48. See *C.J.P.* p. 8 for the location of synagogues in other areas.
49. The actual organization of the Jewish community will be dealt with in the discussion of the Roman occupation of Egypt.
50. *C.J.P.*, nos. 20, 24.
51. *Ibid.*, No. 19.
52. *Ibid.*, No. 4.

citizen, but citizenship conferred no special privileges. While the Jew still kept most of his socio-religious practices, the tendency toward acculturation was soon apparent in his everyday language and in the language of his prayers, and although he still considered himself a Jew, the Jew of Egypt was very different in his 'Jewishness' from the Jew of Palestine or Babylonia.

Origins of Anti-Semitism in Ptolemaic Egypt

Anti-Semitism did not emerge from the first contacts that the Jews had with the Greeks. In fact, the earliest mention of the Jews in the ancient Greek world indicate that they were looked upon as philosophers[53] who spent their time discussing the nature of God and in observing the stars. As a result of the travels of the Greeks throughout the Near East, more and more information concerning the Jews was issued and circulated so that in addition to their being philosophers, they became known as a people who deliberately shut themselves off from society as a whole. This was a rather strange peculiarity to the Greek mind, which prided itself on its social activities in the gymnasium, the theater, assembly, etc. Explanations were offered to account for Jewish exclusiveness and early historians related that Moses, the leaders of the Jews, was responsible for deliberately instituting a number of customs and precepts issued expressly to keep the Jews separated from mankind as a whole.[54]

These early accounts reflect Greek curiosity about the peoples of the world—they were as interested in the Jews as they were in the Egyptians when Herodotus brought back the account of his travels in the Near East. However, following the Jewish Diaspora these people began to settle in Greek cities, and then their seclusiveness and religion were no longer re-

53. Rheinach, *Textes,* nos. 7,9. See also Gill, *Notices of the Jews,* p. 41.
54. Rheinach, *Textes,* no. 9.

garded with the same amusement and curiosity that had been initially aroused when the Jews were confined to their own homelands. Now that the Greek had closer contact with these people this greater familiarity with their *modus vivendi* apparently bred contempt.

Monotheism and Messianism were not familiar concepts in the Greek world. In the Greek mind, all gods had a right to share the pantheon; syncretism was the way of life in the ancient world and not the exception. But the Jewish deity, Yahweh, would not tolerate such an *entente* with pagan gods; in fact, he would not even recognize their existence, which was a serious insult to the Greek, the Egyptian, and to every other polytheistic people. Even though their gods only desired sacrifice as a means of recognition, it did not mean that their followers revered them any less than the Jews did their god. They were prepared to give the same kind of respect to the Jewish god as to their own, but were insulted that he in return was not ready to reciprocate that respect. Furthermore, Yahweh's followers also seemed to consider themselves superior to those who worshipped pagan gods. Yet it was not the Jewish religion as religion that gave rise to anti-Semitism in the Greek world, but rather the obligations of that religion, for it compelled the Jew to remain aloof from his neighbors.[55,56] For example, the orthodox Jew could not take part in the social life of the city, since this centered around recognition of the city's patron gods. This meant that the Greek theater and the festivals that formed an important and cherished part of Greek life could not be attended by the Jew. In addition, the revered Hellenistic institution, the gymnasium,

---

55. See S. Davis, *Race Relations in Ancient Egypt* (London: Methuen Co., 1951), p. 88.
56. Tarn, *Hell. Civil.,* p. 220 suggested that the origin of the ill-feeling that the Greeks felt toward the Jews was a result of the exemption the Jew enjoyed from taking cases involving non-Jews to Greek courts. But this is unlikely, since Jews and Greeks had few legal encounters with each other. Note also the papyrus previously cited that indicates that the Jews themselves often appealed to Greek rather than Jewish courts.

was anathema because the Jew regarded display of the body as immoral and heathen.

Participation in the social life of the city, especially the gymnasium, was an unavoidable antecedent to political life, but though the Jews aspired to politics, they were unwilling to take part in Greek society. Yet during the Roman period they precipitated numerous outbreaks against themselves by insisting that they be treated as citizens and residents of their cities and by demanding the same privileges as were enjoyed by the Greeks, even though they refused to participate in the social life of the Greek community.

These two peoples could not comprehend the resentment each felt toward the other—the Greek could not understand the exclusiveness and unsociableness of the Jews, their religious morality, or the refusal of Yahweh to recognize their gods; for his part, the Jew could not understand why the Greek refused to treat him as an equal or allow him a share in the political life of the city.

As long as there was no attempt to infringe upon the rights of citizenship, the Greeks were willing to tolerate Jewish unsociableness. Although they were resentful that the Jewish god regarded their own gods with contempt, they could just as easily reverse this feeling. But when the Jews eventually did try to maneuver their way into the long-cherished responsibilities of citizenship, Greek resentment and contempt finally turned to hatred.

In the latter half of the Ptolemaic period the social conflict between Jew and Greek within the cities (and especially in Alexandria) raised tempers almost beyond control. However, during this era anti-Semitism only took a characteristic literary form in which the Jew became a target for derision and contempt. Defamatory writings about the Jews came to be widely circulated in the ancient world and as a result, whenever the Jew traveled to a new location, he found that the description given him by his Greek and Egyptian enemies had preceeded him.

Political Contributions to Anti-Semitic Feelings in Egypt

It was a singular characteristic of the Diaspora Jew that he uncategorically supported whichever ruling power was able to maintain supreme power. Thus, whenever there was a local rebellion, the Jew could be counted on to come to the aid of the ruling sovereign. The monarchies were aware of their loyalty and in Egypt the Jews were particularly singled out and given positions of responsibility in the military and the government.[57] But it was because of their loyalty that the Jews often suffered the anger of the Greeks and Egyptians, especially following the rule of Ptolemy VI Philometor (181-145 B.C.), when politics in Egypt became unsettled and rebellion became an almost common occurrence.

When Philometer came to the throne, he was five years old and as a consequence the government of Egypt was in the hands of the young king's courtiers until he was old enough to assume the supreme powers himself. It was unfortunate that so young a boy was made king since the unsettled state of affairs meant that the country was internally weak and open to outside threat. During this period, for instance, Egypt was invaded twice by Antiochus IV and only Roman intervention saved it from imminent overthrow.[58]

Internally the country was also in grave difficulty—Eurgetes II, Philometer's brother, attempted to usurp the throne and after Philometer's death there was the possibility of all-out civil war over the succession between Cleopatra II, Philometer's wife, and Eurgetes, his brother. There was no reason for either side to count on the Egyptians—they were not likely to support either of the Greek kings and they only hoped that the two would kill each other off so that they might get a share in whatever was left over. Cleopatra also could not count

---

57. We have already drawn attention to the numerous Jews who were enrolled in the Ptolemaic army and bureaucracy.
58. The Syrians were even able to conquer and hold on to some areas in the Egyptian realm.

on the Greeks, particularly in Alexandria, because they supported Eurgetes. However, there was another foreign group in Egypt that did have some numerical strength and did have fighting ability—the Jews. Although they were not as strong as either the Egyptians or the Greeks, they were united and could be counted on to come to the support of whichever king promised them a strong and stable government. During Philometer's life, a vast immigration of Jews had entered Egypt under the leadership of Onias, an important Jewish military leader.[59] Philometer allowed these Jews to form a distinctive military colony *(katoika)* and gave them land in the nome of Heliopolis, which was subsequently renamed the "Land of Onias."[60] In return the Jews promised to lend their support to Philometer should he ever need their services.

During Philometer's reign, the Jews were not called upon, but after his death (145 B. C.) when Eurgetes II, backed by the Alexandrians, made his move against Cleopatra II, the queen sent to Onias for his support. The Jews rallied and entered the capital, Onias at the head of a large Jewish force, and the rebellion in Alexandria was crushed.[61] Josephus maintained that on account of their services, Cleopatra came to regard the Jews so highly that she entrusted the whole of her kingdom to two Jewish generals, Onias and Dositheus.[62]

However, Onias' loyalty ultimately resulted in misfortune for the Jews when Eurgetes eventually overthrew Cleopatra and thereby became the new king (145-116 B.C.). One of his first official acts was to punish all those who had opposed him and those Jews who had played an important military role under Onias were singled out for retribution.[63]

59. *Ant.*, 13.3.1; *Wars.*, 1.1.1. This was either Onias III or IV. In *Wars*, he is the III but in *Ant.*, the IV (cf.Tcher., *Hell. Civil.*, p. 276-80).
60. The *katoika* was about 20 miles from Memphis.
61. *C.Ap.* 2.5.
62. *Ibid.*
63. *The Third Book of the Maccabees,* which apparently refers to the time of Ptolemy IV Philopator, more probably dates from the time of Ptolemy Eurgetes (C. W. Emmet in R. H. Charles). We have already made some mention of the book in reference to the history of Palestine (see above). At that time it was pointed out that the author believed that Ptolemy Philopator had visited Jerusalem and had

Fortunately for the Jews, Eurgetes and Cleopatra became re-conciled and with their marriage came the relaxation of the measures Eurgetes had taken against the Jews.[64] In fact, the political conditions that followed Eurgetes' ascendance to the throne were of such a nature that Eurgetes himself was forced to rely on the Jews as an important ally in his effort to deal with the potential threats to his suzerainty.[65] Those threats broke out in open hostility after his death (116 B.C.).

Strangely, Cleopatra was again the victim of a political movement to overthrow her, but this time her rival was her

attempted to enter the Temple but was suddenly paralyzed and had to be carried back by his men. However, the king swore vengeance on the Jews, and it is at this point that the second story in the book begins.

The fact that III Maccabees is composed of two stories has been recognized for some time (cf. Emmet.). The account regarding Ptolemy Philopator comprises the first story; that dealing with the persecution of the Jews relates to the second. This latter story was directed at the state of affairs during the time of Eurgetes, but was placed in the time of Philopator so that it would seem to be a continuation of the king's plan for vengeance.

The author relates that on Philopator's return, he attempted to carry out a census of all Egyptian Jews so as to enslave them, but then changed his mind and decided to exterminate them. Accordingly he ordered the Jews to be brought to the Hippodrome in Alexandria where they were to be trampled by drunken elephants. However, the plan miscarried after the Jewish god intervened, in response to the prayers of his devoted worshippers, and he caused the elephants to turn on the king's own soldiers, thereby averting a great disaster. After hearing of the miracle, the king repented and allowed the Jews to return to their homes. Such was the narrative.

Emmet placed the story at the time of Eurgetes, thus making it contemporary with that king's alleged persecution of the Jews. E. Schürer, *History of the Jews,* however, placed it in the early first century A.D., while H. Ewald, *History of the Jews,* believed it was written during the time of the emperor, Gaius. Although the actual date of its composition is not certain, Emmet's arguments seem the most cogent (cf. also V. Tcherikower, "The Third Book of Maccabees As A Historical Source of Augustus' Time," *Scripta Hierosolymitana* Vol. III (1961): p. 1-26).

The work was apparently written by an orthodox Jew whose purpose was to encourage his coreligionists to remain faithful to their religion and their God. If they did so, he in return would deliver them from all the difficulties and hardships that they were presently suffering or those that they would shortly suffer. It is thus a work very much like the *Book of Esther.*

However, even though the story is fabulous in its imagination, we may agree with Tcherikower *(Hell. Civil.,* p. 274) that there probably is some degree of historicity in the account as far as Ptolemy Eurgetes II's punishment of the Jews is concerned, but the details have been distorted beyond recovery.

64. The deliverance of the Jews at this time was subsequently celebrated as an annual festival (*C.Ap.,* 2.5).
65. See Tcher. and Fuks., *C.J.P.* p. 23.

son, Ptolemy IX Lathyrus. The latter had raised a rebellion in Alexandria against his mother, but this attempt proved abortive and Lathyrus was compelled to withdraw to Cyprus. Sensing that she might be able to put down the rebellion once and for all, Cleopatra sent an army to destroy her son, but instead her generals deserted and went over to Lathyrus.[66] The Jews, however, remained faithful and took a leading part in the civil war, thereby inviting the wrath of those who supported Lathyrus in Alexandria. When Lathyrus was finally able to put himself into power (88 B.C.) there was a not unexpected hunt for those Jews who had opposed him[67] so that here again the political alliance made by the Jews proved to have dangerous ramifications.

By 58 B.C. it may have been apparent that the strength and direction of the central government was about to crumble once and for all. The new power filling the vacuum in the Near East was Rome. Pompey had taken over Palestine in 63 B.C. and it was apparent that Rome had not yet ceased its aggrandizement policy. Thus, when Gabinus, the proconsul of Syria, approached Egypt (55 B.C.) to interfere in the complicated internal problems of the Empire, the Jews who were guarding the strategic entrance at Pelusium, did not challenge his advance and the Romans passed without incident.[68] Following the Roman invasion of Egypt, however, the Jews were regarded as traitors by those who opposed Roman intervention, even though the Romans were supporting the claims of one of the Ptolemies.[69]

Seven years later (48 B.C.) the pro-Roman sentiments of the Jews were again revealed when they came to the aid of Julius Caesar, who was beseiged in Alexandria by an Egyptian army. Caesar was having difficulty holding out against his enemies and seemed to be in desperate need of outside help. Fortu-

66. *Ant.*, 13.10.4.
67. See Tcher. and Fuks., *C.J.P.* p. 25, note 63.
68. *Ant.*, 14.6.2.
69. This was Ptol. XIII Auletes.

nately, Antipater, an influential Palestinian Jew,[70] decided to aid him with armed support. Once again a foreign army approached the Jews who were defending Egypt's borders—this time in the "Land of Onias," midway between Pelusium and Memphis. The Jews at first refused to allow them passage, but after some cogent arguments from Antipater, they changed their minds and even accompanied him in his rescue of the besieged Romans.

No doubt the Jews were again regarded as traitors because of their pro-Roman action, but the accusation was unjust since Egypt was not yet a Roman province, nor one about to be incorporated into the Empire at that time. The Jews were merely backing that Ptolemaic claimant, whom they felt had the greatest chance of emerging as the supreme ruler. The fact that the Romans were in league with Ptolemy XIII Auletes and Cleopatra VI, only lent unqualified prestige to the aspirations of these monarchs and made their cause the more likely to succeed. The Jews were merely playing the roles of *realpolitiks,* not traitors, when they sided with those individuals backed by the Romans.

But to the Greek citizens of Egypt and especially Alexandria, the Jews had betrayed the country. The Alexandrians had uncategorically opposed the later Ptolemaic kings because of their growing tendency to curb the city's political aspirations. They were now incensed at the Jews for allowing the Romans to interfere in Egyptian politics because it was certain that the Romans were extending their conquests in the Near East, and while Rome was not as yet proposing to take over Egypt, it had economic aspirations as far as Egypt's fabulous wealth was concerned. To the Alexandrian, political curtailment was a serious affair, one that involved the emotional makeup of the citizen body. If the Greeks now had to worry about an economic threat also, it would take very little imagination to realize the bitterness these people would feel toward the Ro-

---

70. Antipater was actually an Idumean. We will have much more to say about him when we relate the political situation in Palestine during these times.

mans and all their allies, especially the Jews, whom they had come to hate for many other reasons besides their apparent allegiance to their enemies.

Race relations between the two peoples degenerated with each new monarch, but the violent forms of racial hatred had no ancient precedent and so it was necessary for such precedents to be established. First, however, came the literary attacks aimed at ridiculing and disparaging the Jews and their religion.

Hate Literature in Early Alexandria

The earliest forms of anti-semitic literature fall into two main classes: that which is inspired by hatred of the Jews and tends to be racial in character, and that which deals with the Jews as an unusual people with strange and peculiar customs.

Following the ambiguous accounts that held that the Jews were a nation of philosophers who were possibly descended from the philosophers of India,[71] the Greeks began to write more critically of these odd people. The first history of the Jews was published by Hecataeus of Abdera during the reign of Ptolemy I and contained in some measure a treatise on Jewish origins. According to Hecataeus, a pestilence broke out in Egypt during one of the times when there were a great many foreigners in the country. The Egyptians attributed their misfortune to the wrath of their gods, who were angered because of the strange deities that these foreigners had brought with them into Egypt. The only solution was to drive these people out of Egypt and this was promptly done. The most distinguished of these foreigners, Hecataeus claimed, migrated to Greece. The others entered the country later called Judea, and thereafter became the Jewish nation.

These details were subsequently embellished by an Egyptian

---

71. Reinach, nos. 5, 7.

priest named Manetho, whose claim to history must be as the father of anti-Semitic literature. Manetho wrote that while he was examining the sacred annals in preparation for a history he was planning, he came upon a legend relating that the Jews were identified with some lepers who had been driven out of Egypt by king Amenophis. These lepers, along with other diseased peoples and Egyptian criminals, had been living in the town of Avaris under a priest called Osarseph (Joseph),[72] who passed on to them several laws that they still keep. These were to worship neither the gods (of the Egyptians), nor to abstain from any animals considered sacred in Egypt, but to sacrifice and slay them, nor to intermarry with any people but their own.

Osarseph also ordered them to strengthen the walls of Avaris so that he could make war against Amenophis. At the same time he sent envoys to Jerusalem to ask the Hyksos for aid against the Egyptians. This united force was able to send the Egyptians into exile in Ethiopia for three years, but after this period Amenophis was able to gather a large army, which he used to drive his enemies out of Egypt toward the Syrian border.[73]

The origin of this account is not difficult to discover. Every Passover when the Jewish version of the Exodus was retold, the Egyptians were the victims of a humiliating story. When the Septuagint was finally published, the degrading story could be read by the whole Greek population. It is no wonder that the Egyptian felt a need to answer these abuses, and so Egyptian pride was reasserted by claiming that the Jews were no better than lepers and criminals, and that they had been driven out of the country by the king.[74]

While the Exodus story may (or may not) have infuriated the Egyptians, it was not the sole cause of resentment. We

72. The name was later changed to Moses.
73. Reinach, 10.
74. Although Manetho's narrative is generally regarded as a fiction (as is the Jewish version) it does contain some historical information that serves as a focal point for his propagandistic story.

have already pointed out that the socio-political atmosphere of Egyptian life contributed to the ill-feelings felt toward the Jews, but in the literary attacks it was generally their religion and their peculiar customs that were centered out for derision.

The most conspicuous difference between the Jewish religion and all the other religions of the known world was that the Jews worshipped a single god who was invisible. To the ancient world, the fact that the Jews rejected the known visible gods meant that they were atheists. But even though they were given such a label, it was simply beyond comprehension that this was the true nature of their religion and attempts were made to uncover the "real" form of their god. As a result, a myth arose out of the many stories that must have been current, that within the Temple of Jerusalem was the head of an ass, made of gold, which was worshipped in secret by the Jews. The story was first recorded by Manaseas of Patara, who related that the ass's head was stolen by a man who had secretly entered the Temple.[75] Variants of this story were later embroidered so that the man in question became Antiochus IV,

Giles, p. 15, maintained that it was not even Manetho's main purpose to counteract the Jewish exodus story, which he felt the Egyptians regarded as a harmless myth. The real purpose was to explain the departure of these people from Egypt and Manetho did so by claiming that leprosy, a not-uncommon Egyptian disease, originated with the captive Israelites. This disease was known to have reached almost epidemic proportions and may have been prevalent at the time that the Jews were living in Egypt, hence, it was only a short jump of the embittered imagination to trace its origin to them.

It is also possible that the real cause of resentment between the Egyptians and the Jews stemmed from the association of the Jews with the Hyksos, who had invaded the country and had imposed their domination for approximately one hundred years (ca. 1680-1580). Meek, p. 17ff., concluded that the Hebrews played a significant part in the Hyksos conquest of Egypt and that the Joseph story is to be placed in this context. Moreover the city of Avaris, which Manetho claims was the stronghold of Osarseph, was in fact the ancient Egyptian capital of the Hyksos. Therefore, it is possible that the real source of resentment that the Egyptian felt toward the Jew was a result of the intimate association that the Jews had with the hated conquerors of Egypt. Moreover, the humiliation that the Egyptian felt at hearing the Passover story was not a result of the mythical nature of that narrative but of the remembrance of a time when his country was ruled by a hated foreign power.

75. Reinach, no. 19.

and the statue made of gold was a figure of Moses holding a book and riding on an ass.[76,77]

A somewhat related myth that centered on the Temple cult, held that the Jews practiced ritual murder. This accusation was first leveled at the Jews by Damocritus, who wrote that every seventh year the Jews seized a stranger and dragged him into the Temple where they sacrificed him and cut his flesh into small pieces.[78] This same story was retold by Apion, who placed one such incident in the reign of Antiochus IV. According to Apion's version, when Antiochus entered the Temple in Jerusalem, he found a man lying on a bed in front of which was a table covered with food. As soon as the man recognized the king, he threw himself at his feet and begged for liberty. The king demanded to know what this man was talking about and he was told the following story: The man was a Greek traveler who had been passing through the country when he was suddenly accosted by some strangers and brought to the Temple. There he was shut in a room and was not permitted to see anyone, but was well taken care of and was especially well fed. At first he had been pleased with the treatment, but soon he began to worry and finally he was able to learn from one of began to worry and finally he was able to learn from one of the servants who brought food to him that it was a Jewish custom to seize a Greek traveler and to fatten him for a year, after which the Jews sacrificed him and ate his entrails. Apion added that while they did this they prayed to their god that he grant ill luck to all strangers, especially Greeks.[79]

Some scholars[80] have accepted the explanation that this first

---

76. Reinach, nos. 25, 60, 63.
77. The basis of this story is rather difficult to uncover. Tcher., *Hell. Civil.,* pp. 365-66 proposed that this was an early attempt to defame the Jews by claiming that they in fact did worship a known god and this god was none other than the god of evil, Typhon, whose symbol was an ass.
78. Reinach, 63.
79. Josephus' apologetic rebuttal to this story was that Apion was a flagrant liar since it was impossible for the entrails of one man to feed the entire Jewish nation! (*C. A.P.*, 2-8).
80. J. Trachtenberg, *The Devil and the Jews* (New Haven: Yale University Press, 1943), p. 126.

accusation of ritual murder was merely a piece of Hellenistic propaganda created in order to excuse Antiochus' profanation of the Jewish sanctuary. To the Hellenistic world, any sacrilege against a holy place, Jewish or otherwise, was an anathema that could not be overlooked. Therefore, it was felt necessary by the king or his advisors, to offer some explanation for the nefarious deed.

A more parsimonious explanation is that the entire story was merely a fanciful tale created in order to cast disfavor on the Jews by making them guilty of misoxenia and by suggesting that they took an active role in pursuing a policy of hatred toward mankind.[81]

Charges of inhospitality, hatred of mankind, self-segregation etc. were frequently brought against the Jews. To the citizen of the Hellenic world, hospitality to strangers was an accepted and practiced precept; one would invite guests to eat at one's table and one expected that such an invitation would be reciprocated. Moreover, it was expected that those living in one's city would take part in the festivals and customs of that city and especially in the cult of the patron god. The Jews, of course, could not participate in any of these things because their religion and dietary laws prohibited them from such practices. To the Greek, this refusal to take part in Hellenic life was an insult that he could only interpret as being due to the Jew's hatred for mankind or his desire to keep aloof from non-Jews.

These bitter feelings led to accusations of misoxenia by many authors,[82] particularly Apion, who wrote that the Jews "swore by God, the maker of heaven and earth and sea, to bear no good will to any foreigner, and particularly to none of the Greeks."[83] Poseidonius[84] even claimed that because of their attitude, Antiochus Sidetes had been advised to destroy the entire Jewish nation during his attack on Jerusalem.

81. Tcher., *Hell. Civil.*, p. 367.
82. Reinach, nos. 27, 59, 60, 63.
83. *Ibid.*, no. 63.
84. *Ibid.*, no. 25.

Although these examples do not by any means exhaust the anti-Semitic literature of this period, they are representative of the bitterness and misunderstanding that became focussed on the Jewish community in Alexandria. However, as long as the ill will was confined to pen and paper, the Jewish community was not deeply concerned with these accusations. Hurt and humiliated though he might be, the Jew was still free to go where he wished without fear or danger merely for the fact that he was a Jew. Soon enough, however, pen turned to sword as the anti-Semitism of the Roman period turned the ink of the Ptolemaic era into blood.

3

The Jews in the Seleucid Empire

The Confrontation with Hellenism

ANTIOCHUS III's victory did not initiate any Hellenistic movement in Judea since Hellenization had long preceded the takeover by the Seleucid monarchy. Antiochus, in fact, seemed content to allow the Jews to pursue their own cultural destinies and even went so far as to promise the Jewish community that he would safeguard whatever aspects of Judaism the Jews felt might be threatened.

According to a document preserved by Josephus,[1] the king granted the Jews the right to live according to their ancestral laws. While the actual meaning of this fiat is not known, it probably referred to those religious and social customs, written and unwritten, that were an intregral part of second-century Judaism. Although such practices posed a definite barrier to cultural unification in the Seleucid empire, the fact that the king consented to these and other more detailed privileges[2] showed that he was prepared to offer the military and adminis-

1. *Ant.*, 12.3.3.
2. See R. Marcus' translation of the Antiquities, vol. 7, appendix D, for a discussion of the authenticity of these documents.

trative assistance of the Syrian empire against any acknowledged threat to Judaism.[3]

But though Antiochus did not pursue a policy of Hellenization in Judea, some of the Jews, for example the High Priest and wealthy aristocratic families such as the Tobiads, actively endorsed the movement. Under High Priest Simon the Just, the upper classes flourished and met no opposition in Jerusalem to their adoption of Greek culture. However, following the death of Simon, the new High Priest, Onias III, began to cause difficulties since his sympathies lay with the Ptolemies and Hyrcanus, the ostracized younger brother of the Tobiads. Prior to Antiochus III's victory over the Egyptians, the Tobiads had split into pro-Syrian and pro-Egyptian factions, but this was basically a family dispute. When the High Priest Onias III also began to lean toward the Egyptians, political affairs became very disrupted and civil war among the Jewish ruling classes became imminent.

The Tobiads took the initiative. At first they invited the Syrian governor to storm the Jewish Temple and steal the monies that the pro-Egyptians, and Hyrcanus in particular, had deposited there.[4] When this measure failed, the Tobiads began to spread rumors that Onias was plotting a coup to overthrow the Syrians in Judea.[5] So serious did the situation become that Onias felt that the only way to avert civil war was to assure the Syrian king that the rumors had no validity and he left Jerusalem to confront Antiochus.

The High Priest's departure gave his enemies a chance to usurp his authority; Onias was deposed by the Tobiads and replaced by his more sympathetic and obedient brother, Joshua (Jason). But despite the *de facto* coup, the office still lacked *de jure* authority and to consolidate his position, Jason also went to talk with the king.[6] The new monarch, Antiochus

3. Tcherikower, *Hell. Civil.*, p. 84.
4. *II Mac.*, 3.3.6-8.
5. *II Mac.*, 3.4.1.
6. *II Mac.*, 3.4.5.

IV—a zealous proponent of Hellenism—heard from both men, but a few well-placed bribes made sure that he listened only to Jason.

With all opposition removed, the Tobiads and their figurehead, Jason, began the Greek reforms that were to change Jerusalem from a Jewish to a Hellenistic center. Permission to build a gymnasium and ephebion was granted, Grecian statues were erected on Temple grounds, naked Jews participated in gymnastic games, and the city itself was changed into a *polis* with the name of Antioch[7] (175 B.C.).

Apparently the new reforms had little effect on the common people. Although excluded from the new citizen body and appalled by the physical displays of the young men in the gymnasium, the Jews of the lower class sensed very little actual change. (When the author of *II Maccabees* wrote that Jason abolished the ancestral laws,[8] he did not mean the Mosaic Law, but only some of those intangible aspects of Judaism that had been orally transmitted through the generations and thus came under the rubric of tradition.)

Nevertheless, the Tobiads began to feel that the changes were too slow. They wanted a more extreme form of Hellenism, and when Jason refused to comply completely with their demands, they replaced him with Menelaus, a man who could be counted on to follow orders. The moderates, however, refused to acknowledge the new High Priest and civil war broke out. Because they had Syrian support, behind them, the Tobiads emerged victorious, and in return for the aid that they had received from Antiochus IV, they sent several gold vessels from the Temple treasury to the king.

This gift infuriated the Jewish masses. Up until this time they had generally remained aloof from the internal squabbling, but now they began to realize that the Temple itself was being used as the private coffers of the pro-Hellenists. Whereas the Temple treasury had previously been the property of all Jews and was ostensibly the repository for the wealth of

7. *II Mac.*, 3.4.10. See also p. 59.
8. *II Mac.*, 3.4.11

all Israel, now it was being taken over for the personal and private advancement of a small minority of men who were actively seeking to replace Judaism with a heathen culture. The people rebelled, but leaderless and powerless, their rebellion achieved nothing.[9] However, soon afterward, a leader did emerge among the Jewish masses and subsequently opposition to the Hellenistic movement took a more serious turn.

The Hasmonean Era

The Maccabbean crisis is too well known to describe it in any detail, and therefore in the following discussion we will deal only with those details of the rebellion and subsequent events that seem to have some bearing on the main theme of this study.

Any discussion dealing with anti-Semitism during this period cannot escape the stark reality that in the persecution of Antiochus IV, the Jewish people encountered the first official attempt to exterminate their way of life (but not the Jews as a people). The various hypotheses dealing with Antiochus' motives have been dealt with quite ably by Tcherikower[10] and what follows is only a brief summary of his work on the subject.

One opinion of Antiochus IV was that he was a madman[11] and that his motives for eradicating Judaism were a result of some erratic whim of his personality. A more likely hypothesis holds that he was so devoted to Hellenism and its propagation that he felt that the only way to meet the resistance of the Jews in this area was to exterminate those who refused apostasy. A corollary to this opinion is the belief that Antiochus may have been concerned about the security of his empire, and by unify-

9. *II Mac.*, 3.4.39-42.
10. *Hell. Civil.*, p. 175-86.
11. His name was popularly changed from Antiochus *Epiphanes* (god manifest) to *Epimanes* (madman).

ing it as one cultural mass he hoped to consolidate it politically as well as culturally. A final hypothesis is that Antiochus was motivated by true anti-religious zeal. This latter theory, although attractive to those who seek anti-Semitic actions in anything adverse to the Jews, is almost totally unacceptable since in the Hellenistic age all beliefs and all deities were openly tolerated. It was not until the monotheistic religions gained ground that religious persecutions became fashionable.

Each of these hypotheses has some historical support and each is open to criticism.[12] The essential point is that a war of extermination was launched against Judaism in Palestine——circumcision, observance of the Sabbath and religious holidays, possession of holy books, etc. were all forbidden under penalty of death. The Temple was converted to a pagan shrine and Jerusalem was repopulated with numerous Gentile inhabitants and a new Greek *cleruchy*.[13]

However, the attempt to enforce these edicts met with more than passive resistance. Inspired by the belief that loyalty to their religion and their god would insure their success, the Jews fought desperately and often victoriously against several Syrian armies, until finally the 'foreigners' were driven out of Jerusalem and Judaism was reestablished in the city. It was also during this time that the charismatic nature of the rebellion's leader, Judah Maccabee, and the members of his family, the Hasmoneans, began subtly to pervade Jewish consciousness.

Although the struggle for religious freedom dominates the rebellion, one cannot fail to consider the socio-political situation in Syria and Palestine at the time, especially as it relates to Jewish-Gentile relations. While the Jewish rebellion may initially have been a resistance movement, with no apparent signs of nationalism, it is noteworthy that the Gentile populations of Palestine reacted rather quickly to the Syrian call for aid. Under Apollonius, the first army to march on Jerusalem

12. *Hell. Civil.*, p. 175-86.
13. *I Mac.*, I.34; I.38.

was composed of various peoples besides Syrians. This was also true of Nicanor's army, which contained "troops of all nationalities."[14] Judging from the statements in the *Books of the Maccabees,* it appears that the Syrian army during this crisis was composed mainly of volunteers. Furthermore, the fact that Antiochus had to guarantee his forces a year's pay in advance[15] indicates that it was difficult for the king to hold regular soldiers in service for any length of time, and therefore the king had to depend on untrained volunteers for a significant part of his army.

The motives for these enlistments and for the persecution of the Jews in many Greek cities[16] is not difficult to uncover. In the towns of Palestine, a growing social problem had been created by the expansion of the Jews into the cities of the Diaspora. These sites were already densely populated and when the Jews moved in, they became uncomfortably overcrowded. Needless to say, arguments between Greeks and Jews broke out over property rights as land became increasingly scarce and valuable. For those who were economically minded, the Syrian invasion was a golden opportunity to take over Jewish property and homes.[17] Yet the main difficulty probably rested in the fact that these Jews maintained their own social organization and refused to be assimilated. When the Jewish movement showed signs of nationalism, the Gentiles in the various communities began to fear that the Jewish residents might invite Jewish armies to come and conquer these cities and to include them in their expanding empire.[18] In such situations, fear led to attack and counterattack[19] until many cities either destroyed their Jewish residents or were destroyed by them with the help of the new Jewish army. With regard to the Syrian army, the authors of *I* and *II Maccabees* inform us that the invaders were followed by numerous slave

14. *II Mac.,* 8.9.
15. *I Mac.,* 3.28.
16. *I Mac.,* 3.37; *II Mac.,* 11.3.
17. *I Mac.,* 3.37; *II Mac.,* 11.3.
18. Cf. *Ant.,* 12.8.1.
19. *I Mac.,* 3.41; *II Mac.,* 8.11.

dealers.[20] These retinues accompanied an army only when it was felt that victory was inevitable, and such overconfidence could only lead to disaster in an untrained volunteer army.

Owing to the part played by Judah and his brothers, it is not very surprising that the Hasmonean house became the rulers of the emerging Jewish state. Johnathan, Judah's brother, was subsequently appointed High Priest[21] and the position afterward became hereditary, as did the office of king when it was reestablished in 105 B.C. after Judah Aristobulus appointed himself to the position.[22,23]

Under the Hasmoneans, the Jewish state was built into a powerful and independent nation. The conquests and expansion begun by Johnathan and Simon were furthered by the aggrandizement plans of John Hyrcanus as when both the Samaritans and the Idumeans were forced to submit to circumcision and the Jewish Law. Those who refused were slain without remorse.[23] a Thus the goal of Judean nationalism became territorial expansion and conversion by conquest and proselytism.

After Hyrcanus, however, internal difficulties within the emergent state began to drain the power of the Hasmoneans. The civil war that erupted between the religious and politically minded groups depleted the nation of its manhood and finally the question of kingship was given to an outside source for arbitration. But this eventually proved disastrous to the Judean state for it was none other than Pompey, the Roman general, who was called upon to settle the dispute. Once the Romans were called upon to play a part in Jewish politics, they continued to exert an influence upon Jewish affairs and Judea henceforth became nothing more than one of the Empire's vassal states.

20. *Ant.*, 13.9.1.
21. *I Mac.*, 11.57.
22. *Ant.*, 13.12.1.
23. Although the orthodox Jews, the Hasidim, accepted Johnathan as High Priest, they were not in favor of it because to them a military leader could not rightfully be a spiritual head and they turned away from the Hasmoneans.
23a. See *I Mac.*, 10.15, 12.4, 12.8; *II Mac.*, 10.17, 12.6,7,9.

The Seleucid Empire

Before dealing with the Roman-Jewish confrontation, we must briefly consider relations between the Jews and the Greeks in the Seleucid Empire. This is a rather important topic since it was a policy of Roman government to leave intact whatever social structures already existed in conquered countries. Thus the Jew's position in the Diaspora during this period remained virtually unchanged following the Roman conquest. However, it is a rather curious fact that what little is known concerning the position of the Jews during the Seleucid monarchy is largely inferred from their condition under the Romans since, as previously mentioned, few changes were introduced after the fall of the Seleucids.

Because of the paucity of information regarding the economic, social, and political life under the Seleucids as compared with the impressive material from the Ptolemaic dynasty, the description of conditions in Syria is not really adequate enough to provide an appreciation of the Jew's place among the Greeks and Syrians. However, some attempt will be made to outline the more salient features that may have affected their lives.

Following the death of Seleucis I (the founder of the empire), the Syrian state slowly fell apart as various minor states broke the bonds that tied them to the monarchy. Seleucid power rested on the efficiency of its army and whenever that failed, as in the various Parthian crises, the state diminished in size and influence. Like the Ptolemies, the Seleucids felt that the native Syrian population could not be relied upon, and it was largely relegated to the status of an inferior race while military and political security were entrusted almost solely to the Greco-Macedonian elements. Indeed, the Seleucid aim seemed to be the transference of the former Persian Empire into an isomorphistic Macedonian state copiously dotted with newly founded cities bearing Greek names and populated with Greco-Macedonian immigrants.

The capital of the empire was the city of Antioch. Here rested the offices of the king, his court and advisors, the army and the bureaucracy. Also settled in the capital were Greek and Macedonian merchants, traders, farmers, artisans, etc. along with a large number of native Syrians. The other large cities of the empire, the Apameas, Seleuceias, and Laodiceas were generally smaller replicas of Antioch bearing the same relationship to Antioch as the Greek cities of Egypt bore to Alexandria.

Immediately after the Seleucids founded a city, that city was assigned a territory that was divided into sections. Some of these were presented to the city proper in its function as a corporate body while the remainder was divided among the first settlers of the area.[24] This tended to ensure the loyalty of the settlers and troops, since desertion would have meant abandonment of their landed property.[25] Although the major division between the inhabitants was based on the free-enslaved dichotomy, the division that is of most interest involves the distinction among the free inhabitants between citizens and noncitizens. This is an important issue, because an understanding of the Jew's status would also indicate what kind of position he enjoyed and what kind of attitude developed toward him.

The Social Position of the Jews

Josephus (ca. A.D. 100), staunchly asserted that Seleucus I "granted them [the Jews] citizenship in the cities which he founded in Asia and Lower Syria and in his capital, Antioch itself, and declared them to have equal privileges with the Macedonians and Greeks who were settled in these cities. . . ." But when the Romans took over the government

24. Rostovt. i. 481.
25. A.H.M. Jones, *The Greek City From Alexander to Justinian* (Oxford: Clarendon Press, 1967), p. 8-9.

of Syria, "the Alexandrians and Antiochenes asked that the
Jews should no longer continue to have the rights of citizenship, they did not obtain their request."[26] In his polemic
against Apion, he again wrote "our Jewish residents in Antioch are called Antiochenes, having been granted rights of
citizenship by its founder Seleucus."[27] And in still a third passage he stated that following the reign of Antiochus Epiphanes,
the Syrian kings restored to the Jews all that had been taken
from them and moreover, granted them citizenship rights on an
equality with the Greeks.[28]

Modern historical criticism, however, has challenged the
veracity of Josephus' statements. Marcus[29] points out that it
was unlikely that there were enough Jews in Syria and Asia
during the time of Seleucus I to warrant such action, and after
discussing the three sources quoted above, he concludes that it
was rather unlikely that the Jews received either citizenship or
special privileges from the Seleucids before the time of Antiochus III. Tcherikower[30] asserted that there is no extant
document that confirms Jewish settlement in Syria under
Seleucus and like Marcus, maintained that before 200 B.C. it
was unlikely that the Jews of Palestine or Asia played any important part in the history of those times. As to the Jews of
Babylonia, Tcherikower claimed that Josephus was not interested in that part of the Diaspora and consequently did not
possess any quotable sources concerning the activities of these
peoples. Hence, both conclude that the Jews did not possess
the right of citizenship in the Diaspora during the Hellenistic
period.

Tarn[31] holds that the chief obstacle preventing the Jews
from being classed as citizens was the fact that full citizenship
required worship of the city's gods, which in turn meant apos-

26. *Ant.*, 12.3.1.
27. *C. Ap.*, 2.39.
28. *Wars*, 7.3.3.
29. Josephus, Loeb Library, vol. 7, appendix C.
30. *Hell. Civil.*, p. 328-29.
31. *Hell. Civil.*, p. 221.

tasy. Moreover, he claims that the Jews in a city such as Antioch or Alexandria referred to themselves as a racial community only and not as an enfranchised class. The solution to the problem of citizenship, Tarn claims, is the recognition that in the periods when the kings held power, they had the authority to grant citizenship to anyone demanding it, provided, of course, that he agreed to recognize the city's gods. (This granting of "isopolity"—"potential citizenship"—enabled one to call himself an Antiochene, an Alexandrene, etc. and to appeal to the importance of that status in an emergency.[32])

Despite the fact that reopening the question of Jewish citizenship may be tantamount to beating a dead horse, it seems relevant in this case to show such a fallen animal no mercy. While one may cite the privileges accorded to the Jews as bearing some relation to the anti-Semitic attitude of the Greek populace, it is unlikely that it can assume the importance that the question of citizenship took in the Hellenistic world.

The Greek citizen took pride in his community and zealously participated in the democratic form of government that he had stubbornly won from an obstinate oligarchy. During the Hellenistic era, democracy was firmly established as the way of life in Greek cities, and those colonies and cities that were founded by the Seleucids proved no exception. Anyone possessing citizenship, regardless of his background or present wealth, held the same political rights as any other citizen.[33] While birthright was an important *sine qua non* in the early years of democracy, this status was eventually extended to those who had made some special contribution to the city, and it also became possible for the citizens of one city to exchange their citizenship for another.[34] However, these conditions were common only to the Greek mainland. In Syria and Asia Minor, noncitizens did not have an equal chance of becoming citizens; soldiers were an exception since the king might grant them the

32. Tarn, p. 222-223.
33. Jones, p. 159.
34. *Ibid.*, p. 160.

coveted status in return for a pledge of military service, and by such means the kings established reserve military forces. However, this privilege raised problems in those Greek cities that encouraged racial exclusiveness. To the Greek inhabitants, proud of their bloodlines and jealously preserving their privileges, any attempt to introduce a new foreign element into the citizenship class would be regarded not only as a threat to the autonomy of the city, but as a personal affront. For a barbarian to be admitted to the city as an enfranchised citizen was unthinkable and yet, this is precisely what happened when the king granted various military personnel isopolity. What then was the attitude of these proud people toward the Jews whose claims to citizenship were not based on family, clan, *deme,* etc. but merely the whim of an autocratic monarch? Despite the claim that Josephus did not know enough about the Jewish situation in Babylonia, he would be familiar with the situation in Syria since this area was probably an important source of immigration in Asia Minor.[35] The loyalty of the Jews to the reigning monarch has already been mentioned in connection with Egyptian politics.[36] This seems to have also been the case in the Seleucid empire, for Josephus informs us that Antiochus III settled 2,000 Jewish families in Lydia and Phygia in order to crush the possibilities of rebellion in these areas,[37] and it is entirely within reason to suppose that the king conferred the privilege of citizenship upon these soldiers if they expressed such a desire.[38] Nevertheless, because of the requirement of apostasy it is unlikely that this occurred on any large scale.[39] The privilege, however, never seems to have been revoked[40] and quite possibly the adoption of Hellenism by more and more Jewish immigrants tended to increase the numbers of

35. K. Kraeling, *The Jewish Community at Antioch* (New Haven: Yale University Press, 1932), p. 132, 138; Tarn, p. 219.
36. See Chapter 2.
37. *Ant.,* 12.3.4.
38. V. Ehrenberg, *The Greek State* (New York: W. W. Norton, 1964), p. 40.
39. Kraeling, p. 138.
40. *Ant.,* 12.3.1.

Jews asking for citizenship. It is an interesting possibility that when Jason petitioned Antiochus IV to grant Antiochene citizenship to the Jews of Jerusalem[41] he was not asking the king to simply make Jerusalem a *polis,* but was in fact asking for the right of isopolity whereby the privileges of citizenship in Antioch would be extended to the residents of Jerusalem. This had been practiced in Greece before[42] and during the Hellenistic period.[43] Thus, the number of Jewish citizens must have been substantial, for it is unlikely that the various city-states would have moved to have the status withdrawn from only a tiny minority of their citizen body.[44] The fact that many foreigners were permitted enfranchisement, however, meant that the whole concept of citizenship was degraded,[45] and kinship, brotherhood, and solidarity weakened.[46]

But this was not all. Even within the noncitizen classes, the Jews occupied a special niche and were granted special privileges, such as the right to receive a fixed sum of money to pay for their own oil,[47] and the right to be tried in their own courts[48] once they were enrolled in a *politeuma,* the semi-autonomous socio-religious community. In addition, the community was placed under the personal protection of the monarchy, a rather unusual practice in the Hellenistic democracies. According to Ramsay,[49] the kings purposely extended various privileges to the Jews because in that way he could be sure that they would be even more loyal to the interests of the king. Moreover, as the size of the Jewish communities in the various cities increased, they would provide useful support in quelling any uprisings against the kingdom.[50] This view is not entirely without historical foundation, for on some occa-

41. *II Mac.,* 3.4.10.
42. Ehrenberg, p. 106-7.
43. Jones, p. 160.
44. *Ant.,* 12.3.1.
45. Ehrenberg, p. 40.
46. Ibid., p. 41.
47. *Ant.,* 12.3.1.
48. Tarn, p. 220.
49. *Expositor,* 1902, vol. 5, p. 21.
50. *Ibid.,* p. 22.

sions the population did revolt against the king, and the Jews were in fact called upon to support the monarchy. For example, when the revolt against Demetrius II broke out in Antioch (145 B.C.), the king appealed to the Jews, and with their aid the rebellion was violently crushed.[51] Demetrius himself appears to have been a harsh and unpopular king and his handling of the insurrection in which he murdered the wives and children of some of the rioters, confiscated their property, and burned down a section of the city, did not increase his popularity or that of the Jews who supported him.[52] But as long as the Seleucids (and later the Romans) were able to enforce their rule the populace refrained from venting their frustrations on the Jews. Once the great powers began to weaken, the tendency toward riot in the city of Antioch soon found expression in the attacks against the Jews[53] and there was no one left to whom they could turn for aid. While there were other circumstances that contributed to anti-Semitic feeling in the Seleucid Empire, these mainly came to the fore under Roman occupation.

51. *I Mac.*, 11.45-48.
52. G. Haddad, *Aspects of Social Life in Antioch in the Hellenistic Roman Period* (London: Hofner, 1949), p. 127.
53. *Ibid.*, p. 64-67.

4

The Jews in Rome: Prior to the Jewish War

THE POSITION of the Jews in the Ptolemaic and Seleucid Empires has been inferred from conditions found mainly in the capitals of Alexandria and Antioch. Rome, the third great city-state of the ancient world, eventually conquered both empires and imposed its own authority on the defeated inhabitants of these two great centers. The result of this conquest was that one system of authority now governed where previously there had been two. With this unification came a more or less uniform treatment of subject peoples, for it was a basic principle of Roman government to leave undisturbed all those customs, traditions, laws, etc. already in practice, except of course if they were anti-Roman. Hence, the prevailing legal conditions in the Diaspora following the Roman conquest did not change to any noticeable degree. A few half-hearted attempts were made by some Greek cities to eradicate Jewish privileges after the Roman takeover, but in the main, the Jews could rest assured that whatever status and privileges they had previously enjoyed would be safeguarded by the Romans. Likewise, it also became evident that any attempt to increase their status or privileges would be met with the same resistance. As long as Roman government prevailed, social positions in the various countries would be fixed.

The Mood of Rome

Whereas the Jews of Alexandria and Antioch played a secondary role in the city life of those two great centers, in Rome they constituted an important group and they often influenced the outcome of political rivalries that plagued the city-state. Before these rivalries can be discussed, however, it is first necessary to trace briefly the growth and development of the Roman Empire, for only in this manner can one comprehend Rome's treatment of the different peoples who came under its rule.

The city-state of Rome began inauspiciously enough with the merger of the Latin and Sabine peoples, ca. 600 B.C. Not content with the Palatine area around the Tiber river, the newly formed coalition pressed north and then south, eventually bringing the whole of the peninsula under its jurisdiction. The conquerors proved benign since the defeated were permitted to maintain local autonomy, and they were not required to pay any indemnity; their only obligation was to supply the Roman army with a specified number of men.

Once the peninsula had been secured, the army pushed its way into the west: Carthage, Spain, France, and then England fell to the legions. Close on the heels of the soldiers came the officials who followed the army to administer the conquered lands as decreed by the government in faraway Rome.

Rome now had a western Empire, but oddly enough there was reluctance to expand eastward into the territories of the well-established empires. Although Macedonia was taken over in 148 B.C., it was only after Rome decided to accept the donation of the kingdom of Pergamum in 133 B.C. that the advance into the east began. In 67 B.C. the Seleucid empire was conquered, followed in 30 B.C. by the Ptolemaic. Thereafter Rome was master of almost all of the known world and the city-state located on the Italian peninsula decided the fates of millions. All roads led to Rome and the roads were well trod. The final decision for almost any problem besetting humanity rested with the political body governing in Rome, but decisions often depended to a large extent on the power politics that prevailed in the city at any particular moment.

More often than not, the aristocrats and conservatives ruled the governing bodies. The common people, the plebians, were represented by an Assembly, but even though they formed the majority of the population, they had very little real power. Theoretically, the Assembly's representatives, the Tribunes, had the power to veto any final governmental decision. In practice, however, the Assembly rarely reflected the needs of the common people since the power of aristocratic patronage often stood behind the election of officials, and many of those who held the vote were actually 'clients' of some nobleman and as such were merely puppets.

Although the Senate was legally required to accept decisions passed by the Assembly, it could nearly always thwart any measure by refusing to vote funds for its implementation. Thus, through its control of the state's finances, the Senate had the equivalent of the power of the veto and more often than not, the Senate, which reflected the feelings of the aristocrats, the conservatives, and the wealthy landowners, was able to impose its will on the majority. It was only when the Assembly was firmly united behind some individual who was prepared to use force that the Senate respected the Assembly's legal prerogatives. For instance, when the Gracchian brothers introduced their land reforms, the masses were charged with a great deal of enthusiasm. But the Gracchi held no real power and consequently, the landowners, through the Senate, had little trouble in disposing of the brothers and their reforms.

It was only with the formation of the *Populares* party that the Senate's power began to decline. The *Populares* were a group of ambitious, aggressive individualists who felt that the only way for them to gain a foothold in the government was to ally themselves with the plebians. But even though such illustrious men as Marius, Pompey, and Crassus had joined their cause, it was not until Julius Caesar entered the party that the *Populares* came into real power.

Using the power he had gained through conquest and allegiances, Caesar put the Senate in a position whereby they had to accept his wishes and through him the Assembly forced its will, for Caesar soon became the spokesman for that body. The final blow came when Caesar took personal control of the Treasury for with this new development the Senate was robbed of their veto.[1] Thereafter, the government slowly changed to absolutism, in practice if not in name.

The Early Confrontation of the Jews and Romans

The Roman conquest of the Near East was not the first meeting of Jews and Romans. In 161 B.C. Judas Maccabee had sent an embassy to Rome to establish an entente between Rome and the Jewish state.[2] This pact was renewed three times, once each by Johnathan (142 B.C.),[3] Simon (139 B.C.),[4] and by John Hyrcanus I (132 B.C.).[5] For their part, the Romans enlisted the Jews as *socii* only to embarass the Syrian king, Antiochus IV, not because Rome saw the Jewish state as a formidable military power. Although most of the Jews in these delegations returned to Jerusalem, some of them appear to have remained for they were soon ordered to leave the city. According to the Roman historian Valerius Maximus,[6] who wrote his account 170 years after the actual event, the praetor, Dispalus, expelled the Chaldeans and astrologers from Rome

1. See above.
2. *I Mac.,* 8.17-32.
3. *Ant.,* 13.5.8.
4. *Ibid.,* 14.8.5; *I Mac.,* 12, 1-4.
5. *Ant.,* 13.9.2.
6. Reinach, no. 141.

because they were duping Roman citizens. Valerius claims that the Jews were also banished because they were contaminating the morals of the Romans through the worship of the Jewish god, Jupiter Sabazius.[7] Whatever the actual causes for their expulsion, it is fairly certain that there was no substantial settlement of Jews in Rome during this period. Equally important, this banishment did not establish any precedent for anti-Semitic actions by the Romans. In fact, it is very likely that

---

7. Various hypotheses have been offered in explanation of this juxtaposition of Judaism and the Sabazian cult. The most parsimonious is that a confusion arose in the minds of the Roman officials (or in that of Valerius Maximus) as to the name of the Jewish god and via the synchretistic tendencies of the ancient world the Phrygian god, Sabazius, the Bacchus (Dionysus) of Asia Minor, was identified with the Jewish god, Yahweh (Kyrios Sabaoth) through the similarity of Sabazius with Sabbath or Sabaot. (Vogelstein, *Jews in Rome* (Philadelphia: Jewish Publication Society, 1940), p. 12).

   Following from this we may deduce the explanation for the expulsion from the fact that the Romans pursued a policy that outlawed any cults that offended Roman morality. Such a cult was that of Bacchus-Dionysus-Sabazius, which had been banished in 186 B.C. on the grounds that it introduced crime and immorality into Rome. Any disturbances during the period in question would remind the Senate of previous Phrygian counterpart of Bacchus. The Romans may not have taken the time to discriminate between cultic names or practices and any resemblance to the Bacchanalians, no matter how superficial, may have been dealt with in the same manner.

   Some scholars maintain that there was a direct relationship between the Phrygian and Jewish god. Thus Gressman, "Jewish Life in Ancient Rome," *Jewish Studies in Memory of Israel Abrahams* (1927): p. 170-91, argued that the Jews of Phrygia renounced their Jewish faith for that of Sabazius and actually changed some aspect of that cult. Such a radical notion is offset by the statement of Cicero *(Pro Flacco,* 66-68) that these Jews still sent donations to the Temple in Jerusalem. It is rather unlikely that Jews who had renounced their ancestral religion would continue to send donations to the holy shrine. The possibility still exists, however, that a number of Hellenized Jews did actually participate in the cult and thereby introduced Jewish symbols and beliefs into the cult of Sabazius. For a more lengthy exposition of this view see F. Cumont, "Les mysteres De Sabazius et Le Judaisme," *Comptes-Rendus* Academie des Inscriptions et Belles-Lettres (1906): p. 63-79; and W.O.E. Oesterley, *"The Cult of Sabazius,"* in *The Labyrinth,* ed. by S. Hooke (1935). A more negative statement appears in E.R. Goodenough, *Jewish Symbols in the Graeco-Roman Period.* McClelland and Stewart Ltd., (Toronto: 1953), vol. 2, p. 45-50, especially note 2.

   It is interesting to note that the confusion between the two religions extended as long as A.D. 100 in the classical writers of that period. For example, Plutarch compared the Jewish cult to that of Bacchus with these words: "I think also that the feast of Sabbath is not wholly unconnected with the worship of Bacchus. For even now many persons call the Bacchanals, Sabboi." (Symposium, 4.6.1. in W. Giles *Heathen Records to the Jewish Scripture History* (London: Cornish, 1856), p. 98. Tacitus was more direct in equating the two: "But because their priests performed in concert with the pipe and timbrels, were crowned with ivy,

during this early period the Jews were not even distinguished from the Syrians.[8]

There is no further mention of any Jews in the city until the year 61 B.C. when Pompey, returning from a successful military campaign in the Near East, brought back numerous Jewish captives following the fall of Jerusalem (63 B.C.). This group of Jewish slaves may have formed an important addition to whatever Jews were already present in Rome, but could not have formed the original nucleus since in an impassioned speech made by Cicero in 59 B.C.,[9] the great Roman orator indicated that the Jews were numerous and occupied an influential position in the community. Such notoriety could hardly have been achieved by slaves in less than two years. A more reasonable explanation is that the Jewish slaves brought by Pompey had their freedom purchased by Jews already well established in the community.

But in Rome, the farmer, Jewish or otherwise, could not find work as a freedman since the small farms had disappeared and had been replaced by large estates that were worked by more amenable and adaptable slaves.[10] Therefore, once the Jews obtained their freedom, most of them became part of the

and a golden vine was found in the temple [see *Ant.*, 15.11.3] some have supposed that Bacchus, the conqueror of the East was the object of their [the Jews'] adoration.'' *(Hist.* 5.5 in Giles, p. 111-12).

Whatever the relationship between the two cults, the precipitating factors for the expulsion as far as the Jews are concerned is most likely tied in with the politico-religious conditions of that time. H. Leon, *The Jews of Ancient Rome* (Philadelphia: Jewish Publication Society, 1960), p. 3, suggests that the Jews being referred to were remnants of Simon's embassy who stayed in Rome and began actively proselytizing in the community. This is also the opinion of C. Roth, *Jew of Italy* (Philadelphia: Jewish Publication Society, 1946), p. 4 and S. Guterman, *Religious Toleration and Persecution in Ancient Rome* (London: Aiglon press, 1951), p. 39.

8. M. Radin, *The Jews Among the Greeks and Romans* (Philadelphia: Jewish Publication Society, 1915), p. 39.

9. *Pro Flacco*, 66-68.

10. Following the Punic Wars the economic life of Rome no longer was based on the small farm. Food was now imported from conquered lands and the competition ruined the peasant farmer. Destitute, he had no alternative but to sell out to those who offered a price. Land was bought up by speculators and large estates were formed that were worked not by these dispossessed farmers, but by the increased

Roman mob, since these liberated slaves had no skilled trades.[11]

The Religious Confrontation

Although Judaism made comparatively little impact on the Hellenistic religions, or the society and politics of Alexandria or Antioch, its influence in Rome extended beyond the plebs to many of the city's influential citizens. On more than one occasion the ruling oligarchy had the difficult problem of countermanding this influence, for Judaism plainly undermined the ancient Roman religion because it alerted the people to a new and different morality. Its greatest threat, however, was the possibility that the religion might unify the people against the prevailing political order.

Few historians deny that by the first century B.C., Roman religion held no appeal for the ordinary Roman. Veterans, small farmers, and the various skilled and unskilled laborers were all unable to find permanent gainful employment and were driven to idleness. For them, the philosophical code of the ancient religion was irrelevant. Meaningful religious experience and personal involvement no longer attended the official cults and all that remained for the uneducated masses was the spectacle.[12] For those who sought some new approach to alleviate the plight, the alternatives were either the origastic

number of slaves captured in the foreign wars. The farmer had nowhere else to go in search of work except to Rome. But Rome was not an industrial community. There was little employment available and as a result a large, restless, hungry mob was formed whose frustrations were largely placated by the social and political amusements of the arena and the Assembly.

11. The Palestinian Jews only learned new trades when they ventured into the Diaspora. J. Juster, *Les Juifs dans l'Empire Romain* (Paris: Girard, 1914), vol. 2, p. 292, claimed that when Pompey enslaved the Jews he put them to work in public maintenance projects or in commerce and industry according to their aptitudes. However, it is unlikely that they would surpass in a short time the ability of those peoples who had worked at these professions all their lives. Therefore, we may be fairly certain that if they were not employed by their sympathetic coreligionists at Rome, they were not employed at all.

12. H.H. Scullard, *From the Gracchi to Nero* (London: Methuen Co., 1965), p. 213.

rites of the mystery religions, the philosophical doctrines of Stoicism, or Judaism.

The cults of Cybele, Bacchus, Isis, etc., with their emphasis on emotional catharsis, offered little or nothing toward the moral uplift of the downtrodden society. Their attraction was mainly through the senses and passions.[13] But the excesses of emotionality and immorality of these mystery religions were carefully regulated by the more austere conservative elements and often they were forced underground.[14] Stoicism might bring some peace to the upper classes, but it did not reach the ears of the poor and destitute. The illiterate and many of the educated still felt the need for religious meaning and involvement. On the other hand, Judaism was conscientiously taught to these people and its basic philosophy was freely available to anyone who cared to attend the synagogue service. Here the Roman readily observed some of the revered characteristics of the philosophical schools of Greece, for example the reading of some passage from the Scriptures, followed by a lengthy discourse on its meaning. And missing from Judaism were the cultic excesses of the other Oriental religions. Such sobriety impressed searching minds and created respectability.[15]

In addition, the Jewish religion carried a message that there was one true god who actually cared what happened to mankind and who took an active interest in the welfare and moral good of individual men. He was not a capricious deity who played with humanity as did the ancient gods, but he was a god who rewarded justice, kindness, charity, honesty, and love. These virtues, rather than ritual acts, were the religious duties of Judaism. They bore no resemblance whatsoever to the moral precepts of the heathen religions.

What was there to fear in this new morality?

The opposition came from the upper classes: the aristocrats,

13. F. Cumont, *The Oriental Religions in Roman Paganism* (New York: Dover Publications, 1956), p. 29-35.
14 Scullard, p. 11, 213-14.
15. G.F. Moore, *Judaism in the First Three Centuries of the Christian Era* (Cambridge: Harvard University Press, 1927) vol. II, p. 324.

the nobility, the conservatives, in short, the ruling class. Entrenched in their senatorial seats or influencing those who were, such people viewed with suspicion any new religion that might arouse the masses to reconsider their plight. Besides being a religion of patriotism and chauvinism, Roman religion taught fear, and fear could be used to pacify and discourage free thought. The one great thing that the oligarchy itself feared was the emergence of a united lower class. Such unification might arise through worship of foreign deities and the ruling class was alert to the possibility. For example, Dio Cassius warned his readers with these words: "Those who introduce strange ideas about it [religion] you should both hate and punish, not only for the sake of the gods, but because such persons, by bringing in new divinities persuade many to adopt foreign principles of law from which spring up conspiracies."[16] Penalties were also suggested for those who transgressed: "Those who introduce new kinds of worship, unknown to custom or reason, and thus disturbing weaker minds [that is, the lower classes] are to be punished, if persons of rank, with deportation; if not of rank, with death".[17]

Could the doctrine of Judaism be interpreted as fostering conspiracy?

In 139 B.C. the Chaldeans and astrologers were expelled from Rome probably because of their emphasis on fatalism. According to their beliefs, nothing could save mankind from its preordained fate. Morality went unrewarded.[18] Deliberation and planning were useless since man was ruled by chance.[19] If oracles and sacrifices were useless, then why continue with

16. Dio Cass., 52.36. Polybius, 6.56 asserted that the ancient religion with its emphasis on fear of the gods and punishment in Hades was necessary in order to check the fickleness of the mob, its lawlessness and its potential violence (against those in power). In the same vein, Livy (1.19) wrote that Numa purposely put the fear of the gods over the uneducated multitude so as to check their passions. The same sentiment was expressed by Diodorus Siculus (1.2) when he said that religious fears helped men to be upright and pious.
17. Paulus, *Senten,* 5.21.2, quoted by Guterman, p. 32.
18. Cumont, p. 37.
19. *Ibid.,* p. 179-180.

such practices? Propitiation of the gods had to be accomplished by other means. For some, the alternative took the form of participation in one of the Oriental mystery religions.

Judaism also preached a type of fatalism: Roman society was corrupt and doomed to destruction, its ultimate destiny could not be averted; eventually there would be an upheaval and Rome would be destroyed. But for those who followed the precepts of Yahweh, there was the possibility of deliverance. Yahweh was the one true god and Judaism was destined to become the religion of the world.[20]

The Jewish pronouncements were initially viewed with disdain or mockery—the babbling of beggars. But a number of times Jewish prophesy seemed close to realization: During the seige of Jerusalem (63 B.C.) Pompey took it upon himself to enter the Temple—a sacrilege in Jewish eyes. When an earthquake subsequently shook Asia Minor (and possibly Rome[21]), the Jews interpreted it as a sign of their God's indignation at the pagan's indiscretion. No doubt this and other messianic rumors aroused the populace and made them receptive. It was a fertile time for proselytizing, and many converts were won. Once some kind of a commitment had been made, the convert was likely to remain a proselyte, even through the predicted disasters that brought him into the religion were not realized.[22]

The possibility of disaster having passed, the authorities turned their attention to the originators of such prophesies. In a world solidly imbued with the belief in omens, doctrines such as those that joyously awaited the fall of Rome could not be taken lightly. However, the authorities did not often resort to physical reprisals. Instead, they adopted one of two measures: either banishment (usually from the *pomerium*, the religious center of Rome) or condemnation and ridicule. Banishment or exile from Rome itself was possible only when the Senate was

20. Moore, vol. I, p. 323.
21. F. Huidekoper, *Judaism at Rome* (New York: David G. Francis, 1891), p. 143.
22. Cf. L. Festingers, *et al. When Prophecy Fails* (New York: Harper and Row, 1964, for a psychological interpretation of the motivation influencing proselytic movements.

in complete control of the political situation, and Judaism met its strongest opposition during such periods.[23] Abuses and ridicule went on no matter what the political climate.

The Jews in Early Roman Literature

In Rome, condemnation of the Jews was not penned with the acrimony and hatred that inspired the anti-Semites of Alexandria. The strange practices of Judaism only produced mockery and amusement. At worst, these practices were viewed with contempt, but never with the purpose of inciting the reader to violence.

For example, the religion was called an outright superstition, since it was a Roman tenet that those who did not worship the pagan gods were atheists—a frequent charge, often levied against those observing an unrecognized religion, was "unbelief."

The Jewish Sabbath was often singled out for comment by the Romans even though its nature was not understood. Thus, Horace related that his friend, Fuscus, once met him in the street and was anxious to tell him some news, but refrained since it was a Sabbath day.[24] The verse is enigmatic but indicates that Horace at least had some suspicion that the Jews placed special emphasis on the occasion. The passage has also been cited as substantiating the adoption of Jewish practices by Roman gentry.[25] Seneca held the Jews in contempt because of their Sabbath observance, since it meant that one-seventh of their lives was wasted in idleness.[26] Plutarch believed that the Sabbath was a time of drunkeness,[27] while Suetonius regarded

---

23. See Huidekoper.
24. *Satires*, 1.9.67-72.
25. Leon, p. 13.
26. Quoted by St. Sugustine, *De Civitate Dei* 7.11 in Giles, p. 62.
27. *Symposium*, 4.5. in Giles, p. 96.

it as a fast day,[28] as did Justin.[29] The origin of the holy day was explained in a variety of ways by the ancient historians. Some traced it to the last day of the wanderings in the desert (suggesting that some of them were conversant with Jewish history). Others explained it as a respite that they voluntarily took from their toil[30] or as a practice that had simply been passed on to them.[31] Apion, the Alexandrian anti-Semite, wrote that while the Jews were traveling from Egypt during the Exodus, they acquired buboes[32] and rested on the seventh day of their journey. Realistically, they called that day the Sabbath, because the Egyptian word for buboes was "Sabbatosis"![33]

As puzzling to the Romans as the Sabbath, was the refusal of the Jews to partake of pork and one explanation given by Roman observers was that the pig was a Jewish god and therefore singled out for divine honors.[34] Other practices, however, such as circumcision, were especially regarded by the Romans with contempt[35] because they equated circumcision with castration, a measure of public safety in Rome.

The numerous references to the Jews and their practices indicate that the Romans had fairly definite ideas about the Jewish religion, but probably they felt little resentment toward the Jews, since Rome was not a stranger to foreign peoples or odd customs. The gibes and sneers were meant for the intelligentsia, as entertainment more than anything else, and after Tacitus, anti-Jewish literature declined.

The main factor in Rome (as in all the other gentile centers of the world) creating hostility towards the Jews was not their customs, but their adamant denial of any other deity besides

28. *Octavian,* 16, in Giles, p. 89.
29. Justin, in Giles, p. 132.
30. Tacitus, *Histories,* 5,4.
31. Juvenal, *Satires,* 16.9.7 in Giles, p. 102.
32. A type of venereal disease.
33. Josephus, *Contra Apion,* 2.2.
34. Plutarch, *Sympos.,* 4.5, in Giles, p. 96; Juvenal, *Sat.,* 16.9.7 in Giles, p. 102; Petronius, in Giles, p. 91.
35. Tacitus, *Hist.,* 5,5.

Yahweh.[36] "The first thing that new converts are told is to de-
spise the gods," wrote Tacitus.[37] What Tacitus meant was that
the Jews refused to participate in the state cult (because to
them it was idolatry). They remained aloof from other groups
socially as well as religiously, because of the "implacable
hatred they harbor toward the rest of men." It was their
separatism, their apparent lack of hospitality, that Tacitus and
the other anti-Jewish critics regarded as most disconcerting.

Yes, despite the charges of "atheism," "impiety," "misanthropy," "barbarous superstition," and the condemnation of
their practices as "sinister," "shameful," "contrary to a pro-
ductive life," "rites contrary to those of all other men," "ab-
surd," and "sordid," the religion became so widespread
among the Romans, that Seneca remarked with disdain: "the
conquered have given their laws to the conquerors."[38]

Due to the fact that little was overtly required of them,
Roman women were particularly susceptible to Judaism's
lures.[39,40] Even the Senate was not immune. Around 12 B.C.[41]
a decree was even passed that before each meeting of the august body, frankinsences had to be burnt by each senator in
honor of the ancient gods.[42] The basis for the decree was the
belief that those following Judaism would have to refrain from
such practices and thus reveal themselves. Roman citizens
were warned to remain loyal to the gods of Rome. Guterman[44]
maintains that an edict even existed that forbade Roman citizens the worship, private or public, of any gods not officially
recognized by the state, but no such document has ever been
uncovered.

36. See I. Heinemann, "The Attitude of the Ancient World Towards Judaism,"
    Revue of Religion 4 (1939-1940): 385-400 for a discussion of this viewpoint.
37. *Hist.*, 5.5.
38. Reinach, no. 145.
39. Moore, vol. 1, p. 326. See also the twelfth chapter of J.S. Raisin, *Gentile Reac-
    tions to Jewish Ideals* (New York: Philosophical Library, 1953).
40. Moore, vol. 1. p. 331-32.
41. Huidekoper acknowledges Dio's date.
42. Dio Cass., 54.30.
44. Guterman, p. 30.

The Jews and the Roman Emperors

Due to their large numbers and the influence of their religion over the people of Rome, the participation of the Jews in the city of Rome was viewed with alarm by the Senate during its times of crisis.[45] But once the struggle for political supremacy was finally settled by Julius Caesar, Jewish influence in political matters became neglible. Fortunately, the Jews had supported Caesar during his rise to power and in return they were granted a number of important privileges.[46] These privileges so endeared them to Caesar that it is reported that the Jews wept openly in their sorrow for his assassination.[47]

For his part, Augustus, Julius Caesar's successor, renewed their privileges,[48] adorned their Temple in Jerusalem with costly gifts, and granted them an additional number of special favors.[49] Yet, despite this favorable treatment, there is no reason to believe that either he or Julius Caesar really endorsed the religion of Judaism itself. There is even one reference that indicates that Augustus, at least, did not wish to have his name connected with the practice of Judaism. When the emperor's grandson, Caius, purposely avoided Jerusalem in his itinerary through the religious centers of the Near East, Augustus praised him for his thoughtfulness.[50] The motive was probably due to the custom of followers of Yahweh to visit the holy city whenever they could, and by not doing so, Caius thereby demonstrated that he was not a follower of the monotheistic creed.[51] This attitude was probably common to all the emperors. Whatever privileges were granted to the Jews during this period must not be considered as being granted to the *religio,* but to the *natio,* although religion and nationality

45. Cicero., *Pro Flacco,* 66-68.
46. *Ant.,* 14.10.1-8.
47. Suetonius, *Julius,* 84.5.
48. *Ant.,* 16.6.1-7.
49. Philo, *Legatio ad Caium,* 158.
50. Suetonius, *Augustus,* 93.
51. Huidekoper, p. 175.

were closely connected. Because they had supported the victorious Ceasar as a *natio* in his Egyptian campaign,[52] and because of their status as *socii,* which they held from time of the first Maccabean embassies, they were given special consideration, at least as far as observance of their religion was concerned.

Except for the privileges that he bestowed upon the Jews, there is little to relate about Augustus as far as the Jews or Judaism are concerned. The only noteworthy occurrence was that during his reign a number of Jews achieved close political ties with important Roman personages. For instance, the Jewish king, Herod, became close friends with Asinius Pollo, a prominent Roman official.[53] As a result of this friendship, two of Herod's sons were able to mingle with other influential citizens in Rome.[54] Four of his other sons also spent some time in Rome[55] but their presence had very little effect on the activities of the city's Jewish community. For example, when two of Herod's sons, Alexander and Aristobulus, were murdered, some impersonator claiming to be Alexander was readily accepted as the real son,[56] indicating that the ordinary Jews rarely caught even a glimpse of the more prominent Jews.

Under Augustus' successor, Tiberius, the good fortune that the Jews had enjoyed for a number of years disappeared. Alarmed at the large number of proselytes the Jews were making, the emperor banished all Jewish converts from the city (A.D. 19). Tacitus writes that 4,000 of these proselytes to Judaism were sent to Sardinia, and all the others observing the religion were ordered to leave the Italian peninsula.[57] The banishment is also referred to by Suetonius.[58] Since the prac-

---

52. See ch. 2.
53. L.A. Feldman, "Asinius Pollio and his Jewish Interests," *Transactions of the American Philological Association* 84 (1953): 73-80.
54. *Ant.,* 15.10.1.
55. *Ant.,* 16.3.3; 17.3.2; 17.13.3.
56. *Ant.,* 17.12.1.
57. *Annals,* 2.85.4.
58. *Tiberius,* 36.

tice of Judaism by Jews was not a crime, there is no reason to believe that the Jews were also ordered out of the city.[59]

The laws forbidding anyone to sacrifice in public or in private to a foreign god were meant to apply solely to Roman citizens.[60] The only exception was in the case of citizens who were of Jewish descent.[61] Nevertheless, the only way that these non-Jewish-born citizens could be exiled was through special enactments that superceded traditional legal practices. Such a situation arose in 186 B.C., when the Senate issued a *senatus consulatum* that apparently authorized the consuls to expel the Baccanalians on the grounds that they were corrupting Roman religion and morals.[62] The matter was so urgent that the Assembly was not even consulted,[63] even though the procedure was illegal.[64] Precedents for such harsh steps were readily found, however, in the statements of previous officials that have been preserved by Livy.[65]

The remainder of Tiberius' reign was uneventful for the Jews, except for the fact that Agrippa, the grandson of Herod, was imprisoned for a short time.[66] Under Gaius Caligula, who followed Tiberius, the Jews of Rome suffered no reverses although in the Diaspora their coreligionists fared far worse.[67] Claudius, who succeeded Gaius, also seemed to have left the Jews alone, and except for Suetonius' enigmatic sentence: "Iudaeos impulsore Chresto assidue tumultuantis Roma expulis,"[68] conditions remained unchanged for them.[60]

59. F.L. Abel, "Were the Jews Banished From Rome in 19 A.D.?" *R.E.J.* 127 (1968): 275-79.
60. Guterman, ch. 2.
61. Juster, vol. I, p. 245.
62. Livy, 39.8.
63. *Ibid.*, 39.17.
64. P.M. Schizas, *Offences Against the State in Roman Law* (London: Univ. of London Press, 1926).
65. Livy, 4.30; 25.1; 39.16.
66. *Ant.*, 18.6.6.
67. See ch. 5.
68. *Claudius*, 25.4. For an extensive bibliography on the word *Chrestus* referring to Christ, see references cited by Leon, p. 23-27.
69. Dio Cassius (60.6.6) reported that Claudius prohibited the Jews from holding meetings during the disturbance caused by Chrestus. The author of *Acts* (18.2),

In A.D. 63 a number of earthquakes shook southern Italy and in A.D. 64 a fire almost gutted Rome. One year later, rebellion broke out in Judea and the first Roman attacks were repulsed. It seemed that the vague messianic prophesies of the destruction of Rome were about to be realized, but this time the reaction was not against the Jews, but against the Jewish-Christians, possibly due to the intervention of Nero's pro-Jewish wife, Poppaea.[70] The Jewish war of A.D. 66-70 was not averted, however, and a new era in Jewish-Roman relations was ushered in, affecting not only the Jews of Palestine, but those of the entire world.

on the other hand, maintains that the Jews were banished. The latter source however, may have synonomously equated Jews with Jewish-Christians since this was the only group of interest to himself and his readers. Thus, when the author of Acts spoke of Claudius' banishment of the Jews, the passage is to be understood as the expulsion of all the Jews (who followed Christ).

This would also mean that Claudius was perceptive enough to realize that there was a difference between the Jews who followed Christ and those who did not, a difficult problem for a non-Jew. However, Claudius did have the advice of Agrippa II, a Jew who would have been capable of explaining the difference to him. The fact that a difference was recognized is attested to by Nero's persecution of the Christians alone in response to the fire at Rome.

70. *Ant.*, 20.8.11.

5

The Jewish War: A.D. 66-70

Rome and the Jews of the Diaspora

THE SELEUCID Empire had always been a patchwork of cities, provinces, territories, etc. undefined by any geographical boundary, and only held together by the king's circumscribed influence. By the time Pompey invaded Syria, that influence was at its lowest. Consequently, those cities that had become fully independent and those that were seeking greater independence did not really feel dismayed at the appearance of the Roman legions. Politically at least, they could see the overthrow of an unwanted monarchy, one that sought continued dictatorial power, even though it could only make a show of doing so.

In Judea, the Jews were too preoccupied with their own internal problems to deliberate on what the Roman presence heralded. Tucked away in a small unimportant section of the Near East, they felt that the Romans wanted nothing from them, and they were certain that Judea would be passed by as the legions trod over Asia. Some Jews even looked favorably on the Romans and they called upon Pompey to arbitrate the

1. *Ant.*, 14.3.1.

85

incumbent civil war, which centered around the legal succession to the Hasmonean throne.

Uninterested in their problems, Pompey sent them away promising to settle the disorder after he had dealt with the Arabs to the south. But when Aristobulus began his own preparations to oust his brother, Hyrcanus II, the Roman general became annoyed at the mobilization; his main concern was to preserve peace in Palestine so that he could be sure of untroubled passage through the country. As a result, he gave his support to Hyrcanus and helped him to capture Jerusalem.

From that time on (63 B.C.) Judea became a vassal state and Rome began to regulate the lives of the Jews. Hyrcanus was confirmed high priest but Palestine, and a large number of gentile cities that had been conquered by the earlier Hasmonean kings, were placed under the direction of the Syrian governor.[2] Aristobulus and his family were taken back to Rome and paraded in disgrace at Pompey's triumph.

Yet the actions of the Roman general were not overly vindictive. Josephus maintains that even though he entered the sanctuary of the Temple—an area never before seen by unholy eyes[3]—he took care not to disturb the sacred treasury;[4] rather atypical behavior for a Roman conqueror.[5]

For their part, the Jews felt that they owed no loyalty to Pompey and in the forthcoming civil war in Rome, they found no difficulty in supporting Julius Caesar,[6] a relationship that was mutually advantageous.

In order to further his personal ambitions, Caesar had had to fight the Senate and in this endeavor he was aided by the Jews of Rome, since they too were opposed to the conservative body. The Senate was not unaware of Caesar's plans, and they threw in their lot with Pompey in the hope that he might rid the country of their enemy. Because of this, Caesar and the

2. *Ant.*, 14.3.4.
3. *Ibid.*
4. *Ibid.* Cf. also Cicero, *Pro Flacco.*, 67.
5. Cf. *Ant.*, 14.7.1.
6. *Ant.*, 14.7.1.2.

Jews of Rome were natural allies. The Jews of the Diaspora now also had reason to support Caesar—he was about to do battle with the heathen who had conquered Jerusalem and had defiled the sanctuary. Caesar may even have been regarded as a holy messenger sent by God to punish Pompey. Even had it not been politically expedient to support Julius Caesar, the insult by Pompey could not be forgotten. For his part, Caesar welcomed the assistance both at home and on the battlefield.

Following Caesar's victory, Hyrcanus was confirmed as ethnarch and high priest, and the Jews were permitted to rebuild the walls of Jerusalem.[7,8] To the Jews, the latter meant that the Romans were returning their independence, since the presence of such defensive walls was regarded as a sign of autonomy in the Near East. In Rome, they were allowed the singular privilege of being permitted to assemble for meetings, although other religious societies were forbidden to do so.[9]

These favors were recognized and extended by Caesar's successors such that the Jews were granted exemption from military duty in deference to their religious scruples,[10] and they received a guarantee that the monies that they had been accustomed to send to Jerusalem would be protected both in its collection and its delivery.[11] This latter endorsement was rather important since it had become commonplace in the Greek Diaspora for the various communities to confiscate Jewish donations destined for Jerusalem[12] (after the overthrow of the Seleucid and Ptolemaic kings).

There were also several attempts to deprive them of their property and civil rights now that the Jews seemed to be unprotected. In Delos, Miletus, and Sardis, those collecting Temple donations were robbed and Jews were prevented from

7. *Ant.*, 14.7.5.
8. Cf. A. Büchler, ''The Priestly Dues and the Roman Taxes in the Edicts of Caesar,'' *Studies in Jewish History,* by I. Brodies, and J. Rabbinowitz, (London: Oxford Univ. Press, 1956).
9. *Ant.*, 14. 10.9.
10. *Ibid.*, 14. 10.11.
11. *Ibid.*, 14.10.21.
12. *Ibid.*, 16.6.3-6.

observing their religion.[13] In Laodicea and Miletus not only did the Jews find difficulty in worshipping, they were even attacked in the streets.[14] In Tyre, they were beaten and their property was stolen;[15] and in Ionia, they were forceably made to sacrifice to gentile gods.[16] Everywhere Greek cities either petitioned the Romans to revoke the edicts of toleration granted the Jews by the Seleucids, or else they cancelled them of their own accord.

The Roman officials were quick to act. Stolen property was returned and the Jews were guaranteed protection. When the citizens of Antioch petitioned Mucianus, the governor of Syria, to revoke the privilege whereby the Jews were permitted to receive a fixed stipend to buy their own oil (since they could not use gentile oil), the governor upheld the Jewish prerogative.[17] In all cases the *status quo* was rigidly enforced.

In A.D. 40 a civil disturbance once again broke out in Antioch. For some unknown reason political groups within the city developed such great antagonism toward each other that fighting broke out in the circus and spread throughout the city. Somehow the Jews became involved, and the conflicting parties momentarily forgot their greviances and united to turn against them. The reason for the pogrom is not clear from the testimony of Malalas,[18] a sixth-century historian. It is possible that the disturbance was a manifestation of Greek resentment for the Jews and especially their privileges in the city, since a copy of Claudius' document to Alexandria guaranteeing Jewish privileges (A.D. 41), was also sent to Antioch,[19] no doubt to make the same point.

13. *Ibid.*, 14.10.8,21; 14.6.6.
14. *Ibid.*, 14.10.21.
15. *Ibid.*, 14.12.3-5.
16. *Ibid.*, 12.3.2.
17. *Ant.*, 12.3.1.
18. J. Malalas, *Chronicle*, 10.5.243-246. Trans. by M. Spinka, and G. Downey. (Chicago: Univ. of Chicago Press, 1940).
19. *Ant.*, 19.5.2.

The End of the Hasmonean Dynasty

Although Hyrcanus had been appointed ethnarch and high priest of the Jews, the real power behind the throne was Antipater, the newly appointed procurator.[20] When Hyrcanus finally died his position was not inherited by any Hasmonean but rather by Antipater's sons, Philip, Archelaus, and Antipas. Antipas received Judea, Samaria, and Idumea while Archelaus was made governor of Galilee. Although Philip was the most benevolent of Antipater's sons, little is known of him and at his death the territories that had been consigned to him were added to Syria. Archelaus proved himself so intolerable that the Jews themselves petitioned Augustus to remove him. In A.D. 6 Archelaus was banished to Gaul and his territories were also added to Syria. As a result, a great many Jews were now being directly supervised by the Roman government.

This marked a turning point in the history of Judea that should not be underrated. As long as the Jews governed themselves, be it under a Hasmonean or a descendant of the Idumean, Antipater, the Romans respected their strange and unusual customs and traditions. But once they fell under the aegis of the Roman procurator, they ceased to be *socii* and *amici*. They were now *victi*. No longer were they entitled to any special consideration. If they payed their taxes and obeyed their overlords, they were left in peace. Any sign of unrest, however, was tantamount to rebellion and would be dealt with as such by the Roman army.

At first the Romans tried not to offend the Jews. Yet from his position in far off Rome, Augustus did not have to deal directly with provincial affairs and consequently he was unaware of the niceties that were required in dealing with the Jews. In Rome, religion and administration did not clash; in Judea it was inevitable. Neither side could appreciate the position of the other. The Roman procurators had no insight into the pas-

20. *Ant.*, 14.8.5.

sions with which the Jews held their traditions, or the fanaticism with which they were willing to die to oppose even the smallest infringement against their customs. The Jews, for their part, could not understand Roman administration, nor did they welcome a new foreign ruler. When the confrontation finally came, judgment gave way to emotionality. Every contact seemed to carry Judea and Rome closer to war.

The Procurators

After its incorporation into Syria, Judea was administered by a procurator who officially was subordinate to the Syrian legate, but who in practice had almost complete authority. The army that was entrusted with maintaining order in Judea, contained many peoples conscripted from neighboring areas. The Jews themselves had been exempted from serving in the army on religious grounds,[21] but the Syrians seemed to take pride in the fact that the Roman army was composed mainly of Greeks from Caesarea and Sebaste.[22] Unfortunately, these soldiers had the same prejudices that infected the rest of Syria. Ordinarily, the procurator was stationed in Caesarea, so that Jews and Greeks rarely came into close contact, but on religious holidays, when Jerusalem was overcrowded with devotees, the procurator moved his residence to the holy city to oversee the festivals and to prevent any political disturbances. Naturally, the army went with him.

However, as Schürer[23] points out, the Jews could not complain of any lack of consideration on the part of the Romans in the early days of administration. Their customs and laws, as far as they were understood, were duly recognized, and the procurators were ordered to respect them. But after the first few procurators, the officials who were in charge of Judea

21. *Ant.*, 14.10.13.17.
22. *Ant.*, 20.8.7.
23. *Hist. of the Jew. People,* p. 196.

often did not comply with their orders—the intricacies of the Jewish customs and traditions were beyond their comprehension and in some cases they seemed utterly ridiculous. Such a simple thing as taking an oath of allegiance to the emperor was sometimes refused[24] and of all the peoples of the countries conquered by Rome, only the Jews declined to worship the emperor. The only condescension they would consider was to agree to offer sacrifices on behalf of, not to, the emperor. Furthermore, Jewish law did not permit the display of any images and consequently, those Roman standards that bore a likeness of the emperor had to be left behind when the soldiers entered Jerusalem.[25] The officials even had to comply with a law that demanded death for any gentile who entered the inner court of the Temple, even if he were a Roman citizen.[26]

These were some of the concessions that were officially granted to the Jews. But not all the Roman functionaries were prepared to observe these concessions. To the majority of the procurators, the Jews were base and contemptible people, ignorant and superstitious, who had to be made to accept the fact that they were a conquered nation.

The Prelude to the Jewish War

In the year A.D. 6 Judea was reunited with Syria and it became a Roman province. In order for taxes to be levied, Rome ordered a census of Judea but this immediately sparked rebellion because of a religious belief of the Jews that God would punish them if they allowed themselves to be numbered. According to the *Book of Samuel,* God had been so angered at the census carried out by King David that he sent a plague to punish the Jews for cooperating.[27] Naturally, religious feeling

24. *Ant.*, 17.2.4.
25. *Ant.*, 18.5.3.
26. *Wars*, 6.2.4.
27. *II Sam.*, 24:1-15.

ran high and only the pleas of the High Priest, Joazer, eventually persuaded the Jews to capitulate, thus averting rebellion.

However, in the district of Galilee, Judas of Gamala and a pharisee named Zadok formed a subversive group, known as the Zealots, whose avowed purpose was the overthrow of Roman rule through terrorism. Rome was their enemy and any Jew who refused to join or aid them in the war of liberation was a traitor and a Roman sympathizer, deserving the same fate as the unwary Roman soldier. Such religious fanaticism made reconciliation impossible, no matter what offers the Romans were prepared to make. But the Zealots were still a minority in the early part of the first century A.D. and Rome did not anticipate any great need to augment its forces in the Jewish province.

Not much is known of the early procurators until Pontius Pilate was appointed to the office (A.D. 26-36). This unsympathetic official made an inauspicious entrance into Jewish life very quickly by ordering his soldiers to enter Caesarea without removing the effigies from their standards. Since they entered by night, this sacrilege went unnoticed, but came the morning, the news spread rapidly that the city had been defiled. The Jews of Jerusalem immediately flocked to the procurator's headquarters in Caesarea and begged him to remove the detested images. But Pilate refused to listen to their entreaties until he was convinced that they were willing to die for their demands. Reluctantly he gave in—the images were removed and the Jews returned to Jersualem.[28]

The incident was no sooner ended than Pilate once again aroused the wrath of the Jews. Feeling the need for an improved water supply in Jerusalem he confiscated part of the Temple treasury to finance the building of an aqueduct to the holy city. No matter how necessary the aqueduct may have been, the Jews were only conscious of the fact that he had violated their sacred treasury and again they rose in protest. This time Pilate was overly displeased. Before any outburst could

28. *Ant.*, 18.3.1.

develop, he ordered his soldiers, many of whom had mixed unnoticed among the people, to fall upon the demonstrators at the first sign of disorder. Thus, the opposition to the aqueduct was eliminated. Pilate was by now completely contemptuous of the Jews.

In his first encounter with them, he had given in to their demands to remove the standards because he may have felt that his superiors would not have viewed his actions favorably if he had slaughtered the Jews for their demand that their officially granted privileges be recognized. This time, he planned to place the standards in Jerusalem in such a manner that the officials in Rome could not blame him if he took action to insure their presence. So, in place of effigies, he had his soldiers carry shields bearing only the name of the emperor written on them. Perhaps he had a premonition that the Jews would object. He might have been condemned for bringing images into Judea against the wishes of the Jews, but he was certain that the emperor could not be displeased if only his name appeared on the battle shields. Most likely he even felt that he would be supported should he have to use force against the Jews. This time, however, the Jews protested directly to Tiberius and surprisingly, the emperor ordered Pilate to remove the offensive shields.[29]

Pilate's last act was to arrest and murder a large number of Jews who had gathered at Mt. Gerizen, in Samaria, to watch a would-be prophet reveal the sacred utensils of the Temple that had supposedly been buried there since the time of Moses.[30] The procurator may have felt that a revolution was brewing when he took such actions but the Syrian legate was convinced that Pilate's actions were unwarranted and Pilate was sent back to Rome.

Events continued to move closer to war when Gaius Caligula succeeded Tiberius as emperor. Aware of the new emperor's narcissism, the inhabitants of the Palestinian town of

29. Philo., *Legat. ad Caium.*, 38.
30. *Ant.*, 18.4.1.

Jamnia saw Caligula's appointment as a chance to embarrass the Jews in that area. Knowing full well that Caligula would not tolerate Jewish opposition, the gentile inhabitants built an altar to the emperor, which, as they correctly surmised, the Jews destroyed. When the emperor heard of the insult to his personage, he became furious and ordered a statue of himself to be erected in the Temple in Jerusalem.[31] At the same time an order was issued that any Jews who offered any opposition were to be killed while the rest of the nation was to be thrown into slavery.[32] War would have been inevitable had the decreed been obeyed. Only Caligula's timely assassination checked the outbreak.

The tempo lulled for a time and then continued to mount with the appearance of a criminal band called the Sicarii, so named because of a small dagger (in Latin, *sica*) that its members carried. Their boldness was of such an order that occasionally they made the Zealots appear almost pro-Roman!

Meanwhile, the Roman soldiers were becoming less inhibited about showing their hatred of the Jews. One soldier exposed his genitals in the Temple court[34] while another tore up a Torah roll before the horrified eyes of the Jews.[35] A third incident involved the murder of a number of Jews who were passing through Samaria on their way to Jerusalem. When the Jews demanded vengeance, Cumanus, the procurator, refused to comply since he had been bribed by the guilty to take no action. The Zealots decided to take matters into their own hands and they raided Samaria, killing everyone they could find. This time Cumanus had not been bribed and he marched from Caesarea to punish the Zealot band. The affair was ultimately settled by emperor Claudius. The leaders of the guilty Samaritans were executed and Cumanus was sent into exile.[36]

Schürer[37] placed the crucial point of the opposition move-

31. Philo., *Leg. ad Caium*, 30; *Ant.*, 18.8.2.
32. *Wars*, 2.9.2.
34. *Ant.*, 20.5.3.
35. *Ant.*, 20.5.4.
36. *Ant.*, 20.6.3.
37. Schürer, p. 228.

ment during the office of the next procurator, Felix (A.D. 52-60). Under his predecessors, the uprisings had been sporadic and directed at specific events. Under Felix resistance became a religious virtue in itself. The Zealots gained their greatest following at this time[38] while the Sicarii became so bold as to assassinate the High Priest, Johnathan, at the direction of the procurator.[39]

Tensions mounted. Nothing could stem the tide of unrest. In A.D. 62 Albinus took over from Felix and according to Josephus, he stole, plundered, and burdened the nation with unbearable taxes. His brutality went so far as to accept ransoms on behalf of those who had been imprisoned for crimes by the former procurators.[40] And yet Florus, the next procurator, made Albinus "appear by a comparison a paragon of virtue"[41] The final blow came when Florus favored the gentiles in a dispute they were having with the Jews in Caesarea.[42] As a result of the decision, the Syrians obtained the city and the Jews were forced to evacuate. The Jews of Jerusalem became outraged at this insult to their coreligionists but restrained their feelings. Then the procurator demanded money from the Temple treasury.[43] When the Jews refused, Florus regarded it as a challenge to his authority and he marched to Jerusalem to enforce his demand. As the soldiers began to approach the Temple, the Jews assembled and barred the way, whereupon they were slaughtered where they stood. But the crowd was so great that Florus realized he did not have enough troops to withstand the multitude. Instead he satisfied himself by plundering part of the city and by crucifying a large number of the recalcitrant citizenry.[44]

The Pharisees tried to restore peace and as a gesture of con-

---

38. Schürer, p. 229.
39. *Ant.*, 20.8.5.
40. *Wars*, 2.14.1.
41. *Ibid.*, 2.14.2.
42. *Ant.*, 20.8.7.
43. *Wars*, 2.14.6.
44. *Ibid.*, 2.14.9.

ciliation they persuaded the people to go out to greet a cohort of soldiers who were approaching the city. The Jews reluctantly consented. But tensions were too strained between soldier and Jew for a peaceful gathering to occur, and on some unknown pretext the soldiers broke ranks and attacked the spectators. The attack did not go unanswered and when it was learned that the army was heading for the Temple, street fighting grew intense. Completely outnumbered, the soldiers were forced to withdraw. Once again, the Pharisees tried to restore order, but the Zealots had gained too much influence by this time. Their visions of destruction of Rome flamed the bitterness of the people and at an Assembly that was held in the Temple court, it was formally decided that no further gestures of peace would be made. Rebellion had been declared.

The fighting lasted four years (A.D. 66-70), but it was no contest. The Jews were not united and fought in fragmentary bands. Only in Jerusalem did the Romans meet stiff opposition. However, in the spring of A.D. 70 the Roman army under Titus drove the Jews from the walls and they had to withdraw to the Temple. From this position they held their ground until one of the soldiers hurled a torch at the building and the wooden structure burned into cherished memories. The rebellion was over.

Following the fall of the city the conquerors burned and plundered what remained and took prisoner those Jews that had not been killed. Some of the survivors later met death in the gladitorial arenas of the cities along the coast[45] while the remainder marched in the triumphal procession at Rome before the new emperor, Vespasian. Both the Sanhedrin, the governing body of Jews in Palestine, and the office of High Priest were abolished, and worship at the Temple site was forbidden. Thus the political and religious center of Judaism was materialistically ended. The synagogue henceforth took the place of the holy shrine and the Temple remained only as a symbol, but a powerful one, for its memory was to inspire messianic hopes in the succeeding generations. The new focus for Jewish learning was moved to Jamnia and it was there that Jewish scholars met to decide which books were holy enough to be included in the canon of the Hebrew bible.

Besides the political measures that Rome took against the Jews, a new policy was adopted toward them as a whole. Whatever considerations had been shown them, especially in their religion and customs were reexamined. Vespasian ordered that the Temple tax sent by Jews the world over for the upkeep of Temple services was now to be used for the benefit of Jupiter Capitolinus in Rome and the tax became known as the *fiscus judaicus*. Although the amount paid was insignificant, the principle was important since no other religious group in Roman society paid such a tax. It was clearly discriminatory and marked the beginning of the social deterioration of the Jew in society.

6

Egypt under the Romans

THE CONQUEST of Egypt did not occasion any very dramatic changes in the administration of the country. Local affairs were allowed to continue much as they had under the Ptolemies but the central government, of course, saw the replacement of Greek officials with those of Roman origin. The prefect became the foremost resident official in Egypt and as head of the civil administration, the finances, and the army, he was in a position of virtual dictatorship answerable only to the emperor in far off Rome. And in Rome, Egypt's first emperor, Augustus, deliberately set the pattern for future Roman suzerainty in Egypt by a series of carefully instituted plans that he made sure his officials carried out.

Egypt itself was regarded as the emperor's personal realm. Although the cities of Alexandria, Naucratis, and Ptolemais were allowed to retain some degree of autonomy just as they had under the Ptolemies, some changes were instituted so as to curtail the power that these cities, (especially Alexandria), had wrestled from the Egyptian kings. Measures were also taken to increase the revenue from the potentially prosperous agricultural areas, and the various industries, and trades that had managed to survive under the Ptolemies. All of these general modifications affected the lives of the Jews and contributed to the outbreak of anti-Jewish riots during the middle half of the first century A.D.

Attention should also be drawn to the fact that under the Ptolemaic administration there had been no anti-Jewish disturbances[1] and that these only occurred after the Romans occupied and imposed their administration on the country. Therefore, it seems most likely that the factors underlying the pogroms that began in Egypt after the advent of the Romans were a direct result of the innovations brought about by their government. This hypothesis does not deny that the underlying factors were already present, but it assumes that had the Ptolemies continued to rule the country, there would have been less chance for these factors to precipitate into the violent storm that settled on Alexandria during the reigns of Caligula and Claudius.

Roman Economic Policy and Its Ramifications

In the eyes of Augustus, the main asset of Egypt was its wealth. Egypt was regarded as nothing more than a source of income and a grainary whose main purpose was to feed and clothe the people of Italy, especially those who lived in Rome.[2] Under the later Ptolemies, the Nile irrigation system had not been carefully supervised and it had fallen into disre-

1. The anti-Semitic literature that began with Manetho was confined to paper and never incited any violence. The imaginative *III Maccabees* cannot be regarded as historical testimony of the Ptolemaic period and may in fact be more relevant to the Roman period (See ch. 4). Its main value is allegorical, not historical.

2. M. Rostovtzeff, "Roman Exploitation of Egypt in the First Century A.D." *J. of Economic and Business Hist.* 1 (1929): 337-64.

pair so that the land was not being as fruitfully cultivated as it could have been. One of the emperor's first orders concerned the restoration of the irrigation system and the redevelopment of Egypt's agricultural potential. The immediate effect was an increase in the harvest, but the benefit was not felt by the people of Egypt since the grain was immediately sent to Italy to feed the people of that country. The Ptolemies had been just as guilty of appropriating crops, but they had kept the grain in Egypt, either for sale in that country or abroad. The Romans did not consider Egyptian needs, but merely drained the country's resources indiscriminately. The rape of the country was carried out with great zeal, so much so that the emperor, Tiberius on one occasion had to admonish his prefect to curb his enthusiasm. Shear the sheep, not flay them, he cautioned.[3] To make matters worse, the carrying trade was placed in the hands of Roman and Jewish companies to the exclusion of the Alexandrian Greeks[4] resulting in considerable financial losses to the latter. The Jews, for their part, did not all benefit from this policy. Like any community, they too showed a clear division in their economic and social classes. Although there were the very wealthy such as Alexander, the alabarch, who lent money to the Jewish king, Agrippa I,[5] there were also merchants, artisans, farmers,[6] peasants,[7] and plain destitutes.[8] It is unlikely that the latter three groups would have much to gain from the new monopolies in the shipping trade. In the *chora,* an economic change for the worse greeted the Jews. Under the Ptolemies, the Jews had been government officials and were particularly conspicuous as tax collectors.[9] But the Romans preferred Greeks in their hiring of non-Roman officials and very few Jews found their way into the Roman bureaucracy.

3. *Cass. Dio.*, 57, 10, 5.
4. J. G. Milne, "The Ruin of Egypt by Roman Mismanagement," *J. Rom. Stud.* 17, (1927); 1-13.
5. *Ant.*, 18.6.3.
6. Philo., *In Flacc.*, 57.
7. Tcherikower and Fuks, *C.J.P.*, nos. 142, 145.
8. *Ibid.*, nos. 146, 149.
9. See ch. 2.

Thus Jewish bureaucratic officials disappeared as did Jewish soldiers, both of whom had played a very prominent part in the Ptolemaic era.

By far the most important innovation introduced by Augustus was the *laographia*—the poll tax, which was levied on every male between the ages of 14 and 60. Only Romans, citizens of the autonomous Greek cities, and a limited number of priests and officials were granted exemption from the tax.[10] Some inhabitants of various district capitals were granted a reduction in the amount they had to pay, but only the former groups were given complete exemption. Every 14 years a house-to-house census was carried out for which everyone was required to return to his legal place of domicile.[11] This all-inclusive tax illustrates quite clearly that to the Romans all the inhabitants of Egypt, with the exception of the privileged class, were regarded as "Egyptians."[12] But even if the Egyptian was regarded as an inferior, it does not strictly mean that Augustus imposed the tax as a mark of subjugation and inferiority as some scholars[13] have maintained. True, the egyptian was regarded as inferior but there were those who paid the tax either at the same rate or at a slightly reduced rate who were not Egyptians and who were not at all thought of in the same terms as were the natives. It was only a special privilege that granted exemption from the poll tax, not all taxes. But even though it was not intended as a debasement, this was how it was interpreted by the Greek citizens. The anti-Semites pointed to the fact that Jews were subject to it as proof that they were no better than the main body of despicable Egyptians,[14] so that the whole question of the tax became a

---

10. S.L. Wallace, *Taxation in Egypt from Augustus to Diocletian* (Princeton: Princeton University Press, 1938), p. 109.
11. Milne, *History of Egypt under Roman Rule* (London: Methuen and Co., 1912), p. 158.
12. H.I. Bell, *Egypt From Alexander The Great To The Arab Conquest* (Oxford: Oxford Clarendon Press, 1948), p. 70.
13. See V. Tcherikower, "Syntaxis And Laographia," *J. Juristic Papyrology* 4 (1950): 179-207.
14. Tcherikower and Fuks, *C.J.P.*, no. 156c.

matter of social status and personal integrity. For the Jews this was no petty matter, particularly for those who had turned their backs on most of their Jewish background in their effort to achieve the ranking and prestige of the Greek citizen of Alexandria. By being entered in the tax lists, they were with one blow being humbled back into the very social class from which they were struggling to emerge. Some tried to evade the tax by getting themselves listed in the public records with the *epheboi*[15] and there is fragmentary evidence from the papyri of the period that one Jew petitioned the prefect to grant him exemption since he claimed to be a citizen. When this argument proved invalid, he declared that he was over the age limit of 60 anyway. Some Jews thus tried their utmost to avoid payment of the tax, mainly because of the inferior position in which it cast them, although the high impost itself may have been a factor.[16] These attempts, however, further aggravated Jewish-Greek relations, for the only way the Jews could hope to escape was by gaining citizenship[17] and this was resisted with great emotionality by the Greeks.

Without going into the intracacies of Roman fiscal policy,[18] it is enough to note that the various taxes that the Romans imposed upon the people of Egypt, both privileged and unprivileged classes, did eventually lead to their destitution. The poll tax plagued the Egyptian peasants[19] and the taxes levied

15. *Ibid.*, no. 150.
16. According to Wallace, p. 136 the rate paid by the less-favored classes was as high as 40 drachmae a year and possibly higher, which appears to have been a large sum judging by the flight of people from their homes.
17. Admission to the citizen body was dependent on prior admission to the *ephebate*. Boys who were eligible for admission to the privileged class had to be presented for an examination in which they underwent the *epicrisis*, the determination of their civic status. The main piece of information that the examiners required before they would endorse a boy was documentary evidence that his father belonged to the privileged class since sons of citizens obtained citizenship by birth. (on the *epicrisis* see Wallace, p. 109-10.)
18. The above mentioned *Taxation in Egypt* by S.L. Wallace is the outstanding reference on this subject.
19. Rostovtzeff, "Roman Exploitation Of Egypt," cites documents indicating that the burden of taxation had become too great for some, and by as early as A.D. 19-20 people began to desert their homes in order to evade the taxes.

on trade led to the downfall of the middle classes.[20] Wealthy landowners in many cases lost their holdings due to land taxes and when they or the middle-class businessmen became compelled to undertake public services, such as the collection of public taxes or the guaranteeing of its payment, they became completely ruined because there was no one left from whom to collect payment. It appears that in some cases entire villages were deserted by those seeking to escape their obligations. With the desertion of the peasants from the land, the once prosperous farm areas of Egypt fell into disuse and eventually the entire Roman world was threatened with disastrous famine since Egypt had become the bread basket of the Roman world.

Egypt itself became a turgid scene of unrest, and though authors[21] writing about this period pass over economics as not contributing to anti-Semitism in the early Roman period, the *laographia* incited the Jews to increase their demands for increased privileges. Other subtle economic pressures, imposed on the country through Roman mismanagement, also heavily contributed to political strife in the first century. The revolts against the taxes in the early part of the first century A.D.[22] were not begun by the peasant classes but rather by those who also came into conflict with the Jews, and Rostovtzeff has suggested that the fighting that broke out between the Greeks and the Jews during the time of Caligula and Claudius was really a disguised attack against the Romans, caused by the bitter discontent engendered by the severe economic policy imposed on the people.[23]

---

20. The increase in taxes was immediately resisted by the Alexanderians and those who lived in southern Egypt and the Roman army had to be called in to quell the riots (Strabo, 17,1,53.)
21. See A. Segré, "Antisemites in Hellenistic Allexandria," *Jewish Social Studies* 8 (1946): 127-36.
22. See note 20.
23. Rostovtzeff, "Roman Exploitation of Egypt," p. 352, 360.

Jews and Greeks in Alexandria

When Augustus began his plans for the subjugation of Egypt, he correctly perceived that Alexandria would be the city most likely to cause political unrest and as a guarantee against any disturbances, he stationed a large force of soldiers in the city. At the same time he denied the citizens of Alexandria the right to a senate of their own, probably because he felt that it might serve as a cynosure for resistance. The refusal extremely disappointed the Alexandrians, but what galled them even more was the emperor's favoritism to the Jews. These people had all their rights and privileges confirmed, including the right to regulate their own affairs through their own council,[24] whereas the Alexandrians were denied this privilege. But while they were angry at the slight that had been given them, they were outraged at the fact that the Jews now demanded further privileges, especially that of citizenship in the Alexandria *polis*.[25]

During the Ptolemaic period the desire for citizenship had not been pressed very hard by the Jews since there was little to gain by it except an increase in prestige over fellow Jews and possible assimilation into the Greek community. This was

24. *Ant.*, 14.7.2,19.5.2. maintains that the post of *ethnarch* was continued. But Tcherikower, *C.J.P.*, p. 57, n. 22, on the basis of Philo., *In Flacc.* 74, argues that Josephus' text has been altered and that Philo is more correct in stating that Augustus instituted the Jewish *gerousia* instead.

25. It is generally conceded on the basis of the Letter of Claudius—see H.I. Bell, *Jews And Christians In Egypt* (London: Oxford University Press, 1924)—that the Jews as a whole were not citizens of Alexandria. A. Momigliano, *Claudius* (New York: Barnes and Noble, 1962) p. 96, n. 25, is one of the few modern scholars who still upholds the view that the Jews were citizens, his argument being based on the testimony of Josephus in *Ant.*, 195.2. and the remark of Philo (*In Flacc.* 80) where he states that the Jews had the right to be beaten with the rod like the Alexandrians instead of the flat of the sword as were the Egyptians. Although Josephus' remarks have been attributed either to an error or an intended alteration in his document, the authenticity of Philo's remark has not been satisfactorily challenged. Momigliano, may therefore be singularly correct if this latter privilege was truly the mark of citizenship. The only possible explanation invalidating Philo is that when he is talking about this privilege he is referring to Jews who were citizens but not the Jewish community as a whole. It has never been denied that there were some Jews in the citizen body. What has been challenged has been the assertion that all Jews were enrolled in the citizen lists.

mainly desired by those Jews who felt themselves completely Hellenized. However, with the degradation caused by enrollment in the *laographoumoi*, the Jews (who were an unprivileged class[26]) began a new push to be enrolled in the citizen body especially by those who felt more kinship with the Greeks than with the Egyptians. The Greeks, of course, were unwilling to let the Jews into the citizen body. Unsympathetic though they were to the Romans because of the refusal to permit them a senate, the Greeks were prepared to offer any help in rooting out all those who sought to avoid the *laographia*.

The Alexandrians indicated their citizenship by giving their *phyle* and *deme*[27] and if a Jew claimed citizenship he had to do likewise. No doubt many Jews whose ancestors had been living in Alexandria from its earliest days, regarded themselves as actually possessing citizenship[28] or at the least being entitled to it should they demand it.[29] Membership in the Jewish *politeuma*, which some Jews may have thought equivalent to the Greek *politeuma*,[30] also furthered such ideas, but being enrolled in a *politeuma* meant only that they could not be expelled from the city[31] and little else. It did not mean that they had equality with other *politeuma* although Josephus may have felt this.[32] Although Jews possibly called themselves citizens, they meant citizen of a *politeuma* not a *polis*. The citizen body never recognized them as citizens[33] and even if they had this

26. In Latin, *peregrini dediticii*
27. R. Taubenschlag, *The Law of Graeco-Roman Egypt In The Light Of The Papyri*, (New York: Herald Square Press, 1944). The term Alexandrian did not mean citizen of Alexandria exclusively but could mean one who had the right of *origo*. The *phyle* and *deme* were the proofs the father had to present at the *epicrisis*. See p. 17.
28. H.I. Bell, "Antisemitism in Alexandria," *J. Rom. Study.* 31 (1941): 1-18.
29. Had the Jews been granted *isopolity* this would have been a possibility given that they could enroll in the gymnasium. But since they were not allowed to do so, the possession of such a right did them no good.
30. Segré, "Antisemitism in Hellenistic Alexandria."
31. A. Segré. "The Status Of The Jews In Ptolemaic And Roman Egypt," *Jew. Soc. Stud.* 6 (1944): 375-400.
32. See E.J. Bickerman, "The Colophon Of The Greek Book of Esther," *J. Bib. Lit.* 63 (1944): p. 356.
33. H.S. Jones, "Claudius And The Jewish Question At Alexandria," *J. Rom. Stud.* 16 (1926): 17-35.
34. See n. 25.
35. Tcherikower and Fuks, C.P.J., no. 151.

would not have meant that they were recognized as part of the citizen body. There is a subtle distinction when one considers those who have the right of *origo* to be citizens, that is the right of domicile and those who belong to the citizen body —privileged citizens with special rights. This may explain the anomaly of Philo whereby the Jews had the right to be beaten with the rod[34] since this might have been granted to those possessing *origo,* and the Jews were certainly entitled to that. Even had they been allowed to enter the *ephebate,* citizenship still involved apostasy, which religious Jews would avoid, some even at the alternative of death. Other Jews, however, were prepared to enroll in the gymnasium and those whose ancestors had completed gymnasium training felt that they were in fact citizens by way of their birthright. One papyrus[35] shows that although one Jew was certain of his claim and called himself an "Alexandrian," a scribe changed the term to read a "Jew of Alexandria," thus connoting that he was not a part of the citizen body, since to one not familiar with Alexandrian status systems, an "Alexandrian" might mean one who possessed the franchise.

The Privileges of Citizenship

Up until this point we have discussed the privileges that went with citizenship[36] without actually discussing what these were. According to Taubenschlag,[37] citizenship carried with it the right to vote in the Alexandrian assembly, to pass decrees in public and private matters and the right to apply for identification documents. It was also a guarantee against enslavement and an exemption from the liturgies, the poll tax, and compulsory labor. In addition, the citizen body was allowed to submit

36. We will drop the distinction between citizen and member of the citizen body at this point, keeping in mind that when we refer to citizens, it is to those enrolled in the citizen body.
37. Taubenschlag, *Law of Graeco-Roman Egypt,* p. 576-605.

collective petitions to the emperor while noncitizens could only submit them on an individual basis. Besides these, there were the rights of having one's own laws, courts, cults, officials, and assemblies. Of all these, it seems that the exemption from the poll tax, liturgy, and compulsory labor were the only obvious advantages that the Jews would be interested in. In view of what has been already said regarding the *laographia,* it must become more and more evident that this was the motivating factor behind Jewish attempts to enroll in the citizen body. As long as Augustus and Tiberius ruled, there were no major outbreaks because of the iron hand with which these emperors ruled the country. But when Gaius Caligula became *princeps,* the Alexandrians felt that his partiality toward their city[38] might serve their advantage in dealing with the Jews. On the other hand, the disturbances that broke out may simply have been displaced aggression, the real target being the Romans. It should be recalled that the Alexandrian merchants had suffered serious losses when the Romans took over transportation of exports[39] and though Alexandrian citizens were exempted from the poll tax, they were still required to pay for work involving the restoration of Egypt's economy. Thus, with regard to the refusal by the Romans to grant Alexandria a senate, the economic losses suffered by the merchant class, the confirmation of Jewish privileges, and the further attempt by the Jews to extend these privileges into citizenship, the motivation for the demonstrations that came during Caligula's reign seems clear enough.

The First Pogrom

The anti-Semitic leaders of Alexandria discovered that they had an ally in the Roman prefect Flaccus once they became aware that Flaccus had had a hand in causing the ruin of the new

38. Philo., *In Flacc.* 21-23.
39. See above.

emperor's mother.[40] Since the prefect was in mortal fear of Caligula's vengeance, the anti-Semitic leaders promised that if he would give them a free hand, they would intercede on his behalf with the emperor, who as we have said, had a partiality for the city. At first the prefect consented to discriminate against the Jews in the law suits that appeared before him[41] but then matters got completely out of hand.

The arrival in Alexandria in A.D. 38 of the Jewish king, Agrippa I, marked the occasion for the anti-Semites to stage a demonstration in mockery of this man who shortly before had been a penniless supliant at Alexandrian banking houses. The village idiot was dressed in royal attire and was paraded through the streets in mockery of Agrippa—the beggar raised to royalty. The Jews and Agrippa were naturally offended and they looked to the prefect to punish the outrage. But Flaccus realized his position was precarious. Agrippa was the emperor's friend and not to punish those who had insulted him would anger the unstable Caligula, who only needed the feeblest of excuses to get rid of him anyways. On the other hand, the Alexandrians were prepared to sacrifice him should he not support them. The Greeks then resolved to divert attention away from the insult to the Jewish king by demanding that the emperor's image be set up in Jewish synagogues to show that they were the loyal subjects of the emperor in contrast to the Jews whom they knew would refuse such a demand. Flaccus in turn played along and declared the Jews "aliens and foreigners"[42] thereby setting the stage for the first Jewish pogrom in recorded history. Synagogues were entered and statues of Caligula were placed in them, thereby defiling them and rendering them unfit for worship. The excitement of the crowd mounted and the Jews were then driven from the various parts of the city and were herded into the Delta quarter. Those who moved too slowly were mauled and killed. Flaccus then

40. Philo, *In Flacc.*, 9.
41. *Ibid.*, ch. 24.
42. Philo, *In Flacc.*, 54.

legalized the persecution by passing a decree establishing the Delta as a ghetto area to which the Jews were to be restricted. Jewish homes and businesses outside the area were plundered and burned. Food shortages and overcrowding in the ghetto soon led to starvation and epidemics and when the Jews crept out in search of food they were hanged if unfortunately caught. We are indebted to Philo[43] for all the lurid details of the attrocities to which the Jews were subjected during this time and for the events which followed. According to his narrative, once the rioting was over there was the need to account to Caligula. Those Jews who in the face of all the carnage still sought citizenship amongst those who had helped in their destruction felt that the pogrom had been the work of a small minority who had had the prefect's support. Since these Jews were the most influential, they believed that they spoke for the Jewish community as a whole and it was they who sent the delegation headed by Philo to put forth the Jewish position. The Greeks also sent an embassy, theirs headed by Apion, one of the most literate anti-Semitic leaders of the Alexandrian community.

When the Jews finally met with Caligula, his ridicule left them no hope for redress. The emperor instead preoccupied himself with plans for the erection of his image in Jerusalem, an event that probably would have resulted in rebellion in a large part of the Diaspora as well as in Palestine. His timely assassination prevented the incipient rebellion until Nero's reign.

In the meantime, the lower Jewish classes in Alexandria had been preparing for a counteroffensive by arming themselves and sending to Palestine for Jewish aid. Thus, while Claudius, the new emperor, was settling one riot, another was going on in the same place. To the dismay of the Alexandrians, Claudius was not of the same frame of mind as the mad Caligula; his was the ideology and methodology of Augustus and Tiberius. His decision was to return all the rights that

43. *Legatio ad Gaium* is the account of the riot and the embassy to Gaius.

Flaccus had taken from the Jews while at the same time con-
firming all their privileges and customs. It was a severe blow
to the anti-Semites. An outlet was sought for their frustration
and that outlet took the form of an accusation against Agrippa
on some pretext that was felt would lead to his death and
exile. However, the political winds had changed since the days
of Caligula and Agrippa was exonerated while Isidorus and
Lampon, his accusers, were put to death instead. The death of
these two rabble-rousers seemed to have deeply moved their
Alexandrian supporters and they became martyrs, lauded in a
series of pamphlets called the *Acts of the Pagan Martyrs*.[44]

When the news of the second riot reached Rome, Claudius
was once again met with delegates, but this time the Jews
were represented by two embassies.[45] It was beyond the
emperor's patience to deal with the Alexandrian question
again; the presentation of two embassies from the Jews exasperated him. However, he kept calm and with cool deliberation
he confirmed the Jews in all their rights and privileges, but
warned them once and for all against seeking entrance into the
citizen body of the city. The Alexandrians, for their part, were
admonished to respect the Jewish privileges.[46] It was a hollow
victory for both sides. All that had been done was to invoke
and confirm the *status quo*.

The Alexanderian situation appeared to have been settled
once and for all since Claudius had definitely stated that he
would not tolerate any further outbreaks, and in fact there were
none until A.D.66. According to a report of Josephus,[47] a
number of Alexandrian leaders were debating in the am-

---

44. *C.J.P.*, nos. 154-59.
45. The Jews were not even entitled to send one embassy since it was only a preroga-
    tive of the citizen body to send a collective petition (Taubenschlag, p. 605).
    However, this has generally geen overlooked and attention has been focused on
    the puzzling fact that the Jews had two embassies representing them. In my opin-
    ion, these were two separate delegations, one representing the Hellenized ele-
    ments as typified by Philo, and the other representing the lower classes whose
    main aims were not assimilation into Greek society.
46. For a complete bibliography dealing with Claudius' decision, see Tcherikower and
    Fuks, vol. 2, p. 36-37.

phitheater about a forthcoming embassy they were planning to send to Nero. A number of Jews quietly entered the arena in order to spy on the proceeding. Some of them were caught and burnt alive for their indiscretion. The Jews immediately retaliated and tried to burn down the amphitheater with the Greeks in it. By this time the prefect, Tiberius Alexander (a nephew of Philo's), had learned of the fighting and tried to persuade the Jews to stop, but his appeal went unheeded and he turned instead to his soldiers, giving them permission to kill, burn, and plunder. In this manner the resistance was put down with serious loss to the Jews, a taste of what was about to happen during the catastrophic war of the next four years.

7

The Conflict of the Church and Synagogue

The New Testament and Anti-Semitism.

FEWER EVENTS have had greater impact upon the Jewish world than the death of Jesus, and yet, placed in the context of its time, it was so insignificant as to merit only the slightest attention by contemporary historians. Were it not for the Gospels and the Book of Acts, we would know nothing about the life of Jesus or the early Jewish society that was founded upon the belief that Jesus was the long awaited Messiah. However, there is no way of determining how objective these accounts really are. As one proceeds through their chronological order,[1] it becomes apparent that each author gives greater emphasis to certain events than do others. Mark, for instance, is influenced by the crucifixion to a much greater extent than is Matthew, whose main concern seems to be Pharisaic opposition to Jesus.

Chronologically, the Gospels also appear to be more anti-Jewish in their tone. Although this anti-Jewish tendency has

1. Mark, Matthew, Luke, John.

The Conflict of the Church and Synagogue   113

been denied,[2] it is most evident that it has served as the theological source of Christian anti-Semitism up to and including our present era.[3] This too has been denied.[4] Interestingly, both denials come from well meaning, but apparently uninformed, Catholic priests. Social research into this question is overwhelmingly contrary to their subjective and pristine views.[5]

One need only cite some current Christian Sunday school primers to convince anyone of this point.[6]

The ritual murder charge, for instance, is still leveled at present-day Jews. Among a large sample of members of different Protestant and Catholic denominations, it was found that 60% of the Protestants and 46% of the Catholics interviewed still linked the modern Jew with the crucifixion of Jesus.[7] Obviously there is something in the New Testament upon which this attitude is based or else it would never have been incorporated into Christian teachings in the first place. In the following pages, the origin of this and other anti-Jewish tenets will be examined in light of the events that shaped the Evangelical accounts of the life of Jesus.

2. See G. Baum, *Is The New Testament Anti-Semitic?* (N. J.: Deus Books, 1965).
3. J. Isaac, *The Teaching of Contempt.* (Toronto: McGraw Hill, 1965); D.D. Runes. *The Jew and the Cross.* (N. Y.: Citadel Press, 1966).
4. E.H. Flannery, *The Anguish of the Jews.* (New York: Macmillan Co., 1964).
5. C.Y. Glock and R. Stark, *Christian Beliefs and Anti-Semitism.* (New York: Harper and Row, 1966).
6. James Brown, in his article "Christian Teaching And Anti-Semitism," *Commentary* 24 (1957): pp. 494-501, quotes some of the passages found in religious texts used by teachers. The following is one such passage:
   Do not use the expression 'the wicked soldiers who were ill-treating Jesus,' without taking care that the children do not identify "to be a soldier" with "to be wicked."
   One should not speak of 'wicked soldiers,' but of 'wicked Jews.' In the Passion narrative the soldiers should be treated as simply doing what they are odered to do.
7. Glock and Stark., ch. 4.

Jesus and His Times

A full account of Jesus' life and teaching would be outside the scope of this work. But certain aspects of his ministry must be discussed, if only to put the man into perspective.

Jesus was brought up in the town of Nazareth[8] in Galilee as a carpenter, the profession of his father. Galilee itself was governed by a Jewish king, Herod Antipas, but it contained a rather large Gentile population. In A.D. 26 or 27 John the Baptist appeared proclaiming his message of repentance and declaring that the kingdom of God was near and that the Messiah would soon appear. One of those John attracted was Jesus, but following his baptism, Jesus received a vision that made him believe that he himself was the Messiah John spoke of. Nevertheless, he did nothing about this belief until after John was imprisoned.[9]

Then he began his ministry, directing his message not to those who were already pious and who observed the Law, but to those who were forsaken and were regarded as sinners and outcasts. "They that are whole need not the physician, but they that are sick,"[10] he contended. But while John the Baptist had advocated a turn to more rigid standards, Jesus proclaimed a new morality.

But a new morality and its advocates, then, as today, attracts vigorous opposition. The Pharisees regarded Jesus not as a new teacher, but as a corrupter of the existing morals. To

8. Nazareth is not even mentioned once either in the Old Testament, Josephus, or the Talmud and yet the early Christians were called Nazoreans (Notzrim, Nosrim). Since the village was so insignificant, it is rather curious that early Christianity designated itself by this epithet.

9. There are two distinct themes relating John's death. The Gospels maintain that he was executed because he denounced the incestuous relationship between Herod Antipas and Herod's sister-in-law, Herodias (Luke, 3:19-20). Josephus, on the other hand, relates that John was executed to prevent rebellion since the people seemed ready to follow him in whatever he did (*Ant.*, 18.5.2). The later copyists of Josephus subsequently interpolated a few lines to make John appear the prototype of Christian virtue. According to their additions Antipas murdered John because he preached cleanliness!.

10. Mark, 2:17.

them exactness and precision in fulfilling the Law was the essence of Judaism and they resisted any attempts to lower the religious standards of the day. Jesus accused them of hypocrisy and spiritual blindness. But Pharisaism was not hypocrisy. It was a way of life chosen by a people who wished to preserve their religion in its contemporary form. Without strict observance of the Law, Judaism would probably have disappeared long ago under the influence of the Hellenists and their later counterparts, the Sadducees.

Jesus, however, continued preaching his message throughout Galilee, but the enthusiasm and large crowds that he attracted endangered his life. The fate of John the Baptist was proof enough of that. Most of these followers, in fact, were probably religious patriots, the Zealots,[11] who more than likely misinterpreted his message. To them Jesus was a potential political messiah, one who would overthrow the hated Romans; Galileans were far more concerned with political upheaval than religious reformation. But Jesus, much though he recognized the composition of his followers, did not entertain a military coup. It was his idea that his followers would come to see his purpose in a different light, one not connected with politics.

When Jesus finally came to Jerusalem, he was coming to the heart of Judaism. If his message were to be accepted, it had to be accepted in Jerusalem. Whether or not he was deliberately trying to fulfill some messianic pattern is mere speculation.[12] The immense crowds that the Gospels indicate that he attracted, are more than likely a gross exaggeration. The contemporary writers of the period ignore him. Josephus gives Theudas[13] and the Samaritan false prophet[14] more attention.[15] If Jesus had attracted a large following in the city of Jerusalem surely there would have been a great deal more recorded.

11. See ch. 5.
12. See H. J. Schoenfeld, *The Passover Plot* (New York: Bantam, 1967).
13. *Ant.*, 20.5.1.
14. *Wars*, 6.5.2.
15. The passage in Josephus referring to Jesus (*Ant.*, 18.3.3) has long been recognized as a Christian interpolation.

Should there have been a disturbance at this time, the Roman procurator would not have hesitated to take action since his main purpose in being in Jerusalem at this time was to prevent any Jewish outbreaks.

What finally did bring him to the attention of the authorities was the disturbance he created in the Temple.[16] The Roman police quickly put an end to the outbreak and Jesus had to flee, his Zealot followers,[17] engaging the Romans until he made good his escape. It appeared that Jesus had finally cast the die.

The Jewish authorities in Jerusalem were alarmed. The Sanhedrin, the governing body of the Jewish community, met that night. There would be no mistaking the possibility of a Zealot uprising and they were determined to quell the impending outbreak; prior experiences with the procurator, Pontius Pilate, were still fresh in their minds.[18] It was evident that he would take any excuse to express his hatred against the Jews. Though they collaborated with the Romans to a great extent, the Sadducees (who ruled the Sanhedrin) were not so callous as to allow this to happen. They determined to turn Jesus over to the officials before any disaster. But where could they find him?

At this very time, one of Jesus' followers who was disillusioned that Jesus was not planning a full-scale uprising against the Romans, left the Passover supper table. The agents of the Sanhedrin found him and it was no trouble to convince him to betray Jesus' hiding place. In the garden of Gethsemane Jesus was apprehended and in the morning he was turned over

---

16. Matthew, 21:12; John, 2:14-15.
17. The large number of Zealots among Jesus' own apostles is impressive (cf. J. Carmichael, *The Death of Jesus*. (N. Y.: Macmillan, 1962) and O. Cullmann, *The State in the New Testament* (New York: Charles Scribner's Sons, 1956). Yet it is clear from the Gospel accounts that Jesus expected these Zealots to perceive that his message was not political. But they were incapable of understanding (Mark, 9:6, 10; 10:13-16, 28-31,32). Instead they interpreted his words literally.
18. See ch. 5.

to the procurator before any chance of an insurrection.

The trial was swift. Pilate pointedly asked him if he had any messianic pretentions and Jesus seemed not to deny them. To Jesus, the question had religious priority over political ramifications. Realizing the consequences, he still chose not to deny the accusation, thus condemning himself. The Roman procurator, of course, would not be aware of the religious overtones of messianism. His course was clear.

At the same time he had another man condemned for the cross. However, there was a custom current among the Jews by which they were entitled to have one man pardoned for his crimes during the passover. Pilate, in conformity with the practice, presented the two men, Barrabas and Jesus to the public. The crowd, probably containing many disillusioned Zealots who had heard of Jesus' refusal to lead the expected rebellion, took out their anger by calling for Barrabas. And so, Jesus' fate was sealed.

The Social Psychology of Early Christianity

During the first few decades after Jesus' crucifixion, the belief in his messiahship was spread with incredible fervor. What had begun as a small, disorganized band of disciples was transformed within a minute period of historical time into a dedicated body of missionaries. Just fifty days after the crucifixion, Peter is said to have converted 3,000 at Pentecost (Acts, 2:41) and very soon thereafter, the faithful are reported as numbering 5,000 (Acts, 4:4; cf. 6:7).

The genesis of this activity, however, is still an enigma, for as Carrington[19] noted, "There is no connected account of this critical period and the reconstructions of learned theologians whether they believe in the Resurrection or otherwise, all suffer from the disconnected nature of the evidence." This, of course, reflects the hoary problem of New Testament scholar-

---

19. P. Carrington, *The Early Christian Church* (Cambridge: Cambridge Univ. Press, 1957), vol. I, p. 39.

ship. In tracing the historical origins and growth of a socio-religious movement such as Christianity, one is forced to rely on records which, in some cases, are obviously biased and self-contradictory.

On the other hand, the contradictions, distortions, impossibilities, etc., contained in the early traditions may often illuminate the "life-situation" *(Sitz im Leben)* of the early Christian church. Such analyses have given rise to the discipline of Form Criticism, through which it is believed that important insights may be gained regarding the Church's efforts to defend itself against the defamatory remarks of unfriendly neighbors such as the Jews, and the missionary concerns of the Church during the first Christian century. Despite the gains that have been won by this approach, however, one of the greatest historical puzzles of all time is still the enigma of the origin of the Church.

Most reconstructions of the events tracing the emergence of the Church generally begin their accounts with the Easter appearances. For instance, Branton[20] comments, "the evidence of the Synoptic Gospels shows clearly that without the experience of the Resurrection the demoralized disciples would never have become the apostles of a gospel that swept across the world like wildfire." However, as J. Weiss[21] noted several years ago, although the disciples were disappointed and grieved after the Crucifixion (cf. Mark, 16:10,14; Luke, 24:17,21; John, 20:11,25) this does not necessarily mean that they had completely lost their faith. Mark's statement that the disciples "scattered" after the crucifixion (Mark, 14:27; 16:7) notwithstanding, there is no reference in the entire New Testament to a flight from Jerusalem at that time and in fact Luke (Luke, 29:49; Acts 1:14) explicitly states that the disciples remained in the city after the crucifixion and did not leave until much later. The cycle of traditions that keeps the disciples in

20. R. Branton, "Resurrection In The Early Church." In *Early Christian Origins*, ed. by A. Wikgren (Chicago: Univ. of Chicago Press, 1961), p. 35.
21. J. Weiss, *Earliest Christianity* (New York: Harper Torch-books, 1959).

Jerusalem thus testifies to their abiding faith. The committment of these disciples to the movement spearheaded by Jesus was simply too strong to wither before the ignominy of the Cross.

Consequently, I must agree with Loisy's[22] conclusion that the point of the resurrection stories was *"to transform what was essentially an inward conviction, insight or vision of faith, into external fact* attested by the witness of the senses, and so make the conviction a part of factual history. . .these apparitions fitted with time and place and given material form in the traditional stories, are based upon visions in which *faith was able to find nourishment and confirmation. . . ."*[23]

If we take as our starting point Loisy's argument that the Resurrection and the increased confidence of the disciples followed from their abiding faith, then a number of interesting historical parallels to the proselytizing activities of the early Church become apparent. For example, even though Montanus' prediction (latter half of the second century A.D.) that the Second Coming of Christ would take place at Pepuza, failed to materialize, the Montanist movement did not disappear. Instead, those sincerely committed to Montanus emerged from their disillusion more enthused than ever before. Similarly, after the Anabaptist prediction that the world would come to an end in 1533 A.D. failed to materialize, these people likewise became even more zealous in attempting to win over converts than before the prediction.[24]

The announcement by the Smyrnian cabalist, Sabbatai Zevi, that he was the long awaited Jewish messiah, was hailed with great welcome by many Jews of that time. Even when Sabbatai was imprisoned in 1666 A.D. by the Sultan, faith in him did not wither, for the fact that he had been imprisoned and not executed was taken as proof of his messianic status. Only when Sabbatai unexpectedly renounced his Jewish faith and

22. A. Loisy, *The Birth Of The Christian Religion* (New York: Univ. Books, 1962), p. 95.
23. Italics mine.
24. Cf. R. Heath, *Anabaptism* (London: Alexander and Shepherd, 1895), p. 119.

embraced Islam, did his followers terminate their proselytizing activities.[25]

One of the basic premises of a number of psychological theories is that individuals strive for consistency in their cognitions (beliefs, opinions, attitudes, etc.). Although there are a number of theories that deal exclusively with the problem of cognitive consistency, the most thoroughly tested has been Festinger's theory of cognitive dissonance.[26] Festinger's fundamental argument is that cognitive inconsistency, which he terms dissonance, arises whenever an individual simultaneously holds two cognitions which are psychologically incompatible. For Festinger, cognitions are dissonant if, considering each cognition independently, one would not expect the one to be held in conjunction with the other.

When dissonance does arise, it acts as a state of tension motivating the individual to engage in a reassessment of his cognitions so as to reduce this tension. The conditions that arouse dissonance and the means by which that dissonance may be reduced, comprise the hypotheses from which numerous social scientists have sought to account for much of the complexity of human behavior.

According to the theory, psychological discomfort will occur whenever a person holds an important opinion or belief which he knows is not shared by someone else whom he respects. While Festinger describes a number of important ways in which this kind of dissonance may be reduced, the process which has greatest relevance to the present discussion concerns the role of social support in situations where there is a difference in opinion and no unequivocal information upon which to resolve that difference. To the extent that objective information exists regarding an opinion or belief, differences may be resolved by subjecting those opinions or beliefs to some physical referent. But in cases where no such referent is possible, for example, when two individuals disagree about the imminence of the kingdom of god and/or the messiahship of Jesus, non-physical means of settling the issue must be sought.

In this kind of situation, Festinger contends that the individual experiencing the discomfort may try to persuade those who disagree, to change their beliefs so that they more closely resemble his own. The more people that can be convinced, argues Festinger, the more is one likely to feel that the belief has merit. Consequently, the less ought to be the magnitude of the dissonance stemming from the knowledge that there are others who continue to disagree or disbelieve. In other words, Festinger maintains that an individual may attempt to alleviate dissonance by winning others over to his opinion. On a large scale, this means of dissonance reduction might even take the form of a proselytizing movement, such as that which occurred in early Christianity.

According to Festinger, there are five conditions which must be satisfied before a phenomenon such as increased proselytism will be observed. First, there must be conviction regarding an important belief on the part of the members of a group. Secondly, the group members must each have made some kind of personal commitment or sacrifice stemming from their conviction. Because of these two factors—conviction and commitment—there will be resistance on the part of the group members to admit that they were misled and incorrect in their beliefs.

Pressure to admit such error comes from the fact that the belief which is relatively specific and concerned with the real world (third factor) fails to materialize (fourth factor). A single individual believer might not be able to withstand such psychological pressure and might resolve his inner tension by abandoning his belief. However, given social support (the fifth factor), it might be possible for individual members to derive sufficient psychological strength from the group as a whole, to carry them through this difficult period of disillusionment for some while longer. To continue its existence, however, the members must have some way of counteracting or reassessing the reality of the situation since it is impossible for them to ignore or argue that the disconfirming event did not take place.

Dissonance does not readily occur by ignoring information, but it may be possible to reduce the magnitude of the dissonance created by an event through the addition of new cognitions, so that the proportion of dissonant to consistent (consonant) elements is reduced by some amount. In other words, group members might search for certain kinds of information which, when added to the total, would decrease the weight of the conflicting evidence.

Having presented some of the assumptions and predictions of the theory of cognitive dissonance, we are now in a position to examine the data of the New Testament for any insights that the theory may shed on the origins of the Christian church.

The controversy over whether Jesus regarded himself as the messiah has been argued extensively over the last half-century. The main text having to do with Jesus' messianic self-consciousness is the scene in Caesarea Philippi (Mark, 8:27) where Peter announces, "You are the Christ." However, as Schweizer[27] has noted, there is not a single genuine saying of Jesus' in which he refers to himself either as the messiah, the son of god, or even the servant of god for that matter. Indeed, the evidence seems so incontrovertible on this point that even rather conservative scholars such as E. Stauffer[28] find no basis for concluding that Jesus considered himself as messiah. This does not mean, however, that the disciples were not convinced of his messianism—it is inconceivable that the early Church would have recognized him as such after the crucifixion had this belief not been held beforehand, and the scene at Caesarea Philippi can just as readily be cited as support for this conclusion as it can be for the conclusion that this was the Church putting words into Peter's mouth.[29]

27. E. Schweizer, *Jesus* (London: A.C. Black, 1971), p. 14.
28. E. Stauffer, *Jesus and His Story* (New York: A. Knoff, 1960), p. 131.
29. Cf. R. Bultmann, *History of the Synoptic Tradition* (New York: Harper and Row, 1968), p. 257.

Here, then, is the first factor—conviction. Although the disciples publicly pronounced Jesus as messiah after the ascension, the latter only supported their belief. Moses, Enoch, Elijah, and Isaiah had also been "exalted to heavenly glory" according to Jewish tradition, but none had been regarded as messiah on account of that exaltation. Thus, messiahship need not necessarily have followed from the appearances and resurrection. It is only in light of their conviction that these occurrences were understood as manifestations of Jesus' messianism.

The second factor, commitment, is evident from the cost of discipleship. Materialistically, discipleship involved the renunciation of personal possessions for most of Jesus' followers (Luke, 10:21). Jesus carried no money with him (Mark, 12:15) and he and his disciples had to make do with what little food they had (Mark, 6:38). Besides leaving behind their former way of life (Mark, 1:17-18), however, Jesus' followers had to make an even greater sacrifice, that of living as itinerants, away from the comfort of their families (Mark, 1:19-20). It was not an empty remark when Peter stated, "Lo, we have left all, and have followed thee" (Mark, 10:28). But their committment went further than dedication to a mundane cause. The disciples were preparing themselves for the Kingdom of God and considered it imminent (cf. Mark, 15:43; Matt. 27:57). Not only were they certain of its arrival, they were convinced that by their preparations they would be among the select few who would be saved (Matt., 20:16) and who would share in the bounty of that Kingdom (cf. Luke, 12:32). For the disciples, then, the messiah was not just the King of the Jews, he was their personal teacher (Matt., 23:8f) who, by his example, was preparing them for the Kingdom.

Thus, there was conviction and commitment on the part of the disciples and these factors exerted pressures which were too strong to give way in the face of the disillusionment which the ignominy of the Cross made them face (the third and fourth factors).

According to the tradition of the New Testament, the faith

was created anew by the apparitions experienced by various members of the still intact Christian community. Without the experience of these appearances, the New Testament suggests that the demoralized disciples would not have been able to resolve their dissonance between their belief in Jesus as messiah and his death, Crucifixion was a shameful death, one reserved for political subversives, not messianic deliverers. The socioreligious movement headed by Jesus of Nazareth ought to have collapsed. Why then did the disciples remain together so that there would be an opportunity for these apparitions to be manifested not only to single individuals, but to several disciples, small groups, and even large crowds (I Cor. 15:5-8)?

There can be no doubt that it was the force of Jesus' personality which kept them together immediately following the crucifixion. But without a reappraisal of the character of the messiah, the group could not have maintained its faith in light of the "stumbling block of the cross" (I Cor. 1:23). Why had Jesus died? The question had to be answered. There had to be some purpose in his death. It was at this point that one of the disciples discovered a new meaning in the event. The death on the cross was part of the divine plan, it was necessary for the Christ to suffer and to die because this had been foreordained "according to the Scriptures." The new understanding was that Jesus had not really been a man. Rather, he had been a unique personage, the Son of God, who only took the form of man to accomplish his purposes on earth (cf. Phil. 2:7; Heb. 1:1f.; Col. 1:15f). Jesus had not been an earthly being, instead, he was a transcendant Messiah. This is the "messianic secret." This is the reason why Jesus was not publicly hailed as messiah until sometime after the Crucifixion. It had required time for the disciples to perceive the divine plan.

But this was still only the insight of a few who were already committed to the belief that Jesus was the messiah. Self-confidence in the validity of this belief required more evidence and this was supplied by the appearances of the risen Christ. The effect of these appearances, as Loisy noted, was "to transform what was essentially an inward conviction, insight or vision of faith, into external fact attested by the witness of the senses."[30]

Although their dissonance had now been considerably reduced, there still remained the dissonance caused by the disbelief of the community at large in the messiahship of Jesus. There were two ways that this source of dissonance could be overcome. One was to reevaluate the status of the dissidents. Perhaps their opinion was not really worth cultivating, a position eventually taken by the Church toward the Jews. The other possibility was to persuade more people that the belief was true, in other words, to proselytize and to make new converts. The more people that the early Christians could convince of the validity of their beliefs, the smaller the dissonance stemming from those who refused to acknowledge that the crucified Jesus was the transcendent messiah.

In surveying the growth of the Church, E.F. Scott[31] wrote: "What ever may have happened on the day of Pentecost it only brought to a head the process which had been leading up to it. If we would discover how the church was made and what it was in its essential nature, we must examine with particular care that dim preliminary period when as yet it had no visible existence. The period was a short one, only a few weeks in duration, and yet it counted for almost everything in the after history of the church."

The Gospels and Contemporary Events

To anyone familiar with the content of the Gospel narratives, it must be apparent that each Evangelist approached his subject material in a different frame of mind. Each author has apparently written his work at a different time and for a differ-

---

30. Loisy, p. 95.
31. E.F. Scott, *The Nature of the Early Church* (New York: Longmans Green Co., 1941), p. 10.

ent audience than did the other authors. Consequently, one should not be surprised to find one Evangelist giving due attention to some aspect of his narrative while another Evangelist seems almost uninterested in the same matter.

New Testament scholars of today generally accept the notion that the early Christian communities possessed a book or books that contained a record of Jesus' teaching. This has come to be known as the Q document. The records were sketchy, and each Evangelist attempted to fit what few facts he had into an acceptable biographical record. Matthew and Luke apparently had more material at their disposal than had Mark since they have apparently recorded more of Jesus' message than has Mark. Most likely the mysterious Q document was not available to Mark and instead he contented himself with a more biographical presentation. However, Eusebius, the Church historian, indicates that Mark's source was none other than Peter, one of Jesus' own apostles.[32] Peter, himself, died in the early 60s A.D. and the fact that the destruction of the Temple is not mentioned in Mark's gospel, indicates that the work was composed between A.D. 65-70.

Mark must have faced many difficulties since his source material, namely Peter, would not have recalled all his information in any particular order and he (Mark) had to rearrange many of these unstructured comments into a plausible narrative. Moreover, after Peter's death, he had no way of checking on his own composition as to whether it corresponded to the actual sequence of events. Whenever there was a gap in his information, he would naturally draw upon some fundamental theological tenet that had begun to develop in the Church. Some of these beliefs came from the Jewish Christians living in the community, but the greatest influence was from the Gentile Christians. Thus, the message of salvation recorded in Mark's gospel is Gentile rather than Jewish since it leans heavily on ideas that were current among the Gentiles in the observance of their own pre-Christian religion. For instance, the

32. Eccles. *History*. II, 15:1-2.

doctrine emphasizing Jesus' divinity could only have been due to Gentile influence. At no time could the Jews, even the Jewish Christians, have conceded that God could have a son. But such a conception was not foreign to pagan religions. Many of the pagan gods had also undergone suffering in order to benefit mortals. Thus, the message of Christian salvation, which included the concept of death and resurrection, was a familiar belief of many pagan cults. And yet, the problem of Jesus' death was still a perplexing issue with the early church, judging by the emphasis that the Evangelists, especially Mark, place upon the event. The contradiction between acceptance of pagan doctrine and rejection of Jesus' death in this context, can only be resolved if one examines the historical context in which Mark composed his Gospel.

The first question revolves around the entrance of the Gentiles into the Christian community. Jesus himself had been explicit when he warned his apostles not to go to the Samaritans[33] and it was only after Paul's missionary activity that this admonition came to have less and less importance. It was a characteristic of Paul's attitude that he was not as concerned with fulfilling the Law as with making new converts. Throughout all the areas Paul visited, Jews had already been actively proselytizing and many Gentiles had heard what they had said. But they were unwilling to become full proselytes because of circumcision, dietary laws, or other necessary requirements of the Law. Thus, the goal of the Jewish missionary, namely complete conversion, was rarely accomplished; instead the missionary had to be satisfied with quasi-conversion and the converts were known as "God-fearers," that is, they accepted the Jewish belief in an unseen God but did not practice all the Jewish rites, for example circumcision. Yet it was always impressed upon these Gentiles that they were inferior to the Jews.

When Paul began his proselytizing activities the invitation was extended to the Gentiles not to enter into a new religion

33. Matt., 10:15.

but to an alternative to Judaism; one that was equal to it in its promises for the future but one that did not demand the rigid standards of the parent faith. By removing the obligations and the inferiority feelings of the parent religion, the Gentile could now become the equivalent of the Jew by means of spiritual regeneration through Jesus rather than through fulfillment of the Law.

In some communities, for example Antioch, the Gentile Christians soon outnumbered those of Jewish origin and some of the important Jewish rites ceased to be practiced. When the parent church at Jerusalem learned of the situation at Antioch, emissaries were sent to demand observance of the laws in accord with Jewish precepts. But Paul objected since enforcement of these demands would have meant that the expansion of the church among the Gentiles would have been limited. In the discussion that ensued, Paul triumphed and the decision was reached that the Gentiles who admitted that Jesus was the Messiah could be baptised without having to undergo circumcision or other Jewish rites. Hellenistic Jews who were troubled by this concession were reassured that Jesus had nullified the Law and that it had been replaced with the doctrine of Faith.[34]

But even though Paul declared that he had turned to the Gentiles only because the Jews had rejected Jesus,[35] he still addressed himself to the Jews whenever he came to a new city.[36] His scant successes, however, embittered him. Henceforth, anyone who believed in the divine origin of Jesus was welcomed into the new orthodoxy without regard to his origin. Any sentiments of Jewish superiority were eliminated: "Behold, I, Paul say unto you, that if ye be circumcised, Christ shall profit you nothing. For I testify again to every man that

34. Paul was aware that his explanations differed from traditional interpretation. But he himself had not been converted in the traditional manner, but through divine revelation (Acts, 9:3-20). Not having been converted by the Jerusalem Christians he felt that he owed nothing to their doctrine or description of the historical Jesus and in place of their historical image he substituted the Cross and the Ascension.
35. Acts, 13:46.
36. Acts, 17:1,2.

is circumcised, that he is a debtor to do the whole law. Christ is become of no effect unto you, whosoever of you are justified by the law; yet are fallen from grace."[37] This made Christianity more appealing to the Gentiles and the number of pagan converts increased rapidly.

The first mention we have of any Christian community at Rome is the enigmatic statement recorded by Suetonius: "Since the Jews constantly made disturbances at the instigation of Chrestus, *(impulsore Christo)*, he expelled them from Rome."[38] There has been a lengthy controversy on the interpretation of the word *Chrestus*.[39]. Some scholars still believe that Chrestus was some Jewish agitator, but the consensus of opinion at the present time is that it is a reference to the early Christians. The year of the decree is approximately A.D. 49 and corresponds with the expulsion of Aquila mentioned in Acts (18:2). Apparently the nascent Christian community had come into conflict with the Jews already established in Rome and an internal quarrel developed into such a public disturbance that Claudius took measures to ensure tranquility.

Christianity, however, continued to blossom. In A.D. 64 a great fire broke out in the city and once again the authorities turned on the Christians. All the ancient writers indicate that the persecution was an attempt to shift public anger away from Nero, the emperor, onto the Christians. It was about this time that both Paul and Peter met their deaths.[40]

Shortly after this persecution Mark began to compose his Gospel. His extended preoccupation with the Passion of Jesus no doubt reflects the contemporary problem faced by his followers. This would account for Mark's attempt to strengthen Christian purpose. By dwelling on the sacrifice made by Jesus for his beliefs, Mark was holding out a worthy example for the Church. In addition, the martyrdom of Peter and Paul and the

---

37. Galatians, 5:2-4.
38. Suetonius, *Claudius,* ch. 25.
39. See the work by A. Momigliano, *Claudius,* p. 286 for an extensive bibliography dealing with this question.
40. Sulpicius Severus, *Chronicle,* 2.29.

possibility of death lingering about their meeting places also required some explanation and justification.

No doubt the Jewish community of Rome had turned against them by this time. By not accepting Christians into their synagogues, the Jews had denied them the protection extended to the Jewish cult by the authorities. And if perchance, the Jewish community, through identification with Christianity, was itself in danger of losing precious liberties granted them by the earlier emperors, it would not be surprising to discover Jews collaborating with the Romans in identifying the followers of Chrestus. Therefore, Mark did not find it a difficult problem to relate the persecution of Jesus in Jerusalem to that of his followers in Rome. The whole sequence of the Gospel is merely an introduction to the Passion. Mark prepares us concerning the opposition Jesus is to face[41] and the death that he cannot escape,[42] a death that has more significance than life.[43,44] This is the exhortation to martyrdom: "For whosoever will save his life shall lose it; but whosoever shall lose his life for my sake and the gospel's, the same shall save it."[45]

The significance of this first gospel for Jewish history cannot be underestimated since it established a picture of the Jews in relation to Jesus that was precise and pejorative: The Jews had turned Jesus over to the Romans[46] and although the Romans had found him innocent of any crime[47] the Jews had insisted he be crucified.[47] It is the Jews, and not the Romans,

41. Mark, 3:2.
42. Mark, 8:31.
43. Mark, 10:45.
44. The emphasis on the cross indicates a strong Pauline influence. In the Pauline epistles, a man named Mark is often mentioned. Mark is mentioned in II Timothy, 4:11 and Philemon 24 and in Colossians, 4:10 is described as a cousin of Barnabas and a fellow worker of Paul. In I Peter, 5:13 it appears that he accompanies Peter to Rome ("Babylon"). Thus, we find Mark incorporating Peter's memories of Jesus' teaching (Eccles. Hist., 3.39) and Paul's concept of spiritual revivification into his narrative.
45. Mark, 8:35.
46. Mark, 10:33.
47. Mark, 15:10.
48. Mark, 15:13,14.

who are responsible for all that befell him (and all that was happening in Rome to his followers now).

We have already discussed the anti-Jewish attitude held by the Greek pagan world toward the Jews prior to the Christian era. This animosity was in no way diluted by the message of love preached by Jesus. Rather it was aggravated by the message of hate that pervades the Passion narrative. This is the central fraud of Christianity. It is a religion that preaches love to all who are Christians—and no other. But it is understandable in light of its past history and the contemporary events that shaped its future.

The Impact of the Jewish War on Jewish-Christian Relations: Matthew

Prior to the Roman-Jewish war (A.D. 66-70) the Jewish leaders in Palestine took only a passing interest in the growth of the Christian community. But after the fall of the Temple, Judaism faced an enormous crisis. The symbol of the religion had been destroyed and it seemed to many that Judaism itself might follow. To the leaders of the new center of Judaism located in Jamnia, the most important problem was the consolidation and strengthening of their religion. In an effort to create solidarity, all heresy was condemned and the Jewish Christians were denounced. The Jewish Christians, however, refused to acknowledge this affront. They felt that their acceptance of Jesus as the Messiah did not preclude their following the precepts of Judaism and they continued to attend the synagogue. Since they were Jews themselves, there was no way in which they could be identified unless they personally indicated their beliefs. As a result, the Jewish leaders adopted special methods for the detection of heretics. Foremost among these was the *Birkath-ha-Minim,* which was written by Shemuel ha Qaton around A.D. 80. The *Birkath* was a special liturgical prayer that was inserted into the eighteen benedictions that the

132 THE ROOTS OF ANTI-SEMITISM

Jews repeated every day in their services. Although the original malediction has been lost, Schoeps[49] has constructed the nature of the statement as follows: "may the *nosrim* and *minim* perish suddenly, may they be blotted out of the book of life, not to be recorded there together with the righteous." The *minim,* that is, the Jewish Christians, would of course omit the malediction and would thereby identify themselves. Next, Gamaliel II, the president of the Sanhedrin, sent various letters to the Palestinian communities and to the Diaspora to inform them of the inclusion of the *Birkath* in the services, and to announce the formal separation of Christianity from Judaism. The result of this measure was that the *minim* were cut off from Judaism, Jews, and the synagogue service.

It is in this context that Matthew composed the second gospel. Writing in the Jewish Christian community of Antioch, Matthew reveals the bitter resentment the community felt toward the source of the new legislation enacted against them. Only in this light can we understand the bitterness with which the Pharisees, the Jewish leaders, are condemned. The mark of the Jewish author is everywhere. This is especially apparent when one compares the gospel of Mark, which was written by a Gentile, with that of Matthew. Mark, for instance, discusses the possibility that existed in Roman law that a woman could divorce her husband.[50] This would have been a very foreign concept to the Jews and Matthew completely ignores it. It is only a man's prerogative to gain a divorce,[51] in Jewish law. Moreover, we find Mark explaining Jewish customs and relating information that would be obvious to the Jews.[52] Matthew, on the other hand, finds no need for such interpretation since his readers were primarily Jewish in origin.

The fact that Matthew was motivated to a great extent by the Parisaic persecution is also evident from the gospel itself.[53]

---

49. H.J. Schoeps, *The Jewish-Christian Argument* (New York: Holt, Rinehart, & Winston, 1963), p. 39.
50. Mark, 10:12.
51. Matthew, 5:32.
52. Mark, 1:5, 7:3; 13:3; 15:42.
53. See G.D. Kilpatrick, *The Origins of The Gospel According to St. Matthew* (Oxford: Clarendon Press, 1946).

For example, it is a singular fact that Matthew nearly always places the pronominal genitive "their" in front of the word synagogue. This occurs five times in Matthew,[54] only twice in Mark,[55] only once in Luke,[56] and never in John. Mark refers to "synagogue" six times without the genitive,[57] as compared to three times for Matthew.[58] The use of the pronominal genitive under such different circumstances, can only be accounted for if we understand Matthew's particular point of view:[59] here is the recognition of the new condition whereby he and the Jewish Christians are no longer permitted entrance to "their" synagogues; Jewish Christians can no longer worship as Jews.

Thus, we can understand the venom with which Matthew described the part played by the Pharisees in the persecution of Jesus. Significantly, the antagonism toward the Jews is more marked in those works that were written by Christians who were originally Jews, for example Matthew and John, as compared to those written by Gentiles, for example Mark and Luke. The transition from Mark to Matthew, thus becomes a transition in which the emphasis is shifted from the blindness of Judaism to the blindness of Judaism's teachers, the Pharisees.[60] Throughout the gospel, Matthew collects or invents polemical remarks made by Jesus against the Pharisees; the Sadducees and the Gentiles are almost ignored. This is understandable in view of the fact that after the war of A.D. 66-70 the Sadducees ceased to exist and the Gentiles were being accepted into the church without qualification. Moreover, the important distinction between the Pharisees and the people *('am ha-'arez)* that can be found in Mark[61] is reit-

54. Matthew, 4:32; 9:35; 10:17; 12:9; 13:54.
55. Mark, 1:23,39.
56. Luke, 4:15.
57. Mark, 1:21,29; 3:1; 6:2; 12:39; 13:9.
58. Matthew, 6:2,5; 23:6.
59. Kirkpatrick, p. 110 argues against explaining the use of the genitive pronoun on contextual grounds.
60. "All therefore whatsoever they [the Pharisees] did you observe, that observe and do; but do not yet after their works: for they say and do not." (Matthew, 23:3).
61. Thus Jesus' popularity with the crowds (Mark, 2:12; 3:8; 4:1; 5:24; 6:31-34; 6:55-56; 7:37; 8:1; 10:1; 11:9) is contrasted with the animosity of the Pharisees and scribes (Mark, 2:6;16,18,24; 3:6; 7:1; 8:15,31; 9:30; 10:33).

erated in Matthew.[62] And yet Matthew's own anger seems often uncontrollable and he is carried away in a prophetic condemnation of the entire people: "Then answered *all the people,* and said, His blood be on us, and on our children."[63] It should be apparent, however, that these are not the words of a Jewish Christian but of some Greek editor. The remark is simply not in keeping with Matthew, whose quarrel is not with the Jews, but with their leaders. It is always the leaders who are condemned and despised, not the people. Beginning with John the Baptist, the evangelist makes this clear: "But when he [John] saw many of the Pharisees and Sadducees come to his baptism, he said unto them, 'O generation of vipers, who hath warned you to flee from the wrath to come?' "[64] The people, however, were not slandered.[65] In chapter twenty-three, Jesus explicitly condemns "the scribes and the Pharisees [who] sit in Moses' seat. . .ye are the children of them which killed the prophets." Matthew's touch is clear, but as a result of various interpolated verses (for example 27:25) Matthew's narrative cannot be regarded as a liturgical protest but rather as the first and most significant indictment of the Jews to be registered in Christian doctrine.

Luke the Historian

In Luke we find the schism between the Jews and the Christians almost complete. While Matthew condemns the Pharisees and not the Jews as a whole, Luke does not show this distinction. In the Book of Acts, which was also written by Luke, he notes that Paul had turned to the Gentiles due to the obstinacy of the Jews;[66] the Pharisees are not singled out by Luke. In addition, Luke attempts to demonstrate that the church and the

62. Matthew, 4:24, 25; 7:28; 9:8; 14:13,34-36; 21:11; vs. 11:16; 12:39-45; 16:4.
63. Matthew, 27:25.
64. Matthew, 3:7.
65. Matthew, 3:5,6.
66. Acts, 13:46.

synagogue were separate organizations, although historically they had common origins.

There were several reasons for this turn of events. First, the threat of persecution was still in the air and the Christians were earnestly trying to assure the Roman government that they entertained no subversive plans against it. Every attempt was made to placate Roman opinion.[67] The theme of Pilate's innocence in Jesus' death, which was found in Mark[68] and Matthew,[69] is elaborated by Luke. Neither Herod Antipas nor Pilate could find any guilt in him;[70] therefore the church has no reason to be anti-Roman.

Behind this effort to placate the Roman authorities was the desire to attain for the Christian communities the same protection that was extended to the Jewish communities. The logical extension of the doctrine that the church had superseded the synagogue had to be the idea that the church should also inherit all the privileges that the Romans had extended to the synagogue.

The second reason is less apparent. During the reign of Domitian (A.D. 81-96) there was an effort on the part of some Jews to avoid payment of the poll tax that was imposed upon all Jews after the Jewish war.[71] Since the distinction between Christian and Jew was still unclear in the eyes of the Romans, it may have been possible that Christians, because of their affiliation with Judaism, were being made to pay the tax also. This may be the meaning of Suetonius' enigmatic statement that "those who concealed their origin. . .did not pay the tribute levied upon their people."[72] In other words, those who did not admit to being of Jewish origin, that is, the Christians, were evading the tax. Luke took it upon himself to educate the Romans as to the differences between the Jews and the Christ-

---

67. This can clearly be seen in the gospel of Mark.
68. Mark, 15:1-15.
69. Matthew, 27:1-26.
70. Luke 23:1-25.
71. See ch. 6.
72. Suetonius, *Domitian.*, ch. 12.

ians and perhaps the levying of the poll tax against the Christians was one of his incentives.

Whatever the reasons behind the writing of his books, the growing schism between the church and the synagogue is evident in Luke's writings. By the time of the composition of the final gospel—John, the schism is complete.

John the Angry Man

There is little doubt that John's gospel provided the impetus for much of medieval anti-Semitism. According to Baum,[73] John's Passion narrative was read in the churches during Good Friday and because of its venomous portrayal of them, "the Jews were ordered to stay in their houses to prevent *as much as possible*[74] the flow of blood."[75] Sikes[76] believes that John's gospel may even have been used by the Nazis to stir up anti-Semitic feelings. For his part, Runes[77] feels that the Fourth Gospel is still one of the cornerstones of Christian anti-Semitism.

There is, in fact, no doubt that this is the most anti-Jewish of all the Gospels with all the weight of the crucifix being placed on the back of the Jews. Although the author seems to have been a Jew himself, he emphasizes the animosity of Jesus toward the Jews and suggests that Jesus did not consider himself as such,[78] although John calls him rabbi.[79] It is also evident from his narrative that John is steeped in the election doctrine whereby the Christians have become the true Israel;[80] and in the opening lines of the prologue he defines the division be-

73. Baum, p. 136.
74. Italics mine.
75. Baum, p. 136.
76. W.W. Sikes, "The Anti-Semitism of the Fourth Gospel," *J. Relig.* 21 (1941): pp. 23-30.
77. Runes, *The Jew and the Cross.*
78. Cf. John, 13:33.
79. John, 1:38.
80. For a fuller discussion of the election doctrine, see ch. 8.

tween the Jews and the Christians: "For the law was given by Moses, but grace and truth came by Jesus Christ."[81]

Too much emphasis has probably been placed upon the Fourth Gospel as a testimony to the historical Jesus. Doubtless the evangelist is portraying the events of his own age and as such his work assumes a greater historical import for Jewish-Christian relations during the second century A.D. than it does as a first-century biography.[82] No longer could the Jewish Christians worship alongside the Jews in the synagogues for the *Birkhath-ha-Minim* was in full force at the time John composed his gospel.[83] And no longer do we find the opposition to Jesus in the guise of the Pharisees or the scribes, but simply in "the Jews." The conclusion can only be that the split between Judaism and Christianity was apparent at the time of the gospel's writing. The mission to the Jews had been abandoned and denunciation had begun. The Jews were the devil's offspring,[84] the persecutors of Jesus,[85] and the murderers of the Christ.[86]

Whether John attacked Judaism from within as an embittered Jew struggling to preserve Christianity within Judaism[87] or as an out and out anti-Semite,[88] the result was the same. The Jews were portrayed as the persecutors and murderers of Jesus; accursed forever.

Conclusions

Although there are numerous other works, mainly letters written or ascribed to Paul, comprising the canon of the New

81. John, 1:17.
82. The switch from the singular to the plural in John, 3:11, indicates that it is the Church and not Jesus speaking.
83. Cf. John, 9:22; 12:42.
84. John, 8:44.
85. John, 5:16; 7:1; 8:40.
86. 18:38-40; 19:4-6,12.
87. See J.A.T. Robinson. "The Destination and Purpose of St. John's Gospel," *New Test. Stud.* 6 (1960): 117-131; Sikes, pp. 23-30.
88. M. Hay, *Europe And The Jews.* (Boston: Beacon Press, 1961).

Testament, they have not had the same impact on Jewish-Christian relations as have the gospels and so these have been largely ignored. It also seems to me that far too much attention has been devoted to the life of Jesus as presented in the gospels. These works are not historical or biographical sketches of a man but of a movement. There is no information outside of the gospels to authenticate any aspect of Jesus' life, but there is information dealing with the growth and expansion of the Church, of its attitudes toward the Roman authorities and its parent body, Judaism, and it is only with these topics that one can begin to feel firm ground underfoot.

Although it would take us too far afield to discuss each of these topics, a few words must be devoted to the best known of all these themes, the Passion narrative. Surely there is no other piece of literature that has had greater impact on the Jew. For centuries the Jews have been accused of deicide. This charge has been answered by Jewish apologists such as Jules Isaac[89] but denial is meaningless and Runes[90] has gone so far as to refuse any dialogue on the matter. For our own purposes, which are academic and not apologetic, theological, or polemical, there is only the task of understanding the roots and manifestations of ancient anti-Semitism and not the injustices. In light of this purpose we should note only that the Passion narratives were not originally intended to denounce the Jews as Christ killers. Rather, they were written to strengthen and to give courage to the early Christians in their own hours of persecution. But the metaphor became distorted and misused as the historical milieu changed. When once the Roman eagle fell, there was no longer any dangerous external threat. It was now internal—a threat to the ideology, theology, and the machinery of Christianity. Witness the many heretical movements abounding in the early Church. There was only one way to create in-group cohesion once the Romans were won over and this was to find another common enemy and that enemy was and still is the Jew.

89. Isaac, *The Teaching of Contempt.*
90. Runes, *The Jew and the Cross.*

8

The Jews under the Last Pagan Emperors

The Postwar Years

THE WAR of A.D. 66-70 marked a turning point in the religious makeup of Judaism. The Temple, the long-standing symbol of the religion was gone forever and so were the Sadducees, the priestly class who had supervised its ceremony and who had tried to introduce Roman culture into Jewish life. After the Temple, all attempts at Hellenization ceased and Judaism withdrew into itself for sustinence.

Politically, the national status of the Jews remained unchanged. The war, though won by the Romans, was won at cost, and neither Vespasian nor Titus took the name "Judaicus" although both had conquered Judea.[1] Huidekoper[2] attributes this to the fact that neither of them wished to convey the impression that either had adopted Judaism instead of conquering it, but such an assumption would hardly have been

---

1. It was customary to append the name of a conquered country to the general's name, for example, X. . .the Parthian.
2. *Judaism at Rome*, p. 273.

made by anyone. According to Eusebius,[3] Vespasian in fact ordered a search to be made for all those who might have been of Davidic descent so that any messianic pretenders might be eliminated. Although Eusebius maintains that "a very great persecution was inflicted against the Jews" this is to be doubted since it is not recorded anywhere else. Eusebius mentions three such persecutions against the Jews. Besides Vespasian, Domitian and Trajan are both said to have sought extermination of the house of David.[4] More than likely, Eusebius has conflated history and Christian propaganda. By arguing that the Davidic line had been exterminated, the messianic belief in Jesus would be substantiated since the Romans had ostensibly eliminated any future contenders. The identical theme is found in Tertullian's *Adversos Judaeos* where he extends Hadrian's banishment of the Jews from Jerusalem to include Bethlehem also. The thinking was that since the Jews were not allowed to enter the city of David, the messiah must already have been born because the prophets had clearly stated that the Christ would be born in Bethlehem.[5]

Persecutions may have occurred, but these were not aimed at the Jews, but at any Romans who had adopted Judaism. The idea that the Jews were subject to various religious persecutions by the Romans is completely out of keeping with Roman policy regarding cults that were *religio licta,* such as Judaism. Whenever an ancient historian refers to Jewish persecution, one must distinguish between Jews by birth and Jews by conversion. It is against this latter group that measures were taken.[6] Since the ancient Roman religion was associated with the destiny of Rome,[7] a Roman who worshipped any deities other than those sanctioned by the senate, would be disloyal to

3. *Church Hist.,* 3.12.1.
4. *Ibid.,* 3.19; 3.32.3-4.
5. *Adv. Jud.,* ch. 13.
6. See Abel, "Were the Jews Banished From Rome in 19 A.D.?" *R.E.J.,* 127 (1968): 275-279.
7. W.H.C. Frend, *Martyrdom And Persecution In The Early Church.* (Oxford: B. Blackwell, 1965), p. 115.

the Roman people. Participation in the national religion precluded observance of foreign rites. Hence, one finds throughout the history of the empire, laws passed not against the Jews, but against "Judaizers"—non-Jews observing Jewish practices.

To commemorate the victory over the Jews in A.D. 70 the usual triumph was celebrated and coins were minted recording the conquest of the country. Most of these displayed the legend *Ivdaea Capta* and bore the figure of a woman seated at the foot of a palm tree, and near her the emperor, his foot on a helmet. The first coin commemorating the war was struck in A.D. 71.[8] Four years later a similar coin was minted indicating that the Romans still pointed to their victory over the Jews with pride, (a tribute more to the latter than to the victors). Most of the coins of this genre carried the image of a woman, tied and sitting by a palm tree; occasionally, there are a pile of arms strewn about on the ground. The palm tree symbolized Judea while the female figure called to mind the prophesy, "and she desolate shall sit on the ground."[9]

In order to increase the national treasury, a special tax was levied against all Jews[10] called the *denarii duo Judaeorum* and a special bureau, the *fiscus Judaicus* was created to insure its collection. According to Vespasian's decree, all those who lived in accord with the Jewish way of life were liable to the tax. In Egypt, the tax was to be paid by every Jew, man or woman, from the age of three to sixty-two and masters of Jewish servants were also required to pay for the number of Jews in their service.

This was another blow to Jewish status in that country since

---

8. J.Y. Akerman, *Numismatic Illustrations Of Narrative Portions of The New Testament* (Chicago: Argonaut Press, 1966), p. 23.
9. *Ibid.*
10. Dio (66.4) asserts that Vespasian levied the tax against all Diaspora Jews because of the aid that they had given their co-religionists in Palestine. But there is no evidence to suggest that the insurgents received any outside help and it is more likely that Vespasian's greed was his chief motive in instituting the tax (See M.S. Ginsburg, "Fiscus Judaicus," *J.Q.R.* 21 (1930): 281-91.

the tax served to denigrate Jews a little further in the eyes of non-Jews. Hitherto, Jews had been equated with the Egyptians because they were subject to the *laographia*,[11] but with the implementation of the Jewish tax, their social position was even lower than the lowly Egyptians.

Some scholars[12] have interpreted the tax as a deliberate social disparagement since this was the first time any ethnic group had been made subject to a special tax. The original purpose of the tax, however, was not to stigmatize the Jews and it is doubtful whether it was regarded as an insult outside of Egypt. There is no reason to believe that the tax was levied against the Jews as a *religio*. None of their privileges were cancelled after the war and there is every indication that they were still regarded as a *natio*, as suggested by the coins bearing the inscriptions *Ivdaea Capta* and *Ivdea Devicta*. The other two bureaus, the *fiscus Alexandrinus* and the *fiscus Asiaticus*, which collected taxes from Alexandrians and Asiatics even though they lived outside their native areas, were created for the same purpose as was the *fiscus Judaicus*. All three were founded along similar lines based on the concept of *natio* and hence offered no departure from traditional Roman policy.

Under Domitian, the agents of the *fiscus Judaicus* attempted to collect the tax from all Jews without exemption even though they did not "live in accord with the Jewish life" or even professed to being Jews. Suetonius[13] testifies to the thoroughness with which the agents of the *fiscus* carried out their search for recalcitrant Jews: "I recall being present in my youth when the person of a man ninety years old was examined before the procurator and a very crowded court, to see whether he was circumcised. . . ." Apparently, the tax was collected with immodest thoroughness.

Despite the unfavorable circumstances surrounding the adoption of Judaism, proselytizers still met with some success.

11. See ch. 6.
12. See Baron and Ginsburg.
13. *Domitian*, 12.2.

Eight months before his death, Domitian still found it necessary to reissue the proscription against those who abandoned the ancient religion of Rome.[14] In A.D. 95 he even examined Flavius Clemens and his wife Domitilla, his own relatives, on a charge of Judaizing.[15] The two were found guilty; Clemens was executed and his wife was sent into exile.

In the following year (A.D. 96) Nerva succeeded Domitian as emperor and Judaism had a temporary respite. Proselytes were formally allowed to acknowledge their religion without fear of punishment as atheists and the enthusiasm of the *fiscus Judaicus* was curbed. Accusations against evaders ceased to be made and only those who admitted their religion were required to pay the tax as had originally been decreed by Vespasian. In observance of this change in policy, a special coin was struck bearing the inscription, *Fisci Iudaici Calumnia Sublata* (abolition of the unjust enforcement of the Jewish tax).

The Jewish Wars

The period between A.D. 90-115 was, generally speaking, free of any Roman-Jewish confrontations in the Diaspora.[16] When Trajan came to the throne, Rome once again had an emperor who envisaged aggrandizement. His major campaign was to be against the Parthians, the unconquered enemy of the Romans. Setting out with a strong force, Trajan easily vanquished the disunited peoples of Mesopotamia and it appeared that his chances for ultimate victory were assured. However, in A.D. 115, while he was planning to attack the Parthians, he

14. See above.
15. Dio, 67.14.1-2.
16. Josephus (*Wars*, 7.1-4) relates that some of the *sicarii* who had evaded capture by the Romans after A.D. 70 fled to Egypt and caused a disturbance in the Jewish communities. When Vespasian was informed of the disorders, he ordered Lupus, his governor, to destroy the Jewish Temple that had been erected in the Land of Onias during the Ptolemaic period. It is possible that the *sicarri* advocated continued resistance to the Romans and Vespasian's action may have aimed at destroying any possible rallying symbols.

received word that the Jews had risen in open rebellion in various parts of the Empire and operations against the Parthians had to be temporarily halted while he dealt with the internal menace.

Taking advantage of the emperor's absence, the Jews of Cyrenaica had risen up against their Greek neighbors. The Jewish leader was a self-styled messiah named Loukas or Andreas and his objective was complete annihilation of the hated Greek population because of all the wrongs that the Jews had suffered there on account of Greek malevolence. According to the exaggerated account of the anti-Semite Xiphilinus, upon whom Dio was dependent, the Jews behaved as savages; they ate their victims' flesh and smeared their blood on themselves. Not content with this inhumanity, they cut some of their victims in two while they fed others to wild beasts.[17] In all, 220,000 Greeks and Romans were slain.[18]

Those Greeks who escaped fled to Egypt where fighting had also broken out between the Jews and the Alexandrians. Eusebius[19] implies a close liason between the Jews of Alexandria and Cyrenaica and after the fighting was over in Cyrenaica many Jews came to Alexandria to help their coreligionists defeat the common Greek enemy.[20] But by that time, the Jews in the city had been defeated and instead the Cyrenaican Jews joined forces with those Jews who were still fighting in the countryside. Even the combined forces were no match for both the Greeks and the Romans (who had been sent to put down the rebellion) and the revolt was quenched after severe losses to both sides. In Cyprus, to which the rebellion had also spread, a decree was passed forbidding all Jews from inhabiting the island from that time forth. Thereafter, any Jew found on a Cypriot shore, even if he were the victim of a

17. These atrocities, fantastic though they might seem, were earnestly believed by some and at least one Egyptian mother prayed to the gods that her son would not be roasted alive by the Jews (*C.P.J.*, no. 437).
18. Dio, 68.32.
19. *Church Hist.*, 4.2.1-5.
20. See A. Fuks, "Aspects of the Jewish Revolt in A.D. 115-117, *J.R.S.* 51 (1961): 98-104.

shipwreck, was to be executed on the spot.[21] In Mesopotamia, the Jews at Trajan's rear had caught the spirit too and they had attacked the emperor as he was approaching Ctesiphon, the Parthian capital. It was a most dangerous position for the Romans, for they now had enemies on two fronts. Trajan ordered Lucius Quietus, to relieve him and the general wasted no time in eliminating the threat,[22] and "On account of this success he was appointed governor of Judea by the Emperor."[23]

By the first year of Hadrian's reign (A.D. 117) it was all quiet on the eastern front. Unlike Trajan, Hadrian planned to strengthen the empire not by foreign conquest but by internal renovation. Therefore, the resources of the empire were mobilized not toward extension but toward consolidation. A number of improvements were planned, one of which was the founding of a new city on the site of Jerusalem.[24] Resistance was inevitable. The plan, however, was not put into full operation and this postponed the hostilties for fifteen years. In the meantime, the Jews converted the caves of Judea into fortresses, which they fortified with weapons previously judged unfit for battle by the Romans.

In A.D. 132 work began on the new city and in the same year the Jews attacked the Romans.[25] The Roman governor, T.

21. Dio, 68.32.
22. Schürer, p. 279 points to the seriousness of the Jewish threat by the fact that Trajan called upon a consular legate rather than a general of praetorian rank.
23. Eusebius, *Church Hist.*, 4.2.5.
24. A dubious legend has it that Hadrian gave the Jews permission to rebuild their Temple but later changed his mind on the advice of the Samaritans. Instead, he allowed them a Temple on any site except that occupied by the previous one. The Jews refused and planned to take up arms but were temporarily pacified by one of their rabbis (Beresith rabba ch. 64). The legend is completely without foundations. If for any reason, it was probably started to malign the emperor's character by making it seem that he was easily influenced by those who wished Israel ill will.
25. Spartian (Hadrian, 14) indicates that Hadrian precipitated the war by outlawing the practice of circumcision, which he equated with castration. Whatever his purpose, it is unlikely that the decree contributed to the war since there was no way in which it could have been enforced. Moreover, the decree was not aimed specifically at the Jews but against all people who circumcised themselves or their offspring. Under Antoninus Pius, the Jews were once again permitted to circumcise their children, but the prohibition still extended to non-Jews. Quite possibly, the emperor had in mind the "Judaizers" when he passed the edict, which would suggest that Jewish proselytism was still occurring at this time.

Rufus, was one of the first victims. Confronted by an army of undisciplined religiously fanatic Jews led by Simon Bar Kochba, the newly proclaimed messiah, he was compelled to retreat, leaving the Jews in possession of their country. The most coveted prize, Jerusalem, was captured and the Jews proclaimed a new era. It was a short-lived era. Hadrian sent to Britian for his able general, Julius Severus, and the rebellion was starved into submission as the Romans cut off the Jews' supply lines. Bar Kochba withdrew to Bethar to make his final stand. When the Romans finally attacked, the Jews gave way; Bar Kochba, however, was not found among the prisoners.

According to Dio,[26] 580,000 Jews were killed in the fighting while those who died of fire and disease could not be determined; Roman losses were so numerous, however, that Hadrian did not enclose in his report to the senate the usual formula, "I and the army are well."[27]

After the war, the number of Jewish slaves was so great that men were selling for the same price as horses in the markets of Hebron.[28] Jerusalem was finally converted into a Roman colony called Colonia Aelia Capitolina and on the site of the ancient Temple, a new shrine was built dedicated to Capitoline Jupiter. Henceforth, any Jew even entering the area of the new city could be put to death. With the desolation of their holy city and the loss of their country, the Jews were no longer a *natio*. They were a people without a home, a stranger in every land, with nowhere to turn except to themselves. Whatever privileges had been granted them before, however, they kept after the war. One by one as the emperors of the Christian Roman Empire succumbed to the new Christian movement of the empire these privileges, given to them originally as a *natio*, were to be revoked. But in the meantime, the world was still ruled by pagan emperors, and Jewish privileges remained in force.

26. Dio, 60.14.
27. *Ibid.*
28. Schürer, p. 305.

Following Hadrian, there were no more events of any momentous importance for the Jews for the next two hundred years. Antoninus Pius is said to have relaxed a ban on circumcision so that the Jews could now legally continue the practice,[29] and during Septimius Severus' reign we once again hear of measures taken to forbid conversion to Judaism.[30] The only explanation is that Romans were still being lured by the religion even though those who followed it had been disgraced in three wars. On the other hand, conditions improved somewhat for the Jews for they were allowed to hold public office and were exempted from those duties that might conflict with their religion.[31]

In A.D. 212 Caracalla passed his famous edict, the *constitutio Antonina,* which extended the rights of citizenship to nearly all inhabitants of the empire and the distinction between citizens and noncitizens disappeared. The edict, however, was not such a monumental measure for at this time Roman citizenship no longer conferred the prestige it once had.

When Alexander Severus became emperor (A.D. 222) events seemed to take a favorable turn for the Jews. Severus rescinded Hadrian's edict, which prohibited Jews from entering Jerusalem, and he reaffirmed their existing privileges. Apparently his relations with the Jews were so amiable, he was considered almost a patron and was contemptuously nicknamed the *Syrian archisynagogus*[32] by the Romans.

However, in A.D. 250 a new form of persecution was commenced by emperor Decius. Various lists were prepared of all the inhabitants of the empire and all the citizens were summoned to appear before commissions so that they could express their loyalty to the acknowledged state cults. This form of religious coercion, although leveled mainly at the Christians, did not leave the Jews exempt since they were legally

29. *Digest,* 48.8.11.
30. Spartian, *Severus,* 17.1.
31. *Digest,* 50.2.3.3.
32. Lampridius, *Alex. Severus,* 28.7.

citizens by Caracalla's edict. However, they may have not been included in the emperor's command since they had previously been granted exemption from such acts by Septimius Severus.[33]

The edict of Valerian in A.D. 257 contained the same obligation and even though citizens no longer recognized the gods of Rome, they were still required to perform the symbolic act of sacrifice acknowledging the Roman cult. The reason for these measures was that the empire was in danger and the threat was internal. Judaism's religious rival, Christianity, had been transformed from an ineffective superstition into a monotheistic force that now vied with both Judaism and the emperor for the loyalty of men.

The Jewish-Christian Controversy[34]

At the end of the first century it was evident that Christianity was not just an offshoot of Judaism but a religion unto itself. The pagan world was now confronted with zealous proselytizers from a new religion that offered the same spiritual principles as were inherent in Judaism but that required no prerequisites such as circumcision. To those seeking a new way of coping with human suffering, Christianity offered the promise that in the next life the "have-nots" would become the "haves." The appeal met with great success and Christianity began to spread all over the Greek- and Latin-speaking world. In light of this success, Christians could not understand the obduracy of the Jews in their denial of Jesus as the messiah. Initially, Christian apologies stated that the only difference between Judaism and Christianity was that the former refused to accept Jesus.[35] For their part, the Jews remained aloof. They

33. See note 31.
34. The relations between the pagan emperors and the early Christian movement will not be discussed since it is beyond the scope of this essay. W.H.C. Frend's *Martyrdom And Persecution In The Early Church* is a thorough presentation of the facts.
35. Tertullian, *Apology*, ch. 21.

mocked the Christian claim of messianism by citing the passage from Deuteronomy that stated that anyone hanged on a tree, that is crucified, was accursed by God.[36] More imaginative Jews circulated the rumor that Jesus was really the illigitimate son of Mary and a Roman soldier named Pantheras.[37] He was merely a sorcerer who had tried to lead Israel astray.[38]

The Christians retorted by picking the Old Testament apart verse by verse as they searched for prophecies alluding to Jesus as the messiah. When they felt that they had such authentication they offered the relevant verses as proof of their contention; context and historical background were ignored. The scriptures, they argued, were intended to be allegorically interpreted. When the Jewish teachers attempted to correct their understanding they were accused of erroneous interpretation[39] or of incompetence.[40] Occasionally they were also accused of knowing the scriptures but of deliberately falsifying their real meaning to the Jews.[41]

Bitter at the refusal of the Jews to accept Christianity, the polemicists argued that Christianity was in reality the true Israel. Because of their many sins, dating back to the time of Moses and the golden calf and ending with the rejection of Jesus, they argued that the Jews had forfeited their claim as the "elect" and it had been transferred instead to the Christians.[42] To prove that the election had passed from the Jews, the Christians pointed to the destruction of the Temple and to the banishment of the Jews from Jerusalem under Hadrian.[43] Justin Martyr even argued that the only reason God had left the Jews on earth was to make it clear that they, and

36. *Deut.* 21.23.
37. Origen, *Contra Celsus,* 1.9.1.
38. *Talmud,* Sanh. 43a.
39. Justin, *Dial. with Trypho,* ch. 68,72.
40. *Ibid.* ch. 34, 38.
41. Origen, *Contra Celsus,* 5.60.
42. Justin, *Dial.* ch. 51,85.
43. Tertullian, *Apol.* ch. 21.

not the gentiles, were solely responsible for the crucifixion of Jesus![44]

The Jews generally refrained from argument.[45] Possibly they may have been cautioned by their leaders against having anything to do with the Christians.[46] As far as their taking an active part in the Christians persecutions, there is little evidence indicating such participation. Surveying the grounds for this accusation, Parkes[47] has concluded that these charges were based on "theological exegesis" rather than on historical fact. More than likely there is some truth in this observation. But on the other hand, one cannot dismiss the possibility that the Jews participated in the persecutions of that era even though they themselves may not have begun them.

Although this period is characterized only by accusation and insult between the two religions, it marked one of the most important epochs in Jewish-Christian relations for in this period the church accepted the doctrine that the Jews were responsible for the death of Jesus and that God was punishing (or would continue to punish) them for their malice. It was the age in which theological anti-Semitism was introduced into Christian doctrine[48] to be formulated in what Jules Isaac has called "The Teaching of Contempt."[49]

---

44. Justin, *Dial.* ch. 21.
45. *Ibid.* ch. 112.
46. S. Krauss, "The Jews in the Works of the Church Father," *J.Q.R. 5*, (o.s. 1893): p. 128.
47. J. Parkes, *The Conflict of the Church and the Synagogue* (Cleveland: World Pub. Co., 1961).

9

The Jews under the Christian Emperors

Changes in the Make-Up of the Empire

IN A.D. 284 Diocletian decided that his empire was too vast and unwieldly for him to administer himself and he decided to decentralize his government. Consequently, Maximian, his comrade, was proclaimed "Augustus" and was given control of the western provinces while Diocletian retained control of the east. In A.D. 293 a new system was also instituted whereby each "Augustus" was to choose a subordinate as his immediate administrator to be known as "Caesar." The "Caesar" not only would govern the province but would take over the position of "Augustus" when the latter died, and after his succession, he would proclaim a new "Caesar." In this way Diocletian hoped to do away with the court intrigue and the assassination attempts that usually plagued the empire.

The city of Rome was also abandoned as the seat of government. Instead, each Augustus chose his own capital. Diocletian moved his residence to Nicodemia while Maximian settled in Milan so as to keep an eye on the barbarians who were beginning to encroach upon the borders of the empire.

But the empire was in a greater difficulty than that which came from the barbarians. The forests that had spread from Spain to Palestine had been cut down to provide fuel, leaving large areas arid and unproductive. The once rich lands that had sent overabundances of food to Rome's already full storehouses were exhausted and some of the formerly fertile lands had turned into desert because of poor soil conservation. To combat the serious food shortages, Diocletian ordered that all farmers were to be bound to the land—forbidden to leave under any circumstance. But the unusual hardships forced many to challenge the severe penalties incumbent upon desertion of farm lands. The labor force had also declined due to a decrease in birthrate coupled with a number of disastrous plagues. Whatever labor body remained was conscripted into permanent occupations to be followed by all hereditary descendants. The entire population of the empire was stratified and regimented and a fantastic bureaucracy was created to cope with the empire's greatest threat ever—the scarcity of food.

Two positions of nobility headed the newly formed caste system. The state officials and those with special rank were called the *honestiores* while the city officials, landowners, and merchants made up the *curiales*. The members of the lower caste, such as the farmers, were termed *humiliores*.

Initially the *curiales* were local government officials chosen by fellow citizens to supervise the finances and administration of the various cities. However, the office of the *curia* came to be a hated and ruinous privilege since the *curiales* had to levy and collect taxes from their communities and whenever they were short they had to make up the differences from their own pockets. Here too desertion was common and some cities were entirely depopulated since sooner or later everyone was handed the office. The only way to avoid it was to flee the land or to descend into the labor class.

Following Diocletian's death, civil war broke out when Constantine and Maxentius both refused to accept the pro-

claimed line of succession in the west. Once they overcame
their adversaries they turned against each other to decide who
would rule the western empire. Associated with this battle
there occurred one of the most momentous events in world history. In A.D. 312 Constantine ordered that the symbol of the
cross be placed on the shields of his soldiers, claiming that
Christ was on his side against the heathen Maxentius.[1] Following his victory, Constantine was established as divine
monarch.[2] As a result, Christianity gained the status of being a
tolerated belief. In A.D. 313 the famous Edict of Milan was
issued in which Constantine granted "both to Christians and to
all, the free power to follow the religion of their choice." Although the edict specifically mentioned Christianity, it extended to all religions the same toleration. It was not until A.D.
325 that Christianity was endorsed as the official state religion.

The Legal Position of Judaism in the Christian State

Following its triumph, the Church was no longer in a position of supplication, begging for tolerance and understanding.
The hardships it had experienced were forgotten. With its
newly found authority and power it began to attack all those
who did not belong to the Church and did it with as much in-

1. Numerous legends have been worked around the theme of Constantine's recognition of Christianity. Only one of these concerns our theme. According to this
   story, Constantine adopted Christianity as a result of his witnessing a famous
   dispute between Pope Sylvester I and a number of Jews headed by a Jewish
   magician named Zambri. The discussion between the two led neither side to
   yield and finally a test of power was held to see who was the true favorite of
   God. Zambri whispered the name of God into the ear of a bull and as a result it
   was instantly killed. Undaunted, the Pope followed the feat by restoring the dead
   bull with the name of Christ. As a result, Constantine and all the Jews witnessing the event were so impressed that they all adopted the Christian faith on the
   spot. [See A.L. Williams, *Adversus Judaeos* (Cambridge: Cambridge Univ. Press
   1935), p. 339-47.] The legend was apparently elaborated to such an extent that it
   formed the basis for medieval miracle plays. [J. Trachtenberg, *The Devil And The
   Jews (New Haven: Yale Univ. Press, 1961), p. 65*].
2. In A.D. 323 Constantine ended the dual monarchy by defeating the eastern Augustus and incorporating the total empire under himself.

dignation and coercion as it could summon from the imperial powers.

The Christian emperors, for their part, sought to eliminate all controversy and division that might further weaken the internal structure and they upheld Christianity as the only tolerated belief system. Paganism was suppressed as much as possible and although the Jews suffered no official religious hostility, they were relegated to second-class citizenship. Many of their civil rights were denied them and they were segregated from the Christians so that they would not be able to contaminate them with their "turpitude."

In A.D. 429 the emperor Theodosius II had all the laws from the time of Constantine to his day compiled in a compendium so that these laws could be uniformly observed throughout the Christian world. This was the *Theodosian Code*. Although it does not include every law that was passed during this period, it is extremely valuable for any study of the legal position of the Jews since the laws relating to them are given in full along with the date, place of issue, and the emperor responsible for their promulgation.

One of the main sections of the legislation dealing with the Jews concerns their involvement in the decurionate, which the Jews, like everyone else in the empire, sought to avoid. While the empire had been pagan, the Jews had been exempt from all those public offices whose duties involved some form of sacrifice to pagan deities. However, in the new Christian state, public office no longer included religious duties since these were handled exclusively by the Church. As a result Jews could no longer claim immunity from public office.

Under Constantine, Jews could be obliged to serve as *curiales* if nominated by the municipal senate of their districts, but two or three Jews in each community were extended the perpetual privilege of immunity from such office "in order that something of the former rule may be left them as a solace."[3]

3. *Codex Theodosius.* 16.8.3.

Likewise religious leaders were also granted exemption from compulsory public service.[4] However, this law seems not to have been enforced for another law had to be passed exempting this class of Jews "from every compulsory public service of a corporal nature."[5]

These early laws, which were issued between A.D. 321 and 330, show no signs of anti-Jewish policy since it was only fair that Jews should help shoulder the burdens of the empire; that the Jews were unwilling to participate in the decurionate was only natural in face of the hardships involved.

While the privileges of the Jews were respected to a certain extent by the fourth century emperors, paganism did not fare as well and definite steps were taken toward its abolition. All sacrifices were outlawed[6] and suitable penalties were ordered for those who continued with such rites. Paganism, however, could not be completely eradicated and shortly after the empire became Christian, Julian, a neo-pagan, ascended the throne. For two years (A.D. 361-363) paganism had a brief revival and since he favored almost all beliefs over Christianity his negative attitude earned him the title of the "Apostate," by which he was known to his Christian contemporaries.

Although Julian was not pro-Jewish, he went out of his way to favor Judaism, perhaps only to slight Christianity.[7] In A.D. 362 he sent a letter to the Jews of Antioch concerning the rebuilding of the Temple that seems to indicate a sincere partiality toward Judaism. First he stated that he had destroyed the tax rolls containing the names of all Jews who were liable to the Jewish tax that apparently was still being collected at that time. In destroying these lists Julian in effect was abolishing the *fiscus judaicus*. Secondly, he addressed the patriarch, Hillel II, as "my brother," which indicates more than a favorable attitude toward not only the spiritual leader of the Jews but toward the Jews in general. Finally, he indicated that the

4. *C.T.*, 16.8.2.
5. *C.T.*, 16.8.4.
6. *C.T.*, 16.10.2; 16.10.5.
7. Sozomenus, *Eccl. Hist.*, 5.22.

Temple at Jerusalem might be rebuilt. This seems to be without doubt the expression of a benevolent attitude. But one must consider that at this time Julian was planning a war with the Persians and the battleground would probably be Babylonia—an area densely populated with Jews! These same people had attacked Trajan and Alexander Severus when these generals had advanced into Mesopotamia against the Parthians, and it was possible that they would fight against the Romans a third time unless they could be won over. To lure the Jews to his side, or to make sure that they remained neutral was of strategic importance in any plans he might have for the invasion of the Persian empire. The final sentence of his letter to the Jews shows that his promise was merely an attempt at *realpolitik:* ". . .when I return safely from the Persian war, I may restore the Holy City of Jerusalem, and rebuild it at my own expense, even as you have for so many years desired it to be restored; and therein will I unite with you in giving praise to the Almighty."[8] The campaign was not a success. Julian himself died during the war and needless to say, the Temple was never built.[9]

Whatever incentive Julian gave the Jews to "address still more fervent prayers for my empire to the Almight Creator of the Universe, who has deigned to crown me with his own undefiled right hand. . ." he found Judaism contemptible. He called it a "school of impiety."[10] and while he admitted that he also "worships the God of Abraham, of Isaac, and of

8. Julian, "To the Community of the Jews," *Letters,* no. 25, reprinted in M. Adler, "The Emperor Julian And The Jews," *J.Q.R. 5,* (o.s. 1893); p. 622-24.
9. The legend told by many Christian writers concerning the rebuilding of the Temple in which the Jews were driven off the site after they had begun the construction is traceable to Gregory of Nazianzen (*Oratio* II), according to Adler (Emperor Julian). On the commencement of the construction, the Talmud is completely silent. Since Julian did not survive the Persian campaign, the plan would have had to be implemented some time in the reign of his successors. Needless to say, none of these shared his apparent proclivity toward the Jews and it is unlikely that any of them would have granted the necessary permission.
Besides, the bribe did not work. The Jews of Babylonia remained loyal to the Persians in the struggle.
10. *Letter to Theodore.*

Jacob,"[11] he contended that this god of the Jews was the same Demiurgus he himself worshipped. In one of his writings that is only partially preserved, he states that history had proven that the Jews are a god-forsaken race[12] and compared to the achievements of Greco-Roman culture, the achievements of Judaism were pitiful.[13]

Taken in narrow context, Julian's behavior toward the Jews would suggest a pro-Jewish attitude on the part of the emperor. But it is only because of the context. To say that he was pro-Jewish because of his promise to build the Temple and because he abolished the Jewish tax is more a misconstruction of his objectives than an objective evaluation. He only appears benevolent in comparisons with those who immediately preceeded and followed him.

When Gratian came to the throne[14] he attempted to undo everything Julian had done to defame Christianity.[15] As a consequence, Judaism was placed in as inferior a position as possible. Jewish clergy no longer were permitted the exemption granted Christian leaders regarding service in the decurionate.[16] If they still desired to avoid participation in these duties they had to make up the payment of taxes from their own pockets.[17] Some Jews circumvented serving on the public council by leaving their native cities, but they were ordered to return so that they could accept their lawful duties. Under Arcadius (A.D. 383-408) the eastern emperor,[18] the Jewish clergy was granted the same privileges accorded to the Christian priesthood as far as the decurionate was concerned.[19]

11. *Ibid.*
12. Quoted from *In Galilaeos* by C.N. Cochrane, *Christianity and Classical Culture,* (Oxford: Clarendon Press, 1940), p. 265.
13. *Ibid.*
14. Jovian, who immediately succeeded Julain, only lived for a few months after he became emperor.
15. To Julian, Christianity was a "Galilean superstition" and although he did not persecute the Christians he heaped abuse on them and made it difficult for them to serve in any official capacity.
16. Christian laymen, of course, were not exempt.
17. *C.T.,* 12.1.99.
18. After Theodosius I's death the empire was partitioned again.
19. *C.T.,* 16.8.13.

However, the privilege was shortly revoked,[20] possibly to keep in line with policies in the western half of the empire since Honorius (A.D. 394-423) affirmed that religion was not a suitable excuse for evading the decurionate.[21]

The question was settled once and for all by Theodosius II for in A.D. 438 he passed a law that excluded the Jews not only from the decurionate but from every public office in the empire.[22] Henceforth Jews were allowed no responsibilities in the Christian world. This was no innovation in policy since Honorius in A.D. 404 had barred the Jews from military service and from court rank.[23] In A.D. 418 Honorius reissued the edict along with the order that all Jews serving in the army at that time were to be immediately released from service. The measures were obviously not out of any respect for Jewish protests against bearing arms on the sabbath or eating unclean food, but because it was felt that the Christian world should not be protected by Jews.

Another series of laws were passed concerning apostasy that made it a crime to become a Jew. As early as A.D. 339 conversion to Judaism was made an offense punishable by loss of the convert's property.[24] Nor was Jewish proselytizing permitted "since it is more grevious than death and more cruel than murder if any person of the Christian faith should be polluted by the Jewish faith."[25] Christians were not permitted to marry Jews under any circumstances. Eventually Jews who were found guilty of taking a Christian in marriage were sentenced to death.[26] But under Theodosius I, intermarriage was only regarded as adultery and was punished as such.[27]

These various decrees dealing with intermarriage and conversion were aimed at minimizing interaction between Christ-

20. *C.T.*, 12.1.165.
21. *C.T.*, 12.1.157-58.
22. *C.T.*, Novella, 3.
23. *C.T.*, 16.8.16.
24. *C.T.*, 16.8.7.
25. *C.T.*, 16.8.19.
26. *C.T.*, 16.8.6.
27. *C.T.*, 3.7.2.

ians and Jews. Although Judaism was still a recognized religion within the empire, it was one that was rigidly segregated
and shut up in small communities that were not to be aug-
mented from any outside sources.

Many of the laws passed by the emperors against the Jews
were no doubt made at the urging of the Church. But while
various emperors acceded to most of the Church's demands,
some of them tried to remain fair and tolerant, and Judaism
was assured the position of a legal sect.[28] For example, under
Theodosius I, it was made unlawful to sue a Jew on the sabbath or to compel him to do anything at all on that day.[29] Attempts by non-Jews to disrupt Jewish internal affairs were also
curtailed when governors in the various provinces were ordered
not to interfere in the disciplinary actions taken by Jewish authorities against misbehaving Jews.[30]

A number of laws found in the Theodosian Code concern
the possession of Christian and pagan slaves by Jews. Apparently in the fourth century A.D. Jews had a certain number of
slaves serving in their families and Christian leaders became
very dismayed at the servitude of Christians to Jews. Accordingly, a number of laws were passed by various emperors attempting to either abolish or outlaw Jewish ownership of
Christian slaves but these seem not to have been enforced
since they had constantly to be renewed by successive emperors. Of paramount concern to the Church was the circumcision of slaves that Jews practiced not so much to offer an insult to the Church but to make the slave feel more a part of his
owner's family by allowing him a share in its religion.[31] By
A.D. 336 it became a crime for a Jew to purchase Christian
slaves and if a pagan slave were bought and later circumcised,
he had to be given his freedom.[32] In A.D. 339 Constantius
broadened the consequences of circumcision by making it a

28. *C.T.*, 16.8.9.
29. *C.T.*, 8.8.8.
30. *C.T.*, 16.8.8.
31. Parkes, p. 180.
32. *C.T.*, 16.9.1.

capital offense,[33] but it did not seem to provide a deterrent. Severity against the Jewish ownership of Christian slaves fluctuated depending on economic conditions. During prosperity it was outlawed, in difficult times it was tolerated.[32] Theodosius II finally put an end to the vacillation by explicitly forbidding the purchase of Christian slaves by Jews once and for all.[35]

In addition, economic problems were still contributing to anti-Jewish feelings. In Alexandria, for example, there were many individuals who attempted to impose upon the Jews special hardships particularly when there were economic problems. The Egyptian prefects appear to have been susceptible to pressure from these people for on one occasion a prefect was ordered not to single out the Jews or Samaritans for special taxes in connection with supplying grain to the capitals of the empire. Instead, they were to place the burden of maritime transport on those who could afford it.[36]

The taxes that Jews paid to support their religion had always annoyed non-Jews especially during economic crises. Although the Temple tax was no longer in effect, a new tax, the *aurum coronarium* was now being collected every year and this money was sent to the new spiritual head of Judaism, the Patriarch who lived in Palestine. Honorius feared that the money that was gathered in his domain might enter the eastern provinces of his rival Arcadius and in A.D. 399 he decreed the collection of the tax illegal and those who continued to collect it were to be punished.[37] However, five years later, Honorius reversed himself and the tax continued to be collected until A.D. 429 when Theodosius II declared that all special taxes collected by the Jews were henceforth to go to Christian charities.[38] The final abolition of the Jewish taxation system

33. *C.T.*, 16.9.2.
34. Under Honorius slavery was permitted the Jews provided no attempts were made to convert the slave. At the same time interference with Jewish ownership of slaves was severely punished. (*C.T.*, 16.9.3.).
35. *C.T.*, 16.9.4-5.
36. *C.T.*, 13.5.8.
37. *C.T.*, 16.8.14.
38. *C.T.*, 16.8.29.

meant that the central organization for Judaism in the Roman Empire could no longer exist. Only economic ties had held the various Jewish communities together. Once these ties were severed, the communities ceased to have any affiliation with one another.

Although they were often accused of contributing to the economic problems of the empire, the Jews like most inhabitants found it difficult to meet everyday demands. Many were destitute and sought some means whereby they could escape their misery. Some Jews attempted to escape payment of their debts by conversion to Christianity; others made a business of conversion. Socrates, the Church historian, relates that "a certain Jewish imposter pretending to be a convert to Christianity was in the habit of being baptised often and by that artifice he amassed a good deal of money."[39] How baptism led to wealth we are not told, but the fact that numerous conversions occurred for other than religious reasons is testified to by emperor Honorius: "we have learned that persons bound to the Jewish religion have desired to associate themselves with the Church's fellowship because of evasion of crimes and in view of different necessities, that this is done not through devotion to faith but by surreptitious action of pretenders."[40] Arcadius was also aware of the economic motive behind conversion and he successfully persuaded Honorius to issue with himself a joint declaration stating that Jews would not be allowed into the Church "until they have paid all their debts".[41] Even Christians were not allowed to take sanctuary if they were involved in economic difficulties.[42] Measures such as these were adopted by both Jews and Christians[43] because the economic situation of the period was an unbearable hardship forcing individuals to adopt any means that might alleviate the burden.

---

39. Socrates, *Eccl. Hist.*, 7.17.
40. *C.T.*, 16.8.23.
41. *C.T.*, 9.45.2.
42. *C.T.*, 9.45.4.
43. Christians, of course, would not seek conversion, but sanctuary (cf. *C.T.*, 9.45.1) or possibly entrance into the priesthood.

Apostasy among the Jews occurred early in the Christian empire. Faced with economic nardships and laws that discriminated against them many turned away from Judaism. But apostasy from one monotheistic religion to another posed a danger to the original belief since it was an indication that it had somehow failed and hence was inferior. Therefore, the Jewish leaders tried to discourage such actions. In A.D. 336 Constantine warned the Jewish leaders that they were not to disturb those who had left the Jewish community for Christianity.[44] But the warning did not seem to do any good for three years later he passed another law commanding the deaths of all those found guilty of stoning Jews who had left their religion for Christianity. To encourage such apostasy, former Jews were assured that they could not be disinherited by their parents if they decided to convert.[45] Since the Jews were not known for their wealth at this time, the edict poses an interesting insight into the thinking of the officialdom of this period. Preoccupation with the economy apparently overrided all other considerations, religious or otherwise. As an example, we have Arcadius' reply to a church leader's request for the destruction of pagan temples in Gaza: "I know that this city is full of idols, but it loyally pays its taxes and contributes to the treasury. If we suddenly frighten them they will run away and we shall lose so much in taxes."[46]

The Religious Conception of the Jew

In the laws of the *Theodosian Code* the Jews are described as a "dismal sect"; their meetings are "sacriligious gatherings"; to be a servant to a Jew is a "shameful servitude"; Judaism is a "moral turpitude"; the very name Jew is "detest-

---

44. *C.T.*, 16.8.5.
45. *C.T.*, 16.8.28. However, should a Christian be converted to Judaism, his property was to be confiscated by the fisc (*C.T.*, 16.8.7).
46. Quoted by S. Lieberman, "Palestine In The Third And Fourth Centuries," *J.Q.R. 36*, (1946): p. 343.
47. See ch.8.

able'' and ''offensive.'' If such expressions of contempt are found in the laws of the empire, with what kind of impartiality were offences or attacks against the Jews judged in the courts? From the tenor of these phrases, it is evident that the theological anti-Semitic views of the second and third centuries[47] had found their way into the legislation of the Christianized empire. The voices of the theologians were not silent any more after the conversion of the empire than they had been before it. The problem that prompted the theologian was epitomized by Sozomen, "how is it that other men are very ready to believe in God the Word, while the Jews are so incredulous?"[48] Unable to answer it, they portrayed the Jews as ignorant and forsaken.

Eusebius, the Church Historian, has left us a number of works that illustrate the Church's message concerning the Jews. His was an argument that had grown and flourished in the Church: the origins of Christianity lay not in Judaism, which was founded on the law of Moses, but in the era of the patriarchs, such as Abraham, who exemplified the true Hebrews, the oldest race in the world. The Church historian scorned exegetical methods.[49] The basic method in interpreting the scriptures, according to Eusebius, was to accept as a starting point the assumption that whenever the Old Testament speaks of David or Jacob or any other such notable figure, it is actually speaking of Jesus. Only by leaving aside the literal meaning (which the Jews in their obstinacy refused to do) could the prophecies of the Scriptures be understood. These prophecies were originally given in this obscure manner because the Jews would have destroyed them had they realized how unfavorable these predictions were toward them. Likewise, Sozomen, another Church historian, argued that

---

48. *Eccl. Hist.*, 1.1.
49. Eusebius, unlike many other Christian writers, was quite familiar with a number of Jews and with Jewish life since he lived in Caesarea, which was inhabited by a large number of Jews. Indeed, it was not improbable that he, like Origen, was instructed by them in the Scriptures.

"they were only acquainted with the mere letter of Scriptures and could not, like the Christians and a few of the wisest of the Hebrews [?] observe the hidden meaning."[50] This accusation is so common among the early Church biographers that it almost seems as if it were their motto.

But common though these ideas might be, they were soon abandoned in favor of more vehement statements, such as those uttered by St. John Chrysostom, bishop of Antioch. In A.D. 387 he delivered a number of sermons to his congregation. These sermons, known as the *Homilies Against the Jews,* contain such abuse, invectiveness, hatred, and "violence of language. . . [that they have] never been exceeded by any preacher whose sermons have been recorded."[51]

The reason for his hostility toward the Jews is unknown. The Church was now a leading force in the world and the Jews no longer posed a threat to anyone. It is true that the Antioch community boasted a numerous Jewish population but it was the Church that stood at the heart of the religious structure and not the once-powerful Jewish community. Unlike Eusebius, Chrysostom appears to have been almost totally unacquainted with Judaism or even the Jewish community of his own city. He was, in fact, compelled to invent a Jew of his own making upon whom he could fasten his acrimonious attack. This is evident from the nature of his sermons in which he reveals the grossest ignorance of Jews and Judaism that can be found in the literature of the Christian movement up to his time. But in this he set an important precedent. After Chrysostom, Christian writers would attack the Jews not because of anything that they did, but solely because they were called Jews. "There is no one more miserable than they who have exasperated God by their sin and by their observation of the Law,"[52] he declared.

Biblical passages were readily removed from their context and made to fit Chrysostom's mould of the Jew. Quoting from

50. *Eccl. Hist.,* 5.22.
51. M. Hay, *Europe And The Jews,* p. 27.
52. St. John Chrysostom, *Homilies,* 1.2.

Psalm 106.37 he claimed that they had sacrificed sons and daughters to the devil and had surpassed the animals in their dissoluteness.[53] Plunder, greed, treason, larceny—a day would not suffice to enumerate all their vices.[54] Such is their gluttony and voracity that they belong in butcher shops.[55]

Turning to the synagogues, he claimed that they were an insult to God since the Jews brought actors and circus members to them and "between the circus and the synagogue, there wasn't much of a difference."[56] The synagogue, in fact, was the cavern of thieves and the den of wild savages.[57] This was true not only of their synagogues but it was also true of their souls.[58]

Perhaps Chrysostom was aware of the fantastic influence Judaism had over women. Women were the major contributors to the construction of a synagogue in Apamea[59] and it was known that Christian women used to attend Jewish synagogues and occasionally Jewish feasts. "I know that many people respect the Jews and think that their rites are honourable; this is why I hasten to eradicate this pernicious opinion."[60] Thus, in his malice toward the synagogues—he states that he was merely trying to correct an inaccurate opinion that the Christians had about these Jewish "homes of idolatry." More likely he feared the potential influence of Judaism over Christians. Swearing to a Jewish oath was regarded as more binding than swearing to a Christian oath,[61] and this belief could only undermine Christianity.

When some of his congregation (likely those who visited synagogues) mentioned to Chrysostom that the holy books

53. *Ibid.* 1.6.
54. *Ibid.* 1.7.
55. *Ibid.* 1.6.
56. *Ibid.*, 1,4.
57. *Ibid.*, 1,3.
58. *Ibid.*, 1,3.
59. G. Downey, *Hist. of Antioch in Syria* (Princeton: Princeton Univ. Press, 1961), p. 449.
60. *Homilies*, 1.3.
61. *Ibid.*, 1.3.

were also found there, he replied that the Holy Ark at one time had been captured and had been placed in the temple of Dagon. Was this temple hallowed because of the Ark's presence? Certainly not. In the same way, the presence of the Scriptures in the synagogues did not make the latter any holier. But the Jews were even worse than the heathens, he contended, for they had introduced these books into their synagogues to insult and dishonor them.[62] "If a demon pronounces the words of the Scripture, do these words sanctify his mouth? No, of course not, since he will always have the nature of a demon."[63]

The presence of Christians at the Jewish Passover was especially grevious to the Church.[64] Chrysostom declared that such Christian participation was an insult to Jesus, and to celebrate with the Jews on the same day that they murdered Christ would surely lead to their exclusion from those who were to be saved on the day of Judgment.[65] Because they have slain Christ, God hates them,[66] and since God hates them, Christians should also: "I hate the Jews"![67] On account of their "odious assassination" there is "no expiation possible, no indulgence, no pardon."[68] "He who can never love Christ enough will never have done fighting against those [Jews] who hate Him."[69]

This was the man of whom Cardinal Newman wrote, "a bright cheerful soul, a sensitive heart, a temperament open to emotion and impulse; and all this elevated, refined, transformed by the touch of heaven—such was St. John Chrysostom."[70] Hay's evaluation of the man is rather different: Chrysostom's homilies were the textbooks from which

62. *Ibid.*, 1.5.
63. *Ibid.*, 6.6.
64. See next section of this chapter.
65. *Homilies, 3.5.*
66. *Ibid.*, 6.4.
67. *Ibid.*, 6.6.
68. *Ibid.*, 6.2.
69. *Ibid.*, 7.1.
70. Quoted by Hay, p. 27.

"priests were taught to hate, with St. John Chrysostom as their model."[71] Parkes summarizes his attitude of the man in the following words: "Dealing with the Christians, no text which urges forgiveness is forgotten; dealing with the Jews only one verse of the New Testament is omitted: 'Father, forgive them, for they know not what they do.' "[72]

Although Chrysostom was not the only churchman to rasp the Jews[73] he towers above all the rest because of his thoroughness. Moreover, because of his statement that the Jews ought to be eternally hated, a new policy of intolerance became part of Jewish-Christian relations. His influence on the people and the clergy, no only of his own period but of many eras to follow, has not been determined, but it must have been extensive: after Chrysostom, any violence against the Jews or any act of destruction against their synagogues was regarded as an act of Divine inspiration.

The only Church Father during this period who could claim any acquaintance with both Jews and Judaism, was Jerome. Prompted by the inferiority of the Christian when it came to Biblical exegesis or even pronunciation of the text of the Scriptures, he approached various Jewish teachers in an effort to study Hebrew from the experts: "The Jews boast of their knowledge of the Law when they remember the several names that we generally pronounce in a corrupt way because they are barbaric and we do not know their etymology. And if we happen to make a mistake in the accent and in the length of the syllables. . .they laugh at our ignorance, especially as shown in aspiration and in some letters pronounced with a rasping of the throat."[74] In this passage, Jerome also calls attention to the fantastic memory of many Jews for the names and lists of

71. *Ibid.*, p. 27.
72. *Parkes, Conflict of Church and Synagogue*, p. 163.
73. Gregory of Nyssa described the Jews as "slayers of the Lord, murderers of the prophets, enemies of God, haters of God, adversaries of grace, enemies of their fathers' faith, advocates of the devil, brood of vipers, slanderers, scoffers, men of clouded minds, bread of the Pharisees, congregation of demons, sinners, wicked men, stoners, and haters of goodness" (*Oration on the resurrection, 5*).
74. Jerome, *Commentary on Titus*, 3.

descendants. This ability was not difficult to understand, since Jewish children were taught genealogies from an early age. But Jerome could only comment that "they run to the synagogue every day to study the Law, in their desire to know what Abraham, Isaac and Jacob and the rest of the holy men did, and to learn by heart the books of Moses and the prophets."[75]

In approaching the Jews, Jerome's main purpose was to learn enough so that he could produce a new translation of the Scriptures, one which would be of some help to Christians when they entered into debate with Jews. Christians still relied on the Septuagint, which was strewn with inaccuracies. The Jews, however, were familiar not only with the orginal Hebrew text, but with the Septuagint, Aquila's translation of the Bible, and the Apocrypha, from which they could quote with equal ability. It was Jerome's avowed intent to provide a new translation of the original Hebrew text that the Jews could not mock. Criticized for studying Jewish writings, he answered, "Why should I not be permitted. . .for the purpose of confuting the Jews, to use those copies of the Bible which they admit to be genuine."[76]

Dependant though he was on his Jewish teachers, he did not differ from any of his contemporaries in his feelings for them. Commenting on his association with the Jews, he admitted a strange dislike for them and upon thinking this statement over somewhat, decided that in fact he even loathed them.[77] But his close association with those he loathed gained him access to the Talmudic school of thought and to the methods of rabbinical exegesis. After several years of study, he took up his plan to translate the Hebrew originals into Latin, and because of his text, the Vulgate, Jerome became the leading Christian authority on the Bible; a position that he retained until only very recent times.

75. Jerome, *Comm. on Isaiah, 58.*
76. Jerome, Contra Rufinum, 3.
77. Jerome, *Letters,* 84.

Judging from Jerome's stated purpose in writing the Vulgate, one is struck with the conclusion that Christians and Jews were still arguing about Biblical passages and that the Christians were still faring worse in the interchanges. In some cases, new converts to Christianity may have earnestly been bothered by Jewish reproaches and some Christian leaders even thought it necessary to warn their followers not to engage in debate with Jews over the Bible.[78] The Church may have had men who could bring emperor's to their knees, but it was still unable to challenge the Jews in Biblical exegesis successfully.

The Ecumenical Councils

The legislation enacted against the Jews by the various emperors did not develop *in vacuo* but was a direct result of religious persuasion from the Church. In the fourth century A.D. a number of ecclesiastical councils were held to discuss uniformity and discipline within the Church and inevitably one of the important topics was the religious and social relationship between Christian and Jews. Some of the decisions of these councils were later implemented into the legislation of the empire.

The first of these councils for which we have canonical evidence was held at Elvira, Spain, some time before the accession of Constantine.[79] Four canons dealing with the Jews were drawn up at this meeting. Restrictions governing marriage between Jews and Christians were introduced at this time[80] and not too much later they were included in the Theodosian Code.[81] The only way in which such a marriage could be sanctioned was if the Jew expressed his desire to undergo

---

78. Parkes, p. 172.
79. Ca. A.D. 300 is a likely date. There may have been a number of other such meetings but we can only surmise of their existence since Christians were not able to meet openly or move about freely before Christianity gained acceptance.
80. *Elvira Council,* Canon 16.
81. See above.

conversion.[82] A penalty was also imposed at this time for any-one who was guilty of adultery with a Jewish or pagan woman. Such conduct was to be punished by exclusion from communion for a period of five years.[83]

It appears that relations between Christians and Jews were very cordial in Spain at this time and on occassion Christian clergy were even invited by Jews to partake of their hospital-ity. Such associations were viewed as sinful and dangerous by the members of the Elvira council. Henceforth, all priests and laity were forbidden to have any intercourse whatsoever with the Jews. The penalty imposed upon those who disobeyed was exclusion from the communion service for as long as this con-tamination continued.[84]

The remaining canon deals with the practice of requesting Jews to bless Christian fields. Christian farmers used to bring in poor crops; the Jews, however, were rather successful in their agricultural endeavors and they brought in abundant har-vests. After Elvira appealing to "Jewish magic" was emphati-cally denounced: "Householders are to be warned, that they should not permit their crops, which have been received from God, to be blessed by the Jews, lest they render our blessings fruitless and weak."[85] The penalty for transgressing the ordi-nance was excommunication. It appears that the Church felt its spiritual connection with God being challenged. If Christians turned to Jews to bless their fields, there was no reason why they should not turn to them whenever they needed help. If such practices were to continue, the synagogue would be raised to a higher level than the church regarding direct com-munication with God. But threaten as it may, the Church was never able to eradicate the belief that the Jew possessed special powers not given to the Christian.[86]

In A.D. 325 the first official ecumenical council was sum-

82. Elvira, Canon 16.
83. *Ibid.* Canon 78.
84. *Ibid.* Canon 50.
85. *Ibid.* Canon 49.
86. Cf. Trachtenberg, ch. 3.

moned by Constantine. Its underlying motive was an elimination of all sources of controversy and division within the Church and naturally enough the discussion turned to the place of the Jews in the Christian community. One main concern was a not so idle boast made by the Jews that Christians could not celebrate Easter without the help of the Jewish calendar. This problem was again discussed at the council of Antioch in A.D. 341. It appears that many churches did not attempt to calculate upon what day Easter should be celebrated but instead waited for the Jews to celebrate their Passover. When the Jewish Passover began, the Christian Easter was observed. Some clerics even joined the Jews in their Passover celebrations and Chrysostom occasionally found it necessary to warn his congregation to keep away from such Jewish rites.[87] The emperors tried to prevent such occurrences by prohibiting the Jewish Partiarch from computing the Jewish calendar or by forbidding the Patriarch from sending messengers to the various Jewish communities. To avoid the watchful eye of the government, the Patriarch made his calculations far in advance of the Passover and so his envoys were able to travel without being suspect. Eventually the emperor's intent to abolish the Jewish practice was circumvented with the creation of a permanent calendar. To combat this development a canon was adopted that made excommunication the penalty for any cleric who observed Easter on the same day as Passover.[88]

The "Judaizing" tendencies of some Christians also greatly disturbed the Church officialdom. Accordingly, in A.D. 360 the council of Laodicea stressed that work was compulsory on the Jewish sabbath and any Christian who rested on that day was to be regarded as a "Judaizer."[89] Moreover, it was imperative that the Gospels be read on that day.[90] Participating in Jewish holidays and receiving food from Jews were also prohibited[91]

87. *Homilies*, 1.3.
88. *Antioch*, canon 1.
89. *Laodicea*, Canon, 29.
90. *Ibid.*, Canon 16.
91. *Ibid.*, Canon 37.

and a special order was issued that explicitly forbid Christians to accept unleavened bread from the Jews.[92] It would be extremely interesting to know how common such occurrences were at this time. Judging from these canons, it seems that the Jews had a very popular following in the Christian world.

The final set of ecclesiastical decrees of this nature is a Syrian compilation called the Apostolic Canons. Drawn up in the middle of the fourth century, these canons merely restate or elaborate the earlier canons, especially those dealing with contacts between Christians and Jews. Fasting on the sabbath, celebrating a Jewish festival, or receiving a gift from a Jew meant excommunication.[93] A very interesting edict forbade Christians to bring oil into a synagogue or to light their lamps during Jewish holidays.[94] Jews, of course, were not able to tend the lamps at these times and they required the services of non-Jews to attend to such matters. However, once inside, the Christian was able to observe the Jewish ceremony. By forbidding Christians to aid the Jews, the Church attempted to curtail such participation, even though it might only be visual. More interesting still, is a canon that prohibited clergymen from going to synagogues to pray![95] If this was as common a practice as the canons indicate, the Church had every reason to be alarmed.

It is almost beyond belief, however, that contacts between Jews and Christians were so common or so intimate as the Church canons suggest. Unfortunately, we do not possess the works of any unbiased witness of this period, for it is possible that these canons and the rantings and ravings of men like Chrysostom were a theological inheritance rather than a reflection of contemporary conditions. But no matter how much one questions their reality, one must still face the fact that these canons found their way into the statutes of the empire.

92. *Ibid.*, Canon 38.
93. *Apostolic Canons*, c. 66.70.
94. *Ibid.*, Canon 71.
95. *Ibid.*, Canon 64.

The Decline of the State and the Danger to Judaism

The Jews had always supported a strong government. It was the only way that they could be assured of protection from their hostile neighbors, and as long as the emperor was strong and independent, Jewish privileges could be safeguarded. As the power of the state declined, the position of the Jews became precarious. When the influence of the Church surpassed the power of the emperor, there no longer was any stabilizing force between the Jews and those who sought to do them harm. This is most evident in the conflict between Church and State over the appropriation or destruction of the synagogues in the empire.

As late as A.D. 412 Theodosius II stated that "No one, on the ground that he is a Jew, when he is innocent, should be condemned nor any religion whatsoever should cause a person to be exposed to contumely. Their synagogues or habitations should not be burned indiscriminately or should be damaged wrongfully without any reason. . . ."[96] The fact that the burning or destruction of synagogues was a serious matter is evidenced by seven edicts promulgated by Theodosius II alone. The number of these edicts indicates that looting or appropriating Jewish synagogues was very prevalent while Theodosius was emperor; apparently he was unable to control "those persons who inconsiderately do very many things under the pretext of venerable Christianity."

The first recorded attack against a synagogue occurred in northern Italy under the leadership of the bishop Innocentius. Inspired by religious zeal, the bishop led his congregation in the destruction of the synagogue and the erection of a church on the former site.[97] Some time later, the Christian community of Rome also burned down a synagogue but the authorities ordered them to rebuild it. The official responsible for this setback was labeled a Jew and his later defeat at the hands of the

96. *C.T.*, 16.8.21.
97. Parkes, p. 187.

barbarians was regarded as an act of divine punishment for his unchristian act.[98]

Valentinian,[99] Theodosius I,[100] Honorius,[101] and Arcadius[102] all decreed that religious institutions including synagogues, were not to be violated. But these laws had no effect on Christian leaders, some of whom regarded it as an heroic duty either to appropriate or destroy a synagogue. Hadn't Chrysostom said that "He who can never love Christ enough will never have done fighting against those (Jews) who hate Him"?[103] What better way to fight the Jew than by destroying the meeting place of his religion? The next move was to convince the emperors that the construction of any synagogue was a blasphemous outrage against the Church.

Theodosius I passed a number of decrees that prohibited Christians from molesting Jews,[104] and from appropriating or burning synagogues.[105] If these laws were broken, the Jews were to be compensated for their loss, but in no way were any new synagogues to be built to replace those that had been destroyed.[106] What the emperor in fact did, was to agree that the synagogue had no place in the empire. His laws against the construction of new synagogues meant that eventually the synagogue had to disappear since time would erase them if unnatural causes did not. In essence he was tacitly agreeing with the Church that they had to be eliminated. If this were not the case, he could easily have discouraged such practice by permitting the Jews to rebuild those synagogues that had been taken from them. But the emperor was too frightened of the Church.

In A.D. 338 Theodosius backed his governor's decision that a synagogue that had been burnt in Callinicum at the instiga-

98. St. Ambrose, *Letters,* no. 60.
99. *C.T.,* 7.8.2.
100. *C.T.,* 16.8.9.
101. *C.T.,* 16.8.20.
102. *C.T.,* 16.8.12.
103. See above.
104. *C.T.,* 16.8.21.
105. *C.T.,* 16.8.25-26-27.
106. *C.T.,* 16.8.25.

tion of the bishop, be rebuilt by the bishop himself. When Ambrose, bishop of Milan, learned of the emperor's decision to support the governor, he wrote him a letter warning him that "it is a serious matter to endanger your salvation for the Jews."[107] Initially, Ambrose declared that the accusation against the bishop was false since priests tried to calm disturbances, not create them. Only when they were moved by some insult to the Church, did they take action. Thus, Ambrose intimated that the Jews had provoked the attack and argued that even if the bishop were to blame, if he obeyed the decision and rebuilt the synagogue, he would be regarded as an apostate. If he refused, he would become a martyr. The destruction of the synagogue, he contended, could not even be called a crime, since it was an heroic act to erase any edifice in which Christ was denied. Only his own laxness kept him from destroying the synagogue in Milan. Therefore, there really wasn't any adequate cause for a commotion since it was only the burning of a synagogue—"a home of unbelief, a house of impiety, a receptacle of folly, which God himself has condemned."[108] If the emperor's order were to be respected, it would be celebrated as a triumph by the Jews similar to the celebration of their feast days, and on their walls they would write "The Temple of Impiety, erected from the plunder of Christians."[109]

Thinking Ambrose's argument over somewhat, the emperor softened a little and decided he might have been too harsh in demanding that the bishop should have to rebuild the synagogue out of his own pocket. Instead, he ordered the city to assume the expense, hoping thereby to pacify Ambrose. But the bishop was not satisfied. A short time later he extracted from the emperor a promise to rescind the orders entirely. In return, Ambrose declared that he would offer a prayer to God on his behalf.[110]

107. Ambrose, *Letters,* no. 60.
108. *Ibid.*
109. *Ibid.*
110. *Letters,* no. 61.

This incident established a precedent that continued as long as the Church had any influence in the State. In any collision between the two powers, it was the Church that was to have the last word. According to Ambrose, "civil law must bow before religious devotion."[111] Religious devotion, as we have indicated, took the form of destroying synagogues. Sometimes sanctuaries were not destroyed; instead they were merely converted into Christian shrines. A famous example of this kind of event occurred in A.D. 380 when the Jewish synagogue in Antioch that contained the tomb of the Maccabean martyrs was appropriated by the Church. Disturbed by the large number of Christians who were drawn to the site because of the supposed powers of these martyrs to work miracles, the Christian leaders in Antioch took the most sensible course available to them—they confiscated the synagogue, thereby preventing Christians from exhibiting any interest in Jewish heroes.[112]

Those who felt that Judaism was faring too well, were not content only to confiscate synagogues. Attempts were even made to interfere with Jewish community life and occasionally Christian bishops endeavored to humiliate Jewish leaders by forcing the Patriarch to readmit excommunicated Jews.[113] In the case of legal disputes between Christians and Jews, the Patriarch, of course, could not act as a judge in any proceedings.[114] Moreover, Jews were compelled to follow Roman law at all times except in civil cases where both parties, if they were Jews, could agree to abide by the decision of the religious authorities.[115] It goes without saying that most Jews would choose their own courts wherever possible. If they rejected this alternative and chose Roman law, they were forced to appeal to Christian lawyers since Jews were denied the right to plead cases after A.D. 425.[116]

111. *Ibid.*, no. 40.
112. See Downey, p. 448.
113. *C.T.*, 18.8.8.
114. *C.T.*, 16.8.22.
115. *C.T.*, 2.1.10.
116. Sirmonian Constitution, 6.

When Gamaliel VI died without leaving an heir, the office of Jewish Patriarch was officially ended by the order of Theodosius II (ca. A.D. 429). Thus the House of Hillel, which had provided the Jews with three and a half centuries of spiritual leadership, finally perished. Thereafter Palestine's influence as the center of spiritual Judaism declined and the seat of religious authority was transfered to Babylonia.

Events in the Diaspora

The hatred of the Jews for the later Roman Empire is easily understood in light of the anti-Jewish legislation enacted against them. Rome had always symbolized the forces of evil but it was only in times of severe hardship or religious fervor that the Jews had been ready to physically confront the Roman. Each time the Jews were annihilated. Still they never gave up. In A.D. 355 the Jews of Diocaesarea in Palestine rose up and attacked the Roman governor. The cause of the rebellion may have been either oppressive taxation,[117] the anti-Jewish legislation of Constantine and Constantius,[118] or harsh treatment by the Roman authorities.[119] The result was the same as it had always been. The Jews were massacred and Diocaesarea was destroyed.[120]

Occasionally the Jews foolishly participated in the struggle between Christian orthodoxy and heresy.[121] During the time of Augustine, they chose the side of the Donatists[122] who opposed the Catholic Church on account of its affiliation with the State. Perhaps they hoped to weaken the power of the Church by supporting its enemies but instead they only served to incur the hatred of the Catholic leaders because of their opposition.

117. See Lieberman. Palestine in the Third and Fourth Centuries.
118. See above.
119. Parkes, p. 187.
120. Socrates, *Eccl. Hist.*, 2.33.
121. Theodoret, *Eccl. Hist.*, 4.18.
122. *C.T.*, 16.5.44; 16.5.46.

Contemporary with the Donatists were a group known as the "Caelicoli," a "Judaizing" group who tried to force some Christians to "adopt the foul and degrading name of Jew."[123] The Church appealed to the emperor to put an end to them and the "Caelicoli" were ordered to convert to Christianity proper within one year of the decree. They appear to have obeyed since they were never heard of again.

In A.D. 414 antagonism between Jews and Alexandrians was finally ended following a surprising innovation in Jewish-Christian relations: the bishop simply banished the Jews from the city. According to the Church historian, Socrates, who tends to be somewhat biased, the Jews brought the measure down on themselves: One sabbath, while they were watching some theatrical amusement, a disorder occurred in the theater and Hierax, one of Bishop Cyril's disciples, was seized by the Jews because of some disturbance that he was creating. The Jews handed the man over to the Roman prefect who happened to be on bad terms with Cyril, and the prefect tortured Hierax to death.

When Cyril learned of the incident he approached the Jews threatening them with violence unless they ceased molesting Christians. (Perhaps the bishop felt that the prefect had acted under Jewish orders.) For their part, the Jews feared that an attack was imminent and they decided to take the initiative. Wearing rings made of the "bark of a palm branch" so that they could recognize each other, they waited for night and attacked the Christians. At daybreak Cyril organized a large mob following the Sunday service and attacked the synagogues, driving the Jews out of the city.[124] Naturally, Jewish property and possessions were confiscated. The story of the rings made of bark seems a little fanciful and it is also rather doubtful that the Jews would have been in their synagogues in large numbers on a Sunday morning. In all probability a combination of economic distress, hatred of the Jews, and Cyril's ability to in-

123. *C.T.*, 16.8.9.
124. *Eccl. Hist.*, 7.13.

cite a mob were the causes of the pogrom. In any case, the oldest Jewish colony in the Diaspora to that date was ended.

One year later the Jews of Inmestar in Syria were attacked, but for entirely different reasons. Again Socrates is our main source of information. According to his account, during the Purim celebration a number of drunken Jews kidnapped a Christian boy and hanged him from a cross and then scourged him to death. The explanation was that the Jews used to enact symbolically the hanging of Haman on a gallows during Purim and the gallows tended to resemble a cross. In A.D. 408 Theodosius II, following a complaint of some Christians, actually forbid the Jews to burn these gallows so as to prevent any kind of association with the Christian symbol.[125] But the act was still carried on despite the law. When the Christians of Inmestar learned of the crime it "occassioned a sharp conflict between them [the Jews] and the Christians"[126] by which Socrates means that the Christians attacked the Jews and confiscated their synagogues.

The accusation of ritual murder has been levelled against the Jews in one form or another throughout history beginning as far back as the time of Democritus and Apion.[127] While this Syrian incident is not strictly speaking in the same motif as that found in the charges of ritual murder, it is too similar to be neglected and may have been an early Christian formulation of what later became a frequent medieval charge. Trachtenberg[128] relates that in the eleventh century a Jew who wished to become a Christian had to take an oath renouncing "those who celebrate the festival of Mordecai. . .and those who nail Haman to a piece of wood, and joining it to the sign of the cross, burn them together while hurling various curses and the anathema against the Christians." In A.D. 1191 the Jews of Bray in Northern France, like the Jews of Inmestar, were accused of crucifying a Christian during their Purim

125. *C.T.*, 16.8.18.
126. *Eccl. Hist.*, 7.16.
127. See p. 43.
128. Trachtenberg, *Devil and the Jews*, p. 127.

celebration[129] and in England in 1141 there is an account of "the Jews of Norwich [who] bought a Christian child before Easter and tortured him with all the tortures wherewith our Lord was tortured, and on Long Friday hanged him on a rood in hatred of our Lord, and afterwards buried him."[130] Purim; Easter; Passover—all were heinous celebrations during which the Jews "mix human blood in their unleavened bread, which the preachers of various orders spread among the people."[131]

Because the Jews refused to accept Christianity, they were the enemies of Christ and what more natural thing for an enemy than to act maliciously. A rumor had only to be heard and it was believed. The incident at Inmestar set an important precedent. Hitherto Christian writers had only accused the Jews of theological misantropy: Jews hated Christians. Now there was the charge that the Jews were actively pursuing a policy of ritual murder. Charged with deicide by men like Chrysostom, it was only to be expected that they would annually reenact the drama. The most significant aspect of these events was thus the uncanny control that the lower clergy exercised over the minds of Christians. Whatever the people were told, they listened, they believed, and they obeyed. They listened to impassioned charges of deicide and they believed that God approved of Christians who avenged His son. And they obeyed when their priests told them to eradicate Judaism.

The motive was the weakness of Christianity itself. Unable to win over the Jew, unable to conquer Judaism, fearful of the ever-present "Judaizing" tendency among Christians, hatred of the Jews and Judaism was made an integral aspect of Christian theology. As Runes[132] points out, "no faith in the world in historic times has such a horrible scheme or revulsive hate integrated into its very tenets of belief." Unfortunately, secular authorities were also raised in this atmosphere and they al-

---

129. Trachtenberg, p. 127-28.
130. *Ibid.*, p. 130.
131. *Ibid.*, p. 134.
132. Runes, *The Jew And The Cross*, p. 83.

lowed Christian paranoia to dictate social-political legislation within the empire. The result was a curtailment of the Jew's civil rights, contempt for his very personage, interference with his religion and his everyday life, confinement in segregated areas and occasionally a pogrom to keep him from polluting the rest of mankind.

10

The Barbarian Conquest

The Political Situation in Italy

IN THE FIFTH century A.D. vast hordes of migrating peoples overran western Europe in search of food. Some tribes, like the Vandals, eventually made it to Africa where the harvests could still support the inhabitants. Other tribes fell upon lands formerly controlled by Rome that were not so bountiful but could still support a large influx of people. To insure the security of its borders, Rome called out its army, but the army itself was by this time largely made up of barbarians. As a result, barbarian armies were sent out to halt the encroachment of other barbarian masses. Occasionally, the "loyal" army itself became the new masters of the area it had been sent out to defend, albeit at the "pleasure" of the emperor. This was the case in the Italian peninsula where the Ostrogoths first liberated Italy and then remained as its new overlords.

Before their migration, the Ostrogoths had been living in Illyria to the east of Byzantium. Prior to the ascent of their leader, Theodoric, they had not offered much of a threat to anyone since they still feuded with one another and therefore had no real power with which to confront Roman might.

Under Theodoric, the Ostrogoths finally united and thereby became a potential threat to areas occupied by the empire and its allies. Zeno, the eastern emperor, realized his vulnerability and hit upon a masterful strategm to save his realm: He induced Theodoric to enter the service of the empire and then sent him to Italy in a campaign of liberation. Thus, he removed the threat to the Byzantine areas and at the same time he stood to gain the recapture of Italy, which at that time was also under precarious Roman control.

Supposedly under the aegis of the western emperor, Romulus, Italy was in fact administered by Odovacar, the leader of the emperor's barbarian army in Italy. In A.D. 476 relations between Romulus and Odovacar had become strained to the point where Odovacar had moved his entire army into northern Italy and had taken full possession of that area. It was not unconceivable that he might even extend his influence over the whole peninsula. Although Zeno himself had had amicable dealings with Odovacar, he began to feel unfavorably disposed to the barbarian after the latter broke away from the empire. Thus it was that he sent Theodoric, a barbarian, to deal with another barbarian.

In A.D. 488 Theodoric made plans to leave Illyria. By A.D. 493 he was master of Italy. For his achievement, Zeno conferred upon him the title of Gothic king and he became the emperor's administrator in Italy. The government he established was modeled entirely on the Roman system and Roman law prevailed in all matters. No attempt was made to subordinate native Roman inhabitants. If any decision had to be made, edicts were issued demanding that all current laws be obeyed and warning that those guilty of breaking the laws would be punished in accord with established practice.

Theodoric's Attitude toward the Jews

In evaluating Theodoric's relations with the Jews, one must

admit that the Ostrogothic king conducted himself with an impartiality peculiar to rulers of that era. Most of Theodoric's dealings with the Jews have been recorded by Cassiodorus, a Roman noble who served Theodoric as prime minister, and who preserved much of Theodoric's edicts and correspondence.

Although he is called a barbarian by history, one finds in Theodoric the rare trait of justice, a characteristic that he extended to any and all the inhabitants of Italy. Toward the Jews as toward everyone else, his basic motive was to maintain the *status quo* and in one of his edicts he wrote, "the true mark of *civilitas* is the observance of law. It is this which makes life in communities possible and which separates man from brutes."[1] This was his attitude concerning Roman laws and customs in general. In keeping with this philosophy he remarked, "for the preservation of *civilitas*, the benefits of justice are not to be denied even to those [Jews] who are recognized as wandering from the right way on matters of faith."[2] Here is the uncommon man. The man who is perceptive enough to realize that, "we cannot order a religion, because no one can be forced to believe against his will."[3] Thus, Theodoric is set off as one of the truly enlightened rulers of recorded history. He was an unusually fair and conscientious ruler whose main desire was not to enamor himself among a large and influential segment of his subjects. Rather he attempted to maintain internal harmony as far as possible by following the legal outline that he inherited from the indigent Roman populace. To the Jews he wrote, "we therefore gladly accede to your request that all the privileges which the foresight of antiquity conferred upon the Jewish customs shall be remembered to you, for in truth it is our great desire that the laws of the ancients shall be kept in force to secure the reverence due to us."[4] This was no idle statement as were the pronouncements of other emperors.

1. *The Letters of Cassiordorus*, 4.33, ed. by T. Hodgkin.
2. *Ibid.*, 5.37.
3. *Ibid.*, 2.27.
4. *Ibid.*, 4.33.

In the city of Rome, there was an instance, typical of these times, in which a mob marched on a synagogue and burnt it to the ground. Seemingly, the outbreak was caused when a number of Christian slaves who had murdered their Jewish masters, were brought to task for their crime by the Jews of the community. Apparently Jews were not permitted to discipline Christian slaves no matter what the offence, and the Christians decided to punish the Jews because they had dealt with these guilty Christian slaves on their own. The Jews complained to Theodoric and after examining the complaint he dispatched a message to the ancient senatorial body in Rome to punish those Christians who were at fault.[5]

A similar instance of incendiarism occurred at Ravenna. A number of zealous Christians set upon some Jews and forceably baptised them. When these Jews were then offered some bread that had been blessed by the clergy, they showed their contempt by flinging it into the river. When others in the community heard of the outrage they became so angered that they turned on the synagogues. The Jews naturally complained to Theodoric and he responded by ordering the populace to rebuild the burnt synagogue. Those unable to pay restitution were to be flogged for their crime.[6]

Although Theodoric seemed to be pro-Jewish, he was, in fact, theologically opposed to them. "Why, O Jew, doust thou petition for peace and quietness on earth when thou canst not find that rest which is eternal," he asked. They could expect to have guaranteed all the rights and privileges that the Theodosian Code promised them; but at the same time they could expect nothing beyond. Thus, when the Jews of Genoa petitioned to improve the condition of their synagogue, he gave his assent, but admonished them to take care that they not enlarge it by any means.[7] But even though he showed no special favoritism to them, the Jews of Italy felt indebted to

5. *Ibid.*, 4.33.
6. See Parkes, *Conflict of Church and Synagogue*, p. 207, note 2.
7. *Letters of Cass.*, 2.27.

Theodoric and the Ostrogoths because of their fairness and in the troublesome years that followed, the Jews gave them all their loyalty and support.

The Fall of the Ostrogoths

In A.D. 526, just before he died, Theodoric named his son as regent. But the boy was very young and instead Theodoric's wife acted as ruler with the consent of the eastern emperor. Unlike her husband, the queen tried especially to ingratiate herself to the Catholics of the country. But in doing so she alienated herself from her own people who were Arians. Her second mistake, however, proved more fatal. Attempting to strengthen her position as monarch, the queen married her cousin who also entertained ambitious goals. In the end the queen lost the support of her people by flirting with the Catholics and she lost her life after marrying her ambitious cousin.

Justinian, the new eastern emperor, saw her murder as an excuse to invade Italy. Probably he would have done so without this pretext since his avowed intention was the reunification of the entire empire again under one ruler. With Caesarian dreams, he sent his outstanding general, Belisarius, and 10,000 soldiers to conquer and repossess the country. In A.D. 536 the army set out on its campaign of conquest.

The first signs of opposition occurred in the city of Naples. The inhabitants sent out a delegation to the general asking him to bypass the city since it was of no great strategical importance. Belisarius, however, was too shrewd a tactician to leave any fortified city at his rear. The request was denied and instead he offered a bribe to the deputation promising them a large reward if they would persuade their own people to surrender the city to the invaders. These envoys did just that, but the local Goths refused to comply and the city prepared for the seige. It appears that the Jews had an important hand in the surrender discussions since Procopius, the historian of the campaign, relates that the Jews promised to supply the city with the necessities it would require during the seige if it decided to fight.[8]

Despite the determination of the inhabitants, the seige lasted only a short time. Again, Procopius informs us that the Jews played a prominent part in the defense of the city, so much so that the Romans were unable to scale the walls guarded directly by them. If not superior Jewish fighting ability, then it was probably Jewish desperation that kept the Romans back. Procopius relates that "the Jews had already given offense to the enemy by having opposed their efforts to capture the city without a fight and for this reason they had no hope if they should fall into their hands, so they continued fighting stubbornly."[9] Only when the Romans breached the walls in another part of the city and attacked the Jews from the rear, did they leave their posts to flee the fallen city.

Although Procopius does not inform us of the fate of those Jews who were captured, it is likely that they were either slaughtered or taken back to Constantinople as slaves. The rest of the campaign was also a success and Italy once again was in Roman hands, but the occupation was only short-lived. A few years later, another barbarian tribe, the Lombards, invaded and overran the peninsula tearing it forever from the arm of the empire.

The war of reunification resulted in an effete Italy. The population of Rome was literally decimated[10] and the magnificent architectural structures toppled and crumbled as a result of neglect. Even the senate, that august body of history that had had only a perfunctory existence during the last centuries, disappeared. The entire peninsula went the way of the legendary city—protected, ruined, despoiled, exhausted.

8. Procopius, *History of the Wars,* 5.8.41.
9. Procopius, *Wars,* 5.10.24-26.
10. F. Lot, *The End of the Ancient World.* (New York: Harper Torch books, 1961), p. 268.

It is a moot point whether the inhabitants welcomed the new barbarian invasion from the Lombards; certainly conditions could not get much worse, and should a strong ruler take power, some semblance of order might be created. The Lombards first attacked in A.D. 568. One year later they were settled but not firmly entrenched. It would not have taken a large force to dislodge them from their feeble positions, but like Italy, the entire empire was tired. So the Lombards remained and like the Ostrogoths, they assimilated into the ancient Roman system of government, economy, and urban society instead of trying to make Italy accept barbarian standards. Arianism put up a half-hearted struggle but the Arian clergy was no match for the numerous and vociferous Catholics in the country.

Gregory the Great and the Jewish Question

Following the supremacy of Catholicism in the barbarian state, came the rise to power of the Papacy. In Rome and in those areas not directly controlled by the Lombards,[11] the Pope encountered little secular resistance and his influence flourished and spread throughout the peninsula and beyond. Since the Papal See at this time owned more land than any single conqueror,[12] the Papacy became the patron of Catholic Italy and undertook the support of needy followers. The position of the Pope in relation to the life of his Catholic subjects was, metaphorically speaking, similar to that of the human heart in relation to the body. Papal arteries supported the inhabitants with alms and food, they fed the military with supplies for the fortifications of various towns, they delivered advice to legal officials who ultimately came to the Pope for im-

11. The Lombards were mainly confined to the interior of Italy. Coastal areas were largely free of their influence.
12. Lot, p. 305.

portant judgments. In return, the people tilled the episcopal soil and paid taxes to the Holy See. Devout members of the Church donated presents and finally their own estates upon their deaths. In any matter concerning a religious or secular question, it was quite natural for the inhabitants of the land to look to the Papacy for support and authority.

A number of historians who have addressed themselves to this period and to the condition of the Jews in the early Middle Ages have asserted that Pope Gregory I (A.D. 590-604) played a very definite role in the condition of the Jews not only in Italy but throughout the Christian world at this time. Many of the barbarian states had endorsed Christianity and in those states that followed Catholicism, the various rulers frequently had episcopal advisors or else they listened to and incorporated ecclesiastical laws and decisions into their own civil laws. Since the Pope was the head of the Church he could thus influence the secular potentates via his bishops, some of whom held important stations in the newly Catholicized states. However, this influence went only so far as those bishops or those rulers were willing to let their daily conduct be governed by the Pope in faraway Italy. More often than not, bishops at least, acted independently and emotionally as the spirit moved them. Communication being as slow as it was, if the Pope did request any redress or did state an opinion, it was after the religious fervor of an act had already occurred. One could not unburn a synagogue or unbaptise Jews. Papal pronouncements could also be overlooked or ignored on the grounds of religious enthusiasm. Thus, in evaluating the official position of the Church and its ability to enforce its authority, one can only state that it could exert a definite influence only in and near the Papal estates. The farther removed a country was from this immediate center, the less the observance, obedience, and cogency of the Pope's decrees. A review of some of the letters written by Gregory to his officers will illustrate this discontinuity in the Pope's authority.

The practice of forceably baptising Jews was initiated by

Bishop Severus of Minorca in A.D. 418.[13] Eventually it evolved into one of the most popular expressions of zealous Christianity in the medieval Christian world. Gregory himself had a negative attitude toward forced baptism. On numerous occasions he expressed both his disapproval and his doubt as to its efficacy. Once, a number of Jews from Rome petitioned him on behalf of the Jewish community of Marseilles, which had been won over to the Church by anything less than verbal persuasion. The Pope listened to the complaint and agreed that a grievance had been committed and he attempted to correct the situation. Writing to both the bishop of Arles and the bishop of Marseilles, he commended them on their intentions, but advised them that their methods may not have been the most profitable since the converts would probably return to their former "superstition" at the first opportunity. Thereafter they would be unreachable even if the inclination to conversion might have been present in the first place. The only way to win permanent converts, he advised, was through "the sweetness of their teacher."[14]

Although Gregory objected to violent methods of conversion, he was not adverse to monetary persuasions and on one occasion he wrote to his agent in Sicily that a reduction in rents should be offered to anyone who consented to baptism, the argument being that although the converts acted out of worldly considerations, their children would also have to be baptised. Even if the parents were not sincere, their children would develop the faith and so would be won to the Church.[15] Gregory's reasoning is difficult to understand since it is unlikely that he also intended to have the children removed from the influence of their parents who undoubtably would continue to educate their offspring in their ancient religion.

The desire of the Pope to convert the Jews was manifested

---

13. See Parkes, p. 203-5.
14. Gregory the Great, *Selected Letters,* 1.47 in Nicene and Post-Nicene Fathers.
15. Gregory, *Letters,* 5.8. This particular letter appears in F.H. Holmes-Dudden, *Pope Gregory the Great* (New York: Longmans, Green, and Co., 1905).

in still another instance. Apparently a number of Jews in the province of Agrigentum wanted to convert to Christianity, but according to Church policy, converts had to wait eight months as catechumens before they were allowed to take the rites. Gregory felt that the long delay might prove discouraging and he wrote to Fantinus, who was Defensor of Agrigentum, that if it seemed that the delay might in fact give them second thoughts, he should undermine the law and allow them to be baptized before the prescribed time. In addition, he advised him to supply the Jews with baptismal vestments and to pay for them out of the Church's treasury if the Jews were too poor to purchase them on their own account.[16] Gregory's enthusiasm to win the Jews could not have been more manifest. In these two letters he shows that he was willing to break Church law and to pay for the necessary garments in order not to discourage their entry. He was even willing to bribe them to convert.

The explanation for his attitude and the attitude of the bishops and other Christians who sought the conversion of the Jew is part and parcel of the contemporary uncertainty of the early Christian leaders about their own religion. It is a theme that is woven throughout the history of the Church's dealings with the Jews. If Christianity were the true religion of God, why did the Jews resist? In the physical world one can solve a problem of means of some measuring device, a ruler, a thermometer, etc. If two people disagree, they can easily settle their disagreement by resorting to some tool. But what kind of tool is it that can measure the truth of a belief? Where social reality is at stake, the only way to be right is to convince others that you are right. The more people who agree with you, the more likely your assumptions and beliefs are true. And when one who enjoys a great heritage endorses your viewpoint, then it is almost certain that you have hit upon an undisputable truth. For the Christian thinker, the resistance of the

16. *Letters*, 8.23.

Jew posed an overwhelming difficulty to his scheme of social reality. Hence one finds many attempts, violent or otherwise, to influence the Jews toward the acceptance of Christianity.

Despite the Papal realization that the Jews could not be forceably won over, there was little way in which the various bishops could be convinced. If the Jews could not be converted, the least one could do would be to make their lives miserable in payment for the grief they had brought upon the Christian community through their reputed persecution of Christ. In various communities, bishops seemed to vie with one another to see who could do more to molest the Jews. In Naples, the bishop attempted to prevent the Jews of that city from celebrating their religious festivals;[17] in Palermo, the bishop drove the Jews out of their synagogues and claimed them for the Church along with the guest chambers that were attached to these buildings.[18] When Pope Gregory was informed of these injustices, he wrote to his bishops to return the synagogues to their rightful owners and to allow them to follow their ceremonies without interference. But Victor, the bishop of Naples, chose to assert his independence. Ignoring the Pope's letter, he consecrated the synagogue on his own initiative. When Gregory learned of his bishops's insubordination, he ordered him to recompense the Jews monetarily for their loss. The synagogue, of course, could not be returned, since any edifice that had been consecrated to the Church could not be placed in Jewish hands. However, he did order Victor to return any books or ornaments that he had confiscated when he had seized the synagogues. For some strange reason the Pope could break the law concerning the waiting period for Jewish catechumens, but he could not take it upon himself to restore their synagogues. Moreover, he did not even permit the Jews to evaluate their own losses. Instead the Patrician, and the abbot of the city were entrusted with the evaluation of the stolen properties.

17. Gregory, *Letters,* 13.12.
18. *Ibid.,* 9.55.

We do not know whether the compensation was fair or not, since this would depend on the two officials. But more importantly, one can see in this incident the unquestionable independence of the bishop. Gregory I may have stood at the head of the Church, but the influence that he exercised was dependent upon the personalities of the bishops who theoretically were his ministers. If a bishop chose to ignore a papal injunction, there was little that could be done or would be done. The consecration of the Palermo synagogues clearly illustrates the state of papal-bishop relations.

Misplaced fervor, however, was not peculiar to the clergy alone, for there are also instances of recently converted Jews wishing to show their zealousness for their newly adopted religion. In Caliari, a converted Jew named Peter entered the Jewish synagogue on the day after his baptism and placed within it a number of Christian images along with his own baptismal vestments. It appears that the Jews were not allowed to touch these articles for either legal or religious reasons and they had to ask one of the Christian clergy in the city to remove them. Everyone refused. Consequently the Jews appealed to the Pope and Gregory in turn wrote to the bishop in Caliari ordering him to remove the articles and to restore the building to the Jews.[19]

This discrepancy between the attitude of the Pope and the behavior of the clergy can probably be ascribed to the different approaches each championed as a means of converting or plaguing the Jews. The Pope believed that the Jews could only be won over by peaceful persuasion, argument and sermon; the latter believed that force and oppression would bring them into the Church. The Pope's attitude was the *de jure* position of the Church; the behavior characteristic of bishops Victor and Paschasius illustrates the actual *de facto* policy.[20]

Although Gregory earnestly desired the conversion of the

19. Gregory, *Letters,* 9.6.
20. Cf. S. Katz, "Pope Gregory the Great and the Jews," *J.Q.R. 24* (1933-34): p. 113-36.

Jews he scorned violence as a means to that end. In this attitude he differed from most of the clergy. But on occasion he could be just as hostile in his attitude toward the Jews as they were. An interesting example occurred in Visiogothic Spain where the Catholic King, Recarred, attempted to convert all the Jews in his domains to Christianity. To those refusing the fiat he gave the option of death or exile. The Jews attempted to appease the king by offering him a bribe to change his mind; the attempt failed and the king remained firm. When the incident was related to Gregory he was delighted at the king's integrity and he personally informed him that he (Gregory) "had been led to praise God the more for your work."[21] Although Gregory himself was not adverse to offering a bribe to convert Jews, he severely condemned those Jews who offered bribes not to be converted. How does one reconcile Gregory's actions here with his other feelings about forced conversions? The only possible answer is that while he shunned violent methods he was even more strongly against any attempts by the Jews to discourage such measures. Perhaps he felt that he alone should have the last word in these matters.

Having thus brought to attention this contradiction in Gregory's conversion policy, let us include one more example of his tolerance. In Terracina, the Jews petitioned the Pope for a license to continue possession of their synagogue at its present location. However, the synagogue was so near to one of the churches in that vicinity that the sound of the Jews as they sang their hymns was audible in the church. At the same time that the Jews wrote to the Pope, the bishop sent him a letter asking him not to grant the petition because of the synagogue's proximity to the church and because of the disturbance it was causing. Gregory asked for further information. If the synagogue were indeed so close to the church that the Jews could be heard, they were not to be allowed to hold their services at its present site. However, if the synagogue were taken

21. Gregory, *Letters*, 9.122.

from them they were not to be deprived of a new site.[22] No mention was made of compensation.

While civil rights and religion occupied an important place in Gregory's correspondence dealing with the Jews, the topic that drew his greatest attention concerned the possession of Christian slaves by the Jews. On many occasions, the various emperors had expressly forbid this practice, but for sundry economic reasons, these laws were not always observed. Slaves were very abundant in these times due to the numerous barbarian invasions and wars, and although the Jews were not the only slave traders, they occupied a very prominent position in supplying this economic commodity. The pressing need for these slaves in agrarian communities caused land owners who were in need of cheap labor to bring pressure against those officials who attempted to enforce the laws against Jewish ownership of slaves. In some cases the local authorities also owned vast landed areas and for these wealthy individuals it would be economic suicide to enforce the law. If Jews could not purchase slaves, they would not be able to bring any into the slave markets and hence the landowners would not be able to procure them. Since these laws were unpopular among the wealthy, they were judiciously ignored. However, those who had theological impracticality instead of economic interests at heart, were vehement and unrelenting in their criticism. It was not the mere ownership of Christians by Jews that bothered them, it was the often successful attempts of Jewish slave owners to convert their stock to Judaism. The slaves themselves preferred to remain with their Jewish masters because the Jews treated them humanely. Slaves were often converted to Judaism because there was a Talmudic ordinance stating that servants should either be circumcised or resold so that the Jewish family would not be hindered in the practice of their religion by the presence of foreigners in their homes.[23] It was this aspect of slavery that disturbed the Church. To the bishop

22. *Ibid.*, 1.10.
23. H. Graetz, *History of the Jews* (Phil.: Jew Pub. Soc., 1946), vol. 3, p. 29.

of Luna in Etruria, Gregory wrote, "Wherefore we extort thy Fraternity that, according to the course laid down by the most pious laws, no Jews be allowed to retain a Christian slave in his possession, but if any are found in their power, let liberty be secured to them by protection under the sanction of the law."[24] Yet for practical purposes, the restriction pertained only to such slaves as lived in the city of Luna since Gregory qualified his exhortation by permitting those Jews who were engaged in agriculture to keep Christian slaves; but only if they permitted them to observe their religion.

On at least three occasions, Gregory wrote to the Frankish rulers, Theodoric, Theodobert, and Brunichild that he was "altogether astonished that in your kingdom you allow Jews to possess Christian slaves" and he asked Theodoric to pass "an ordinance of your excellency [that] may remove the evil of this wrong-doing from your kingdom."[25] In view of the obvious tolerance of the secular authorities it was ridiculous of Gregory to order the practice outlawed, yet he continued to address himself to what was, in those times, an insoluble embarassment. Gregory even proposed a comprise so that the secular officials would not be angered by the Church's interference. The plan was to have certain Church officials make careful observance of the return of Jewish dealers from the various territories of Gaul so that they could make sure that any Christian slaves in their possession would be sold only to other Christians. Transactions and final deliveries were not to take longer than forty days. After this period, the slaves were to be seized from the Jews.[26] In the same letter, Gregory relates a very interesting case in which a Jewish slave owner seemingly attempted to get around the slave-owning law by transferring ownership of his slaves to his sons, who were Christians. By this means he hoped to have possession of them in all but legal title. Furthermore, he would also protect himself from loss be-

---

24. Gregory, *Letters*, 4.21.
25. Gregory, *Letters*, o.110.
26. *Ibid.*, 9.36.

cause if any of them attempted to claim sanctuary from the Church they would not be allowed their freedom since they would legally be fleeing from Christian owners. Gregory's solution to this circuitry of the law was to order his officials to make sure that the slaves did not live in the father's house although he permitted them to work for the father. Here again one sees that the greatest fear of the Church was the possibility of conversion toward Judaism and not mere ownership of Christians by Jews.

In this matter of slavery, we must once again emphasize that the population of the western world had fallen drastically. The labor shortage was a very real social and economic problem, hence the obvious necessity of ignoring those laws relating to Jewish possession of Christian slaves, especially where food production was concerned. Had the Jews been prevented from owning slaves it is likely that they would have given up the slave trade and had they done this the labor shortage that would have been created might have caused an unestimable loss of life through sheer starvation.

The final letter worth mentioning in Gregory's relations with the Jews concerns a certain Nasas, "a most wicked Jew, [who] has, with a termerity that calls for punishment, erected an altar under the name of the Blessed Elijah, and by sacrilegious seduction had enticed many Christians to worship there."[27] This may have been another "Judaizing" movement by a sincere individual,[28] but Gregory had absolutely no toleration for it and he promptly ordered the prefect of Sicily to look into the matter and to break up the movement, "lest, (God forbid) the Christian religion should be polluted by being subjected to Jews."[29]

Turning from these letters to his theological writings, one encounters in Gregory nothing that would differentiate him

27. Gregory, *Letters*, 3.38.
28. See L.I. Newman's *Jewish Influence on Christian Reform Movements*. (New York: Columbia Univ. Press, 1925), p. 410-11.
29. *Letters*, 3.38.

from the theologians who preceeded or followed him with regard to the Jews. To Gregory, Judaism was a "foolishness," a "corruption," an "infidelity," a "sin," and an "insanity." But despite their adherence to their "superstitio,"[30] the Jews ought not to be molested, for one day Gregory believed they too would see the ultimate truth of the Christian religion. On the one hand the Pope thus endorsed a policy of toleration, on the other, he spoke and thought of the Jews in anything but tolerant terms.

Parkes' summary of the Pope's self-contradiction is as follows: "it is a curious picture to think of Gregory turning from the dictation of one of his more flowery denunciations of their diabolical perversity and detestable characteristics to deal with his correspondence, and writing to a bishop who has only been carrying these denunciations into logical action, to remind him that it is by love and charity alone that we can hope to win them. . . ."[31]

In evaluating Gregory's contribution to the events of his period and to the period that followed, it might seem that due to his influence, forceable conversions were seriously discouraged by the Papal authorities as a Christian policy. But this does not mean that the Jews were left alone. Instead of using force or threatening violence, they were often given the option of voluntarily submitting to baptism and hence conversion, or else they were permitted to leave the country. The truth of the matter is that the Pope exercised very little influence over events in faraway countries. The Pope may have been the spiritual head of the Church, but the bishops and priests were not concerned with spiritual matters. When it came to practical matters, they more often than not acted independently of Papal authority.

30. This is the term Roman society had formerly used to describe Christianity.
31. Parkes, p. 220-21.

11

The Ordeal of the Jews in Visigothic Spain

Church and State in Visigothic Spain

IN A.D. 415 the Visigoths invaded Spain and eventually conquered the entire peninsula except for a few small areas that remained under direct Roman control. Like the Ostrogoths who conquered Italy, the Visigoths wisely decided to maintain as many of the institutions and laws of the empire as they thought practical, hence the change in power was peacefully accepted.

The Visigoths were a tribal society headed by several chieftains who chose a king for their nations by means of an election. This electoral choice was a jealously guarded national right, and far from being an absolute monarch, the king's power was seriously limited by this electorate. Occasionally some kings attempted to establish a dynasty, but these attempts were never successful; their main effect was to arouse the nobles against all the political machinations of their kings, and in nearly every attempt to strengthen the country or the monarchy, the kings were frustrated by rebellious nobles.

Religiously, the conquering Visigoths were Arians and this

brought them into conflict with the Catholics who formed the majority of the native population. As long as the country remained internally divided, there was no possibility of real unification, and it was with an eye to rectifying this situation that Reccared officially adopted Catholicism and made it the state religion in Spain. Thereafter the country was religiously united (except for the Jews); politically, it was far from soldered.

Independent and unruly, the nobles had constantly made and unmade kings as the various soverigns pleased or displeased them. Hoping to keep the nobles in place once the Catholics were behind him, Reccared converted, thereby uniting Church and State in the government of Spain. Although they opposed their kings on most important issues, the nobles followed Reccared and also converted to Catholicism, but unlike Recarred, they felt no need to cultivate the Church as a political ally.

From the time of Reccared, there was a close similarity between the laws of the kingdom and the canons of the Church councils, so much so that they became interrelated, each finding their way into the other. Legislation, though technically in the hands of the king, was in fact shared with the Church, whose frequent ecclesiastical councils turned into small civil parliaments.[1] On several occasions, the king even approached the synods to ask the Church's aid in revising the laws of the land. Only infrequently were such requests refused. For their part, the bishops were well aware of the general situation and they realized that the king was dependent upon them for support against the nobles. More often than not, the Church sided with the kings, but occasionally it withheld its support when it felt that its own interests might suffer.

In the end the power struggle between king, nobles, and Church seriously weakened the country. Ineffective government, a myriad of contradictory laws, the collapse of trade,

1. Cf. A. Ziegler, *Church and State in Visigothic Spain* (Washington, D.C.: Catholic Univ. Press, 1930), p. 53.

and a small army of Moorish invaders eventually ended the Visigothic reign in Spain. During this long era of internal strife and power struggles, the Jews experienced countless pressures designed to alienate them from their Christian neighbors, and to deprive them of their property, and their freedom.

The Jews under the Arian Kings

There have been claims that the Jews came to Spain at the time of Vespasian[2] or even earlier,[3] but the only early piece of information that reliably places them in that country is the canons of the Council of Elvira that was held sometime around A.D. 300. Four of these canons[4] show that relations between Jews and Christians were friendly and cordial at this time and intermarriage and eating meals together were not uncommon occurrences. However, the higher officials of the Catholic clergy frowned upon this situation since they felt it might prove a danger to Christianity, which itself had only recently gained a foothold in Spain. Hence the Council of Elvira passed four anti-Jewish canons in an effort to minimize any form of society between Jews and Christians. As the Church gained in stature, further measures were taken to segregate the Jews completely from Christians living in Spain.

Before Spain turned Catholic, it was ruled by Arian kings who treated the Jews no better or worse than they had been treated in other Roman societies. Catholics, however, were made to feel uncomfortable by the Arians since they were thought of as theological enemies if not as out-and-out political enemies.

2. S. Katz, *Jews in the Visigothic and Frankish Kingdoms of Spain and Gaul* (Cambridge: Medieval Academy of America, 1937), p. 3-5.
3. Jews were often plagued by the anti-Jewish fervor of the Catholic kings who accused them of being "Christ killers." Some Spanish Jews felt that if they could prove that their ancestors had left Palestine before the Christian era, they might successfully evade the accusation, hence they concocted various inscriptions to prove their antiquity in Spain and in other places (Baron, *Social and Religious History of the Jews,* vol. III, p. 34).
4. See ch. 9.

In the difficult process of taking over the country, the Visigoths found it advantageous to incorporate as much of the legacy left them by the Romans as they possibly could. The Jews were considered as Roman citizens and since the Visigoths adopted the Theodosian Code, Jews were still governed by Roman law. Under Alaric II (A.D. 484-507), the promulgations dealing with the Jews in the Code were reduced from fifty-three to ten by Alaric so as to eliminate much of the redundancy inherent in the laws. In A.D. 506 he issued an entirely new revision of the Roman Code called the Breviary *(Lex Romana Visigothorum)*. In essence it was only a simplified version of the Theodosian Code supplemented by a collection of other laws called the Third Novella of Theodosius and the Sentences of Paul.

Fundamentally, the position of the Jews remained unchanged. Christian tribunals had to be resorted to in cases of disputes between Jews and Christians, but if both parties were Jews, they could still take their quarrel to a Jewish court. However, Jewish courts still did not have the power of capital punishment.[5] But no matter what the cause for litigation, Jews could not be brought to court on their sabbath or during religious holidays.[6] Regarding slavery, Jews were neither permitted to buy or acquire slaves as a gift, and any Christian could purchase a Christian slave who belonged to a Jew even after the slave had accepted Judaism.[7] The only means by which a Jew might retain ownership of a Christian slave was through inheritance or by means of a trusteeship.[8] A slave who had been circumcised was considered to have submitted forceably to the rite and was to be given his freedom.[9] Those guilty of performing the operation were to be sentenced to death.[10]

Intermarriage between Christians and Jews was still regarded

5. *Breviary*, 2.1.10.
6. *Ibid.*, 2.8.3.
7. *Ibid.*, 3.1.5.
8. *Ibid.*, 16.4.2.
9. *Ibid.*, 16.4.1.
10. *Ibid.*, 16.4.2.

as an adulterous relationship[11] and Christians converting to Judaism were to be punished by intestability.[12] A five-year period was allowed for legitimate heirs to make their denunciations public if a man's conversion to Judaism was unknown at the time of his death. A Jew was not allowed to proselytize. The penalty was confiscation of property and death for this "heinous" offence.[13] On the other hand, if a Jew converted to Christianity, other Jews were warned not to molest him for his choice.[14] Denied public office, only the decurionate and guard duties were left for Jews to occupy.[15]

The clauses restricting construction of new synagogues were also included in the Breviary with the stipulation that any violation of the edict would result in the confiscation of said synagogues by the Catholic Church.[16] Parkes[17] explains this surprising qualification, regarding the turning of synagogues over to the Catholic rather than the Arian Church, by suggesting that Roman lawyers worked on the Breviary and being Catholics themselves, they would see no reason for changing the law designating the Catholic Church as the appointed receiver.

The Breviary continued in effect for at least eighty more years after its promulgation. Its importance, as far as the Jews of Spain are concerned, was that it set the stage for the later legislation that was passed by the Catholic kings.[18] The Breviary, although it only reiterated the Theodosian Code, tolerated the existence of the Jewish religion and the practice of its

11. *Ibid.*, 3.7.2.; 9.4.4.
12. *Ibid.*, 16.2.1.
13. *Ibid.*. 16.3.2.
14. *Ibid.*. 16.3.1.
15. *Ibid.*, Third Novella 2.
16. *Ibid.*, Third Novella 3.5.
17. Parkes, *Conflict of Church and Synagogues*, p. 352.
18. If the Breviary guaranteed the Jews some prerogative, this would not be violated, generally. However, if there were some clauses found in the Code but not in the Breviary, the kings would naturally follow the Breviary and the Jews might find themselves in difficulty. For example, the Theodosian Code allowed relapsed Jews who converted to Christianity to return to their former religion, while the Breviary did not.

rites. However, the omission of the sundry laws that prohibited violence against the Jews in the Theodosian Code, is very noticeable in Alaric's abridgement. This was probably not due to any anti-Jewish bias on the part of the king, but simply was an expression of his own confidence that the police powers of his state could provide and maintain the necessary guarantees of internal peace.[19] Missing too, were the privileges granted the Jewish clergy along with the laws that permitted Jews to return to their own religion if they so desired. This latter point turns out to be the most important of these omissions since it was picked up by the later Catholic kings who legislated specifically and harshly against any Jews who converted to Christianity and then tried to come back to Judaism.

The Church councils of the Arian period were, to use Juster's[20] term, "cautious" in that they did not manifest concern and readiness to deal with problems relating to the association of Jews and Christians. Possibly this was because the Catholic Church felt that its position in Arian Spain was not firm enough to have its enactments carried out in other than religious matters. The Council of Agde, held in A.D. 506, passed only three canons relating to the Jews. Clerics and laymen were told not to share any meals with the Jews[21] and all Christians were ordered to fast on Lent. Emphasis was placed on fasting on Saturdays; Sundays were exempted.[22] The other canon deals with relapsed converts who at that time did not present the difficulty they were to prove in the seventh century. In reference to these individuals, it was ruled that Jews who wished to become Catholics would have to spend eight months as catechumens before they could receive baptism. Only the approach of death could shorten the waiting period.[23] The ordinance turned out to be more beneficial to the Jews

19. Parkes, p. 353; Ziegler, p. 188.
20. *La Condition légale des Juifs sous les Rois Visigoths* (Paris: Giraud, 1912), p. 3.
21. Council of Agde, canon 40.
22. *Ibid.,* canon 12.
23. *Ibid.,* canon 34.

than the Church realised for it served to discourage early attempts at forced baptisms.[24]

There is practically nothing that is known about the general condition of the Jews during this period other than that which is mentioned in the laws and the Church canons. These are the prime sources of information since no chroniclers have left us any contemporary descriptions of Jewish life in Spain during the Arian period. All that can be put together is a patchwork of details derived from canon and law.

Under the Arians, the Jews seemed to have lived amidst the Christians in relative peace, possibly because there were no attempts at this time to unite the kingdom religiously.[25] Intermarriage between Jews and Christians was common,[26] as was the sharing of meals.[27] Their religion, which had enjoyed a certain tolerated status in the empire, continued to be tolerated by the Arian kings and there is no evidence that the Jews were molested in any way during this period.

The economic basis of the Visigothic kingdom was agriculture and the Jews probably had large tracts of land that they farmed with the aid of Christian slaves. So abundant were their harvests, Christian farmers used to come to them to ask their divine help for their own farms.[28] Evidently, the Jews were suspected of enjoying powers not experienced by the Catholic or Arian clergy. According to Dopsch,[29] the Jews were very prominent in the commercial side of Visigothic society, but other than numerous references to their slave-trading ventures, there is little documentary evidence for this assertion.

Beyond these remarks, there is little more that can be said. While Spain remained under the control of the Arians, the Jews lived in relative peace. Reccared's conversion to Catholicism in A.D. 587 altered their position quite drastically.

24. Baron, vol. III, p. 245, note 43.
25. Ziegler, p. 188, note 112.
26. Council of Elvira, canon 16.
27. *Ibid.,* canon 50; Council of Agde, canon 40.
28. Council of Elvira, canon 49.
29. A. Dopsch, *The Economic and Social Foundations of European Civilization* (London: K. Paul, Trench, Trubner and Co., 1937), p. 344.

The Jews of Spain under the Catholic Kings

Reccared (A.D. 586-601) recognized that his power as king would always be limited as a result of his dependency on the Visigothic nobles. To offset their influence, he had to have the support of a powerful group of individuals who would rally behind him in case the nobles tried to pressure him. The nobles and the Catholics were in no way united and the king realized that by playing the one off against the other, he would be able to retain his own position without fear of a united popular uprising against him.

Thus, the various Church councils (which met frequently and which rarely failed to incorporate at least one anti-Jewish canon in its laws) came to have the status of civil legislators since the king typically agreed to all of their decisions.[30] Church and State were now united and legislation concerning the Jews at once became more extensive and more hostile. The decision of the Third Council of Toledo, held in A.D. 589, introduced for the first time the fiat ordering the compulsory baptism of Jewish children who were born of mixed marriages.[31] Likewise, Jews were prohibited from exercising any public offices, from acquiring Christian slaves and from intermarriage with Christians.[32] All of these pronouncements automatically became the law of the land. Recarred himself, issued a law that forbid Jews from buying or receiving Christian slaves as gifts. Guilty Jews were to be deprived of these slaves without compensation and if a Jew happened to circumcise the slave or any slaves he owned, he was to forfeit all his property.[33]

This was a very grave economic restriction since slaves were very important to those engaged in agriculture. If the Jews were to be deprived of these slaves, they would not be able to

30. Juster, *Juifs sous les rois Vis.*, p. 4.
31. Capit., 14.
32. *Ibid.*
33. Leg. Vis., 12.2.12.

look after their farms and would be at a considerable disadvantage. Realizing the oppressiveness of the measure, a number of wealthy Jews who were directly affected by the law, gathered a large sum of money and approached the king with a bribe to induce him to rescind the law. Reccared, however, refused and for his integrity he was earnestly commended by Pope Gregory.[34]

In the same year that the Third Council of Toledo was held, another council sat at Narbonne and here too Jewish questions were discussed. The conciliar resolutions adopted at Narbonne ruled that Jews should not be permitted to work on Sundays[35] or to sing psalms at their funerals[36] since this was a practice that the Church reserved for itself. Consultation with Jewish fortune-tellers was also forbidden,[37] probably because of the influence that these Jews might exercise over those who came to consult them.[38] But unlike the Council of Toledo, the decisions reached at Narbonne did not receive royal sanction in the Visigothic empire and hence did not become civil law.

The passage of canons and laws involved very little difficulty; enforcement was another matter. The situation in Visigothic Spain, as described above, was such that the king owed his station to the nobles who elected him and who retained complete independence in their own provinces. Any plans the king wished to inaugurate had to be endorsed by the nobles. Luckily for the Jews, this was no easy undertaking.

The political endorsement of the Church that Reccared accepted was not shared by the nobles or by the people at large. Consequently, the Jews were able to evade many of the discriminatory laws with a number of well-placed bribes that the nobles and even the clergy were willing to accept, even if Reccared was not. Jews may not have been allowed to purchase Christian slaves legally, but the fact was that they did so.

34. Gregory, *Letters,* 9.
35. Council of Narbonne, canon 4.
36. *Ibid.,* canon 9.
37. *Ibid.,* canon 14.
38. Cf. Council of Elvira, canon 49.

Bribery and minimal cooperation kept the laws from being observed and Reccared's inability to follow through with their enforcement eventually led to their disuse.

Following Reccared, there was a rapid succession of kings[39] but until Sisebut (A.D. 612-620) came to the throne, no new anti-Jewish legislation was promulgated. Immediately upon being crowned, this king reissued Reccared's law concerning the compulsory baptism of children born of mixed marriages. Not content with half measures, one year later (A.D. 613) he decreed that all Jews living in Spain had either to convert to Christianity or else go into exile.[40] The number of Jews who left the country is not known, but certainly there must have

---

39. Liuwa II (A.D. 601-604), Witteric (A.D. 604-610), Gundemar (A.D. 610-612), filled the gap between Reccared and Sisebut.

40. A number of historians have attempted to explain Sisebut's actions. Katz, suggests that Sisebut was motivated by either the thought of obtaining the property Jews would leave behind, or else by some unexplainable personal vagary. B. Blumenkranz *Juifs et Chrétiens Dans La Monde Occidental* (Paris: Mouton, 1960), on the other hand, suggests that Sisebut was concerned with the fact that the country was still not united and felt that by bringing the Jews into the Church, unification might be possible. For their part, the Jews could remain where they were and could continue to live as they had before, except that they had to divest themselves of their ancestral religion, which still distinguished them from their Christian neighbors. According to Blumenkranz's hypothesis, the Jews were too numerous and had too much economically at stake for Sisebut to think that they would even consider mass exodus (p. 107-108).

   The Church itself was not behind Sisebut. Indeed, Isidore of Seville, who presided over the Fourth Council of Toledo (A.D. 633), advised Sisebut against such a policy and one of the canons passed by the Council expressly forbade forceable conversion of the Jews (canon 57). However, Parkes (p. 355) points out that once they had been converted Isidore was quite happy over the turn of events and he was of the opinion that they should not be allowed to return to their former religion.

   Baron offers a more interesting interpretation of the king's motives: Sisebut was at that time attempting to free the peninsula completely from Roman-Byzantine occupation. Due to the fact that the empire was also seriously engaged in a war with the Persians, Sisebut almost succeeded in driving the emperor's token army out of Spain. At the same time he heard a rumor that the Byzantine Jews were betraying the empire to the Persians and were also using the chaos of war to massacre large numbers of Christians in Antioch and Jerusalem. To prevent the possibility of a fifth column in his own ranks, Sisebut determined to eradicate the threat by exprelling the Jews. Baron is quick to mention that there are no sources that confirm this hypothesis of a connection between Sisebut's policy and contemporary events, but nevertheless he feels that it is a "reasonable explanation" (vol. III, p. 37-38; p. 246, note 46). Jews did, in fact, play an active part in an insurrection centered in Narbonne, and they were active participants in the downfall of the Visigoths, but this does not mean that Sisebut

been many thousands. Those who remained were obliged to adopt Christianity, at least outwardly. The social position of these Jews under Sisebut is difficult to determine. Many of them secretly practiced their ancient customs and suspicion of their relapsing back to Judaism was not uncommon. Neither Jews nor Christians, they were simply called baptised Jews.

The exile lasted until A.D. 621 when Swinthila came to the throne. During his reign the Jews were allowed to return to Spain and the baptised Jews were permitted to revert back to Judaism if they had relapsed or not.[41] However, the law itself was not repealed and could be invoked at any time. While Swinthila was king there was no anti-Jewish legislation passed nor did the Church exert much influence in the government. But in A.D. 631 there was an insurrection and Swinthila was removed and was replaced by Sisenand (A.D. 631-636).

Under the new king, the Church held the Fourth Council of Toledo in A.D. 633 and ten canons from that meeting dealt with the Jews. Again Isidore of Seville presided and again the Church affirmed the view that no Jew ought to be compelled to accept Christianity. Isidore, like Gregory, was of the opin-

really considered them as a fifth column. The opposite conclusion could even be drawn since the Jews, like the Visigoths, were also fighting against the Byzantine emperor.

Emperor Heraclius himself was a fanatical anti-Semite and he and Sisebut eventually came to terms in A.D. 616 but it is unlikely that the emperor influenced Sisebut to persecute the Jews since the treaty was signed three years after Sisebut ordered the conversion of the Jews.

Graetz (vol. III, p. 48) believes that Sisebut was aroused because the Jews still retained possession of Christian slaves despite Reccared's law to the contrary. Just before ordering the conversion of the Jews, he had ordered that the Jews had to give up all Christian slaves in their employ. Only Jews who adopted Christianity were allowed retention or could claim those slaves which their Jewish relatives had to give up (Leg. Vis., 12.3.13, 12.3.14). Although he attempted to put this law into effect, he appears to have met with the same success as had Reccared. The nobles would not collaborate with him either out of defiance or because of bribery and the bishops seemed not to interest themselves in this law. Frustrated by the inability to implement his policies, Sisebut issued his edict to settle the problem once and for all. If there were no Jews, there could be no evasion of the slave ownership law.

At the present time there is no way of determining which, if any, of these hypothesis is correct. Perhaps it was a combination of all of them. For the Jews, it was the same no matter what the reasons.

41. Joseph ha-Kohen, quoted by Katz, p. 13.

ion that the only way to win the Jews was through persuasion not force. But not too surprisingly, he was also of the opinion that once a Jew had received the sacraments, forceably or otherwise, he should not be permitted to return to his former religion nor should he be allowed to fraternize with unbaptised Jews.[42] Likewise, the sons of these Jews, if they had been circumcised, ought to be separated from their parents and be placed in convents or in Christian homes.[43] In addition, their slaves ought to be given their freedom since Jews were not allowed to own Christian slaves.[44] Another canon sought to lure the children of relapsed baptised Jews back into the Church by offering them the guaranteed inheritance of their parents' property even though they might be disinherited for entering the Church on their own.[45] Jews who had married Christian women could only continue living with them if they adopted Christianity. Upon refusal, the couple were to be separated, the children going to the mother.[46]

Parkes[47] maintains that the children of unbaptised Jews were to be taken from their parents so that they could be placed in monasteries or in Christian homes. But this would have been an extraordinary measure and would have been in contradiction to Isidore's avowed intention of discouraging forceable conversion. Parkes bases his view on canon sixty of the Fourth Council of Toledo. But the word used to describe the parents of these children is *Iudaei,* which was also the term used for baptised Jews. This decision, moreover, was merely a continuation of canon fifty-nine, which had ordered that circumcised sons of elapsed Jews be separated from their parents. Were it to have been as Parkes suggests, the decision would have been the signal for another mass departure of Jews from Spain.

The remaining canons ruled that Jews could not hold public

42. Fourth Council of Toledo, canon 57, canon 62.
43. *Ibid.,* canon 59.
44. *Ibid.*
45. *Ibid.,* canon 61.
46. *Ibid.,* canon 63.
47. Parkes, p. 356.

office[48] nor be witnesses in any legal disputes.[49] These prohib-
itions were likewise extended to baptised Jews because their
devotion was always suspect. The baptised Jew could not be
relied upon or trusted to remain faithful to Christianity. If he
had had any kind of sincerity in him in the first place, he
would not have had to be forced into Christianity; ergo, he
must be watched continuously. Dominated by this sentiment of
mistrust, the Church treated the baptised Jews as a special
group of Christians even though some had faithfully proved
their integrity. Soon their special designation disappeared and
they became simply Jews to be distinguished in no manner
from those Jews who had remained faithful to the ancient
religion.[50]

Chintilla (A.D. 636-639), Sisenand's successor, approved all
the anti-Jewish canons of the Fourth Council of Toledo and in
addition decreed that only Catholics would be allowed to live
in his kingdom, a principle which was quickly adopted by the
Sixth Council of Toledo held in A.D. 638. In addition, the
Council declared that "in the future, every king, before as-
cending the throne, together with other oaths, should be required to take this, that he should not tolerate Jewish unbelief
and should uprightly maintain the present laws."[51] If any king
dared to violate this oath, he would be anathematized.

According to Loeb,[52] a *placitum* was found in the archives
at Leon that purports to be a declaration of faith taken by baptised Jews under Chintilla by which these individuals vowed
to believe in God, the Son, and the Holy Ghost and to aban-
don Jewish rites, observances, and superstitions, such as the
sabbath and circumcision. They also promised to eat those
foods that Christians ate and to have nothing to do with the
Jews; they had to turn over any Jewish books in their posses-

48. Fourth Council of Toledo, canon 65.
49. *Ibid.,* canon 64.
50. Blumenkranz, p. 112.
51. Sixth Council of Toledo, canon 3.
52. I. Loeb, "Notes Sur L'Histoire Et Les Antiquities Juives En Espagne," *R.E.J.* 2,
(1881): p. 137-38.

sion and if they knew of any baptised Jews who transgressed this oath, they were to denounce them to either the king, a clergyman, or one of the public officials.

In Blumenkranz's[53] view, the purpose of the *placitum* was to alienate converted Jews from those who went into hiding or who left the country since it was felt that those who signed it would be despised and hated by the nonconverted Jews. But this is unlikely, since these Jews could not have been more alienated from exiled Jews than they were before taking the oath. Rather it was merely an expression of the suspicion with which the Church eyed the baptised Jews. Even though they had sworn their sincerity to this oath, it was always felt that these Jews would backslide. The *placitum* was an attempt to prevent this from happening. Proud of their determination, the bishops attending the Sixth Council, headed by bishop Braulio, wrote to Pope Honorius I informing him of their magnanimous deed and criticizing him for his own laxness in allowing relapsed baptised Jews to return to Judaism. With the deepest conviction, they assured the pontiff that there would be no such relapses in Spain.[54]

Alas for them, when Chindaswinth (A.D. 641-649) became king, Jewish converts were allowed to practice Judaism again and exiled Jews were permitted to return to Spain. It was a blow, no doubt, to the pride of the Spanish clergy and so wounded were they, that at the Seventh Council of Toledo held during Chindaswinth's monarchy, not a single reference was made to the Jews. The only consolation left them was Chindaswinth's directive that no person who had been born a Christian would be allowed to circumcise his sons. The penalty for such an offence was death.[55]

Chindaswinth was succeeded by his son Recceswinth (A.D. 649-672) and unlike the father, the son pursued an active anti-Jewish policy. In his opening speech to the Eighth Council of

53. Blumenkranz, p. 114.
54. Loeb, p. 137.
55. Leg. Vis., 12.2.16.

Toledo (A.D.) he exclaimed: "I denounce the customs and the life of the Jews who, by their contagious disease, pollute the land over which I rule." In A.D. 654 the Breviary, which still contained a number of laws safeguarding the Jewish religion, was abrogated and in its place the Leges Visigothorum was introduced: Whatever safeguards the Jews had legally possessed under the ancient Arian Code were no longer binding in Catholic Visigothic Spain.

While reconfirming canon fifty-seven of the Fourth Council of Toledo that ruled against forced baptism, Recceswinth also ordered the return to Catholicism of those Jews who had been baptised under former kings.[56] Most likely this was directed at the baptised Jews who had returned to Judaism under his father, Chindaswinth. To reaffirm their faith, the baptised Jews were compelled to sign another *placitum,*[57] the opening lines of which are as follows:

> To our most merciful and tranquil lord Recceswinth the king, from us the Jews of Toledo as witnessed or signed below. . .because our pertinacious lack of faith and the ancient errors of our fathers held us back from believing wholly in Our Lord Jesus Christ or accepting the Catholic truth with all our hearts, we therefore make these promises to your greater glory, on behalf both of ourselves and our wives and children.

Then follows a list of practices that they claim they will not adhere to in the future:

> not to become involved in any Jewish rites or customs nor to associate with the accursed Jews who remain unbaptised. We will not follow our habit of contracting incestuous unions or practicing fornication with our own relatives to

---

56. Eighth Council of Toledo, canon 12.
57. Leg. Vis., 12.2.17. The entire text is reproduced in Parkes, Appendix Three.

the sixth degree. We will not on any pretext, either ourselves, our children or our descendants, choose wives from
our own race; but in the case of both sexes we will always
link ourselves in matrimony with Christians. We will not
practice carnal circumcision, or celebrate the Passover, the
Sabbath or the other feast days connected with the Jewish
religion. We will not keep to our old habit of discrimination
in the matter of food. We will do none of the things which
the evil tradition of long custom and intercourse urges upon
us as Jews. . . .With regard to swine's flesh we promise to
observe this rule, that if through long custom we are hardly
able to eat it, we shall not through fastidiousness or error
refuse the things that are cooked with it. And if in all the
matters touched on above we are found in any way to
transgress . . . we swear . . . [Christian oath]. . .that whoever
of us is found to transgress shall either perish by the hands
of our fellows, by burning or stoning, or if your splendid
piety shall have spared our lives, we shall at once lose our
liberty and you shall give us along with all our property to
whomever you please into perpetual slavery.''

Recceswinth, however, was still unsatisfied. Chindaswinth
had allowed the exiled Jews to return and he wanted to rid the
kingdom of them. But at the same time he was unwilling to
challenge the leaders of the Eighth Council who, like Isidore,
were opposed to forced baptism. Moreover, the Church at this
time was not completely in support of Recceswinth and he had
to take care not to be offensive. Instead, he adopted a plan that
would not arouse the Church but that would at the same time
force the Jews to accept conversion or else leave the country.

The first step was abrogation of the Breviary, which cancelled all outstanding Jewish privileges. No one, even in his
heart, was to have the slightest doubts about the Catholic faith,
according to the king.[58] Although they were not to be forced

58. Leg. Vis., 12.2.2.

into baptism, all the laws enacted against the Jews by his predecessors were to have the same force as before.[59] Oddly enough, Recceswinth failed to see that he was contradicting himself since this last statement meant that he was reintroducing the laws that decreed forced baptism! But without bothering about the oversight, he forbade all Jewish rites, such as circumcision, Sabbath, and Passover observances, etc.,[60] which was tantamount to outlawing Judaism. Christians were forbidden to protect or aid a Jew in any manner in the observance of his rites[61] while baptised Jews were prohibited from attempting to avoid their Christian duties.[62] If any of the baptised Jews relapsed, they were to be stoned by their fellow Jewish-Christians, and failure to punish the relapsed Jews would result in harsh penalties for those derelict in their duties.[63]

Recceswinth's plan was clear. If he could prohibit the Jews from practicing their religion and at the same time deny them any civil rights, they would be compelled to leave the country or else to approach the Church of their own accord. But like the other kings before him, he could not depend on the compliance of the people to carry out his laws. The authorities were especially unwilling to cooperate and if the officials set a poor example, it was unlikely that those who served them would be more zealous in carrying out his commands. Recceswinth lashed out in the only manner he could: he passed another law. Bishops and nobles were threatened with confiscation of one-quarter of their property and excommunication if they aided or protected the Jews.

Confronted by failure, Recceswinth decided to adopt more rigorous means of surveillance to overcome the obstacles he encountered in enforcing his law. At the Ninth Council of Toledo, held in A.D. 655, those in sympathy with his concern for

59. *Ibid.*, 12.2.3.
60. *Ibid.*, 12.2.5-8.
61. *Ibid.*, 12,2,15.
62. *Ibid.*, 12.2.4.
63. *Ibid.*, 12.2.11.

the sincerity of the converted Jews passed a number of measures designed to support the previous laws. To discourage any
"judaizing" by these Jews, especially concerning their observance of Jewish holidays, a canon was passed ordering baptised Jews to attend all Christian festivals and to be present at
the episcopal divine service during Jewish holidays.[64] This was
to indicate to the various bishops the degree of their fidelity to
their new faith.

The more often Recceswinth passed new legislation, the
more the laws were broken. Imagine Recceswinth's anger and
frustration when he had to deal with the fact that some slave
owners were selling Christian slaves to Jews! This had been
strictly forbidden long ago. To add insult, among those found
guilty of breaking the law were some members of the clergy!
Catholic priests selling Christian slaves to Jews! And the Jews
were even circumcising these slaves!! Moreover, marriages between Jews and Christians were reoccuring and in all these
things the Jews were being aided by Catholic clergymen. What
chance had Recceswinth of enforcing his new laws if the previous decrees had proven so ineffective?

The Tenth Council of Toledo (A.D. 656) was summoned to
deal with these matters and though it positively forbade these
practices, the only effect it was to have was to allow some un-
scrupulous officials the chance to blackmail Jews by threatening to expose their illegal activities. The difficulties in curtail-
ing Jewish rights were as great as they had been under those
other anti-Jewish kings whom Recceswinth had succeeded. It
is not clear why this was so except for the fact that the kings
never enjoyed the undivided loyalty of the Church, the people,
or the nobles.

The only possible effect was to drive the baptised Jews
farther from Christianity and closer to Judaism, given of
course, that these Jews were initially sincere in their conversion. But no matter how sincere, in face of the distrust and

---

64. Ninth Council of Toldedo, canon 17.

suspicion that enveloped them, they had little incentive to remain Christians. Nonconverted Jews who were supposed to be inferior, and who should have had less freedom, were in fact, much better off. They may have been despised, but they were still respected more than the Jewish convert to Christianity would ever be.

Under the next king, Wamba (A.D. 672-680), Recceswinth's discriminatory laws remained theoretically in force but Wamba probably had the same degree of success in enforcing them as had his predecessor. Oddly enough, however, Wamba did not himself promulgate any new anti-Jewish laws although he, unlike most of the other Visigothic kings, had good reason for doing so since the Jews took part in a revolt to overthrow him. This came about as a result of an insurrection headed by the governor of Nimes, Hilderic. Encouraged by promises of religious freedom should he be successful, Hilderic was able to win over a sizable number of Jews to his cause and the rebellion began to gather some momentum especially when Paul, Wamba's general, himself switched his allegiance to Hilderic. But Wamba was able to meet the emergency and he gathered a large enough force to put down the movement. As a result, the Jews were driven out of Narbonne if not out of the whole province of Septimania.

If Wamba failed to chastise the Jews, the next king, Erwig (A.D. 680-687) more than made up for his predecessor's neglect. Three months after he became king, Erwig summoned the Twelfth Council of Toledo and submitted to it a revised edition of Recceswinth's code in which the laws relating to the Jews were much harsher. Poignantly, Erwig declared: "It is with tears in my eyes that I implore this venerable assembly to use all its zeal in order to purify this country of this plague or corruption and I cry to you: arise, destroy the guilty and amend the dishonest ways of the renegades, and above all, extirpate with its roots the Jewish plague." Thus did he beg the assembly to adopt his uncompromising laws. They did.

Contrary to the canons of the Fourth Council of Toledo, the

Twelfth Council approved Erwig's plan of forced baptism along with the twenty-eight other anti-Jewish laws he submitted to it. Moreover, Erwig introduced a new hierarchy of punishments designed to fit the gravity of future crimes. Among these, *decalvatio* stands as the most difficult to explain. *Decalvatio* means to make bald, that is to shave the scalp. It was a degrading punishment among the Goths who had long hair[65] and it was also applied to Jews who broke the law. Apparently the Jews had adopted the Gothic custom of long hair, and the punishment was now deemed appropriate to them as well.

Within one year, Erwig ordered every Jew to give up Judaism[66] and to swear to a declaration[67] similar to the *placitum* of Recceswinth. The Jew then had to be baptised and he had to swear an oath of fidelity to the Christian religion that was signed and kept in the archives of each parish.

The penalty for those who chose exile over baptism, was confiscation of goods, *decalvatio*, one hundred lashes, and then and only then, permission to leave the country. The same punishment was to be levied on all baptised Jews from the age of ten years if they were found guilty of observing any Jewish religious rites. Again the kingdom was to contain only two classes of people: those who were born Christian, and the *Iudaei*, the baptised Jews. The latter were prohibited from observing anything that smacked of "judaizing," from circumcision to the possession of Jewish books.[68] Castration was the penalty inflicted upon men who either practiced or submitted to circumcision; women who allowed their children to be circumcised were to have their noses cut off. In both cases the goods of the guilty party were to be confiscated by the fiscus (read Erwig).[69]

---

65. Cf. Blumenkranz, p. 122 and F.S. Lear, "The Public Law of the Visigothic Code," *Speculum* 26 (1951): p. 15.
66. Leg. Vis., 12.3.3.
67. *Ibid.*, 12.3.14.
68. *Ibid.*, 12.3.4,5,7,8,11.
69. *Ibid.*, 12.3.5.

Intermarriage between Jews of the sixth or nearer degree of consanguinity were to be dissolved, and each party was to receive the usual prescription of *decalvatio,* confiscation of property, one hundred lashes, and exile. If there were children from the union, they might inherit the property, providing they did not observe Jewish rites and did not marry "incestuously." If there were no children, the property went, of course, to the fiscus.[70]

Erwig also had a plan to make sure that the baptised Jew actually followed the Christian way of life and did not merely give it lip service: "Every colony of [baptised] Jews in whatever city or province they may be situated, shall visit the bishop or priest of the diocese upon the sabbath and upon other festival days when they are accustomed to celebrate their [Jewish] festival rites; they shall not be permitted to wander about on said days; and during all such festivals when they are suspected of performing these rites, they shall under no circumstances leave their homes without permission of the priest."[71] All Christian priests were ordered to assemble the baptised Jews in their churches and were required to read to them a copy of the law. Following this, a written copy of the same was placed in every Jewish community so that ignorance of the law could not be relied upon as an excuse.[72]

Working on Sundays or other Christian holidays was punished with the lash or a fine;[73] attempting to escape the discipline of the Church or knowing of others attempting it and not reporting such offences was punishable by confiscation of property and exile.[74] All Jews had to sell their Christian slaves unless they could obtain a statement from a bishop as to their sincerity regarding conversion. If the slaves were not sold within a sixty-day time limit, they were to be confiscated. On no account were the Jews allowed to free Christian slaves

70. *Ibid.,* 12.3.8.
71. *Ibid.,* 12.3.21.
72. *Ibid.,* 12.3.28.
73. *Ibid.,* 12.3.6.
74. *Ibid.,* 12.3.2,9.

since this would be an insult to a Christian.[75] For their part, Christian slaves had to declare their Christianity.[76] Harsh penalties were decreed for those who refused to comply with any of these laws.[77]

Celebration of Christian holidays was mandatory for all baptised Jews and laws were passed that compelled them to spend these days in the presence of a bishop or with an orthodox Christian;[78] Christians who hired Jews had to make sure that these regulations were observed by their employees.[79] Needless to say, these latter laws were not forceably observed by economically minded employers.

The denigration of the Jews was furthered by laws that forbid them to hold any kind of public office or position where they might have any authority over Christian workers.[80] Even their right of free travel within the country was severely restricted. Before the baptised Jew could set out on a journey, he had to obtain a passport from the local priest in his area along with letters of introduction to each place that he intended to visit or pass through. Each priest in these places had to acknowledge these letters and had to testify as to the time and departure of the Jew and he had to sign a statement as to his visitor's Christian orthodoxy during his stay.[81]

Because he distrusted the nobles, Erwig prohibited them from serving as patrons for the baptised Jews; for each Jew thus protected, the noble was liable to a fine of three pounds of gold and excommunication from the Church.[82] Believing that the clergy would be the most zealous in observing his laws, Erwig entrusted them more than any other group with putting the laws into practice.[83] But in fact, Erwig trusted no

75. However, a Jew who chose to remain a Jew faced confiscation of his property anyway.
76. Christian slaves preferred to serve Jewish masters than those of their own faith.
77. Leg. Vis., 12.3.12,13,16.
78. *Ibid.*, 12.3.21.
79. *Ibid.*, 12.3.22.
80. *Ibid.*, 12.3.16; 12.3.19.
81. *Ibid.*, 12.3.21.
82. *Ibid.*, 12.3.22.
83. *Ibid.*, 12.3.23.

one. Everyone was liable to suspicion and not without cause. For example, some priests took advantage of their positions to compel baptised Jewesses to have sexual relations with them: "and as priests are sometimes influenced by the execrable temptations of the flesh, it is hereby especially informed, that they shall not take advantage of opportunities of this kind, for indulgence of the same."[84]

The protection that the nobles and some of the clergy extended to the Jews was not motivated by any altruistic feelings. Rather, it had its root in the self-interests of these people. The nobles, for their part, received a sizable gain in the form of bribery from baptised Jews seeking to evade the laws. Moreover, they were also showing the king that they were independent of his sovereignty. The clergy also sought to gain from protecting the Jews since priests were often helped in their trading ventures by the Jews. Erwig was somewhat misguided when he exclaimed, "the perfidy and cunning of the Jewish heresy increases in criminality in the same proportion as attempts are made to abolish it by law."[85] But this cunning lasted only as long as the baptised Jews had economic wedges. Once they were stripped of all their possessions, as occurred under Egica, the protection formerly extended to them disappeared.

To minimize complicity, Erwig required magistrates to judge cases involving Jews in the presence of a clergyman. Only if there were no priests in his district could the magistrate officiate alone.[86] By this gambit, Erwig sought to nullify bribery attempts since he felt that the clergy would not succumb to bribery as readily as would the magistrates. But even so, he distrusted the priests and he ordered them to spy on one another for signs of indifference. The punishment for a priest found less than diligent in his duties regarding the Jews was a fine of one pound of gold and excommunication for a period

84. *Ibid.*, 12.3.21.
85. *Ibid.*, 12.3.1.
86. *Ibid.*, 12.3.25.

of three months; if the priest were poor, there was to be no fine, but the excommunication period was increased to six months. In the case of bishops, who like most of the nobles were not adverse to accepting bribes, Erwig decreed that one bishop might obtain the other's See if one could detect indifference in the other.[87]

The probability that these laws would be observed was ridiculously meager. Neither the nobles nor the clergy cooperated with Erwig in his endeavor to eliminate "judaizing," and their assistance was mandatory for any chance of success. Erwig's attempt to legislate against the Jews was simply a weak and impractical effort. In his passion to eliminate Judaism, he ended by "finally legislating against everyone. In order to punish all ways of avoiding the law he managed to reveal the impotence of the legislator,"[88] an impotence that extended to all facets of government for by the end of his reign the Visigothic empire was on the verge of collapse.

Egica (A.D. 687-702), who succeeded Erwig, realized that the baptised Jews had not been treated too well. Under the earlier kings, Christians and the faithful Jews (when they were not forced into exile) were the privileged groups, while the baptised Jews, because of the distrust and suspicion aimed at them, suffered the most. Egica felt that they might be won to Christianity permanently if the baptised Jews were not so oppressed, and he tried to win their loyalty by removing whatever disabilities they had been subjected to in return for their promise to remain faithful Christians. At the Sixteenth Council of Toledo (A.D. 693), he decreed that the baptised Jews no longer had to pay the special tax that they had formerly paid as Jews, and they were henceforth allowed to participate in commercial transactions with Christians. On the other hand, baptised Jews who wished to revert back to their old religion were allowed to do so.

---

87. *Ibid.,* 12.3.24.
88. Juster, *Condition legale des Juifs,* p. 20.

Before he could implement his policies, however, Egica realized that he would need the support of the nobles and the clergy and the only way he could obtain this support in the conversion of the Jews was to eliminate the most potent weapon the latter possessed—the bribe. Accordingly, Jews were ordered to sell to the fiscus, at a set price, all slaves, buildings, vineyards, olive groves, and houses that had been acquired from Christians. Attempts to trade with Christians of the kingdom or with people in countries across the sea were prohibited and were punishable by confiscation of property and perpetual slavery. Finally, after making sure that they would have no means to pay, he increased the taxes for the Jews.[89]

The baptised Jews fared only a little better. On the surface, it appeared that under Egica they would be left alone, but just the opposite occurred. Any Christian might question the sincerity of the baptised Jew and many did since eliminating the baptised Jews meant that one could take over their trading interests. Capitalizing on the baptised Jew's repugnance for pork, one law stated that a Christian who came into a new area had to begin trading discussions by reciting the Lord's Prayer before witnesses followed by the eating of a dish of pork.[90] The subtle distinction between converted and unconverted Jew quickly became obscured; the baptised Jew was still "a Jew".

The only means of escape for the Jews, both baptised and unbaptised, seemed to be across the sea in North Africa where there were many other Jews living under Moorish rule. Apparently, some messages were intercepted by the Visigothic authorities that indicated that the Jews were in fact hinting at an alliance between themselves and the Moors.

The Seventeenth Council of Toledo (A.D. 694) was immediately called by Egica. All the important men of the realm were invited to attend and the plot was disclosed; severe punishment was demanded for the discovered act of treason.

There was no hesitation on the part of the council. All Jews,

89. Leg. Vis., 12.2.18.
90. *Ibid.*

baptised or otherwise (with the exception of those living in Septimania guarding the mountain passes and agreeing to remain Christians) were deprived of all their property and were reduced to perpetual slavery. Various Christian masters throughout Spain swore to make sure that these slaves would never be allowed to practice any of their Jewish rites and they promised to take from them any children that these slaves might conceive and send them to Christian schools. When these children were older, they would only be allowed to marry Christians.[91]

Naturally enough, many Jews tried to escape, but only a fraction were able to make their way out of the country. However, the Jews who stayed did not remain as slaves for very long. In A.D. 711, the Moors finally invaded Spain and the Visigothic empire was overthrown. More than likely, they found in every village a sizable population that was hospitable and loyal—the Jewish slaves.[92]

91. Seventeenth Council of Toldo, canon 8.
92. Cf. Juster, *Condition legale des Juifs,* p. 23.

12

Jewish Fortunes in Gaul

Jewish Settlement in Roman Gaul

THE HISTORY of the Jews in Gaul prior to its conquest by the Franks (c. A.D. 440) is very fragmentary, the only sources being a patchwork of legal proscriptions, Church canons, and cursory and usually unreliable anecdotes connected with the lives of various saints who lived in Gaul. The earliest legendary notice of their entrance is found only after the destruction of the Temple in Jerusalem (A.D. 70) when Vespasian commanded that many of the defeated Jews be placed into a number of ships without captains or seamen so that they would be at the mercy of the winds to be carried wherever their destinies might lead them. According to this legend, three of the ships beached on the shores of Gaul—one at Lyons, one at Arles, and a third at Bordeaux. Upon landing, these exiles were allowed to leave their ships in peace and were given tracts of land to live on by the prefects in the various towns to which they had come.[1]

First acceptable historical mention of Jewish settlement in

---

1. The legend is cited in A. Neubauer, "The Early Settlement of the Jews in Southern Italy," *J.Q.R.* 4 (o.s. 1892): 606-25.

Gaul occurs in reference to the banishment of Archelaus to Vienna in the year A.D. 6.[2] Thirty-three years later, Herod Antipas was likewise banished to Lyons.[3] Neither of these events allow one to conclude that there was any sizable community of Jews in Gaul at this time and one must be content with Katz's[4] conclusion that the first incontrovertible evidence of large numbers of Jews in Gaul is located in one of the laws passed by Constantine in A.D. 321. This law was addressed to the Jews of Cologne and it cautioned them not to shirk from their curial responsibilities.[5]

More than likely, most of the Jews living in this area originally entered the country in the footsteps of the Roman legions that were garrisoned in the western provinces. The close association of the Jews with the Roman bureaucratic system led many of them to settle in administrative centers located along the main routes of communication, and their close affinity with the Roman social and political structure led both the Visigoths and the Franks to regard the Jews as Roman citizens. Consequently, they were governed by the same ancient laws as were other Romans.

If there were any Jews in the western Roman army stationed in Gaul, they were not long to remain in it for in A.D. 425 the Jews of Gaul were forbidden to carry arms.[7] The same law also ended the public careers of most Jews in this province, since Amatius, the prefect, was instructed to prohibit Jews and pagans from practicing the profession of law and from holding public office on the grounds that some occasion might arise wherein Christians might have to serve these Jews or pagans.

In the second half of the fifth century A.D., Roman control of the west slipped away and was taken over by the Visigoths, who initially ruled almost all of Spain and a large part of

2. Josephus, *Antiquities of the Jews,* 17.13.2; *Wars of the Jews,* 2.7.3.
3. *Ant.,* 18.7.2. In *Wars,* 2.9.6., Josephus places the site of exile in Spain.
4. Katz, *The Jews in the Visigothic and Frankish Kingdoms of Spain and Gaul,* p. 9.
5. Codex Theodosius, 16.8.3,4.
6. Baron, vol. III, p. 49.
7. *C.T., Const. Sirm.,* 6.

Gaul, an area stretching from the Pyrenees to the Loire.[8] But though the Visigoths ruled nearly half of Gaul for a time, their hold was a tenuous one. In the north, in the valley of the Rhone and in the plains of Champagne, squatted the Burgundians, a weak nation in its own right, but one that could still offer some resistance to the Visigoths, especially if allied with another tribe.

The Visigoths, however, sought to conquer lands but not inhabitants. In southern France, they left local power in the hands of the ancient Gallo-Roman families and they still preserved and honored Roman titles. The Catholic religion was also left unmolested and in A.D. 506 the Catholic clergy were given permission to meet in council at Agde. For their part, the Jews of Gaul were treated like the Jews of Spain and there is not much to relate that has not already been discussed in the previous chapter regarding the Arian period. Therefore the following comments will be directed at events dealing exclusively with their condition in Gaul.

In A.D. 465 the Church in Gaul began to legislate against the Jews because it was disturbed at the comradeship that had developed between Christians and Jews during these early times. At the Council of Vannes, clergymen were expressly forbidden to eat with Jews.[9] It was felt that Christian priests who accepted Jewish invitations would be admitting their inferiority to Jews who invited them because the Jews declined invitations to eat at Christian tables. This injunction was later extended to Christian laymen in A.D. 506 by the Council of Agde.[10]

Seemingly, social relations between Christians and Jews in Gaul were not at all restricted although some Christians were aware of their religious differences. In the letters of Sidonius Appolinaris, a Catholic priest, one finds actual trust being extended to one Jew, named Gonzales, to carry messages to the

8. *Ibid.*
9. Council of Vannes, canon 12.
10. Council of Agde, canon 40.

prefect of Gaul. Although Sidonius felt little sympathy toward the Jews, he mentions offhand that Gonzales would be a very dear friend of his except for the fact that he was a Jew.[11] In general, Sidonius displayed an unusual tolerance and on one occasion he wrote to the bishop of Eleutherius that, "In the transactions and disputes of the present world, a Jew has often as good a cause as anyone; however much you may attack his heresy, you can fairly defend him as a man."[12] But though he recommended toleration, he still maintained the traditional Christian predilection for speculating on the possibility of converting the Jews. In his letter to the same bishop he added the opinion that, "while there is any possibility of converting them, there is always a hope of their redemption."

From the evidence of the early canons and Sidonius' letters, it appears that there were few instances of hostility directed toward the Jews in Gaul while the Arian Visigoths were in power.[13] But the Visigoths did not rule Gaul for very long. The Franks soon crossed the Rhine and rapidly became a formidable power in the west. In A.D. 463 Clovis, their youthful leader, decided that it was time to expand and he confronted the Visigoths near Orleans. The Visigoths were no match for Clovis and they were driven back while Toulouse, their capital, was razed to the ground. The next major campaign against the Visigoths was in A.D. 508 when the Franks and Burgundians beseiged Arles. The Visigoths were still in possession of the area but king Alaric II was dead and Theodoric, the king of the Ostrogoths, came to defend the remains of the Vis-

---

11. *Sidonius, Letters,* ed. by O.M. Dalton (Oxford: Clarendon Press, 1915), no. 3.4.1 (A.D. 473).
12. *Ibid.,* 11.11.1 (A.D. 472).
13. There is one account, however doubtful it may be, that tells of the death of the bishop of Auvergne, named Austremonius, by a Jew who was moved to murder because the bishop had succeeded in converting his son to Christianity *(Acta Sanctorum,* Apr. 3, Vita S. Austremonii). The murder did not go unpunished for Urbicus, the new bishop, called a meeting of the Roman authorities immediately after the funeral, and secured permission to put the Jews in the area to death if they refused to be baptised *(Acta Sanctorum,* Nov. 1, Vita S. Urbici). The story has been questioned because at the time the event is supposed to have taken place (c. A.D. 310). Judaism was a *religio licta* while Christianity was not.

igothic kingdom against the two aggressors. The seige merits special interest because one of the historians of the event, St. Cesarius, relates that the Jews attempted to betray the city to the Franks. The recorded events are as follows: During the seige, a relative of Caesarius lowered himself from the wall that surrounded the city and came into the enemy lines apparently offering to betray the city. When his absence was noticed and news of the possible treason spread through the city, the Goths, accompanied by the Jews of Arles, rushed to the home of bishop Caesarius believing that he was behind the treason. The bishop's home was forceably entered and Caesarius was seized. The fury of the mob was bent on either drowning him in the Rhone or in locking him in the fortress at Beaucaire, but all attempts to cast the boat off failed and the mob was forced to bring him back into the city. In the meantime, one of the Jews who was guarding a section of the wall was accused along with the entire community of Jews within the city of the similar crime of treason when a rock with a note attached was found by a Visigothic soldier just short of the Frankish lines. The note gave the soldier's name and his sect and indicated a certain area where the Jews were in charge of the wall and thus could be easily scaled. In return, he asked freedom for the Jews and respect for their property. When the letter was brought to official attention, Cesarius was released and the guilty Jew was convicted and punished for his crime.[14]

It is regrettable that we do not have any other rendition of this affair except that given by Caesarius' biographer, who tends to be rather overzealous in his extollment of the bishop's virtues and in his condemnation of the Jews. There can be little doubt that the latter part of the fable that concerns the alleged treasonable activities of the Jewish soldier was an imaginative creation of the biographer. In his discussion of this event, Levi[15] points to a number of facts that should arouse suspicion. The fact that a kinsman of the bishop originally

14. S. Cyprian, *Vita S. Caesarii*. Patrologia Latina, 67, 1011.
15. I. Levi, "Saint Cesare et les Juifs d'Arles," *R.E.J.* 30 (1895): 295-98.

leaps the walls to the enemy should not have been any proof that the bishop himself was involved in the plot nor should the accusation against the Jews free Caesarius from suspicion. The opportune time in which the crime was committed, namely just after Caesarius had been seized, along with the information that the soldier was a Jew and that he gave not only his name, but also his sect, suggests a complete fabrication. Whatever the outcome of the arguments for or against Jewish involvement[16] we may cull one important fact from the entire incident, namely when the security of a city was in danger, the Jews were often entrusted with the defense of one of the more important areas in the line of attack. This was probably be-

---

16. If the story were true, it is difficult to understand why the Jews would want to betray the city to the Catholics. Moreover, the Theodosian Code (16.8.16; 16.8.24) had forbidden Jews to bear arms and yet in a time of crisis they were stationed at one of the strategic points in the city. It is unlikely that Theodoric coerced them into serving in his army and if he entertained any doubts about their loyalty, he would hardly have entrusted them with guarding one of the walls. Moreover, the Jews would not have had cause to betray the Arians to the Catholics; they would have been especially loathe to betray a man like Theodoric, who on many occasions had shown the Jews a tolerance not usually found in those times (see ch. 10). Given a choice between the Catholics and the Arians, the Jews would most certainly choose the latter as was the case when Belisarius beseiged Naples a number of years later (see ch. 10).

The fact that the incident was chronicled indicates that some form of treason occurred; despite the author's bias, it is likely that Caesarius was the main culprit. The incriminating evidence, circumstantial though it might be, is as follows: (1) Caesarius was originally accused of the crime. Three years earlier he had been accused, by his own bishop secretary, of the same crime—attempting to deliver the city to the Burgundians (*Monumenta Germaniae Historica, Scriptores rerum Merovingicarum*, III, 459-60). (2) The Burgundians were again beseiging the city and Caesarius could not have been a disinterested party since he himself was a Burgundian by birth. (3) The beseigers were Catholics, the beseiged were Arians. Caesarius was a Catholic bishop.

The evidence, although not conclusive, is highly suggestive. It is more than likely that Caesarius would have done all he could to aid his fellow countrymen and correligionists and he had already shown his inclination to do so on a previous occasion.

However, all these points do not explain the part of the Jews in the incident. Juster's solution (*Empire*, vol. II, p. 213), which Katz (p. 115) discredits as unjustified, is that the bishop arranged for the note to be found in order to throw off suspicion from himself. The reason for Katz's objection is one that we have already mentioned, namely how could the Jews' complicity negate the part played by Caesarius?

All the evidence points to the conclusion that the Jews were not guilty of the crime. Therefore, the only possible solution to this question, is that Cyprian, our only source for this incident, is the originator of the accusation against the Jews.

cause they had a lot more to lose than did other inhabitants if a city fell to Catholic invaders.

The Jews under the Merovingians

Although the Franks were not successful in their seige of Arles, they ultimately defeated the Visigoths and drove them out of Gaul while they themselves moved into the power vacuum. Their first major victory was at Tournai in A.D. 446 and this became the eventual capital of the Frankish kingdom. One of the first leaders of the Franks when they began their expansion was a man named Meroveus and it was from his name that the dynasty that succeeded him came to be called Merovingian.

The Franks, however, were not a formidable power until Clovis became their leader in A.D. 482. Although he was only fifteen at the time, he was able to gather the support of his tribesmen behind him and in a number of successful campaigns he managed to establish without question the Frankish claim to Gaul. Following his dynamic conquest, the new ruler encountered the same problem that had previously faced the Visigoths, namely how to secure the loyalty of the Gallic inhabitants. This was a difficult problem, for Gaul contained many different races of people. In the country areas there were large numbers of Celts and Germans while in the cities there were substantial enclaves of Graeco-Syrians and Gallo-Romans. The only means whereby they might be united was religion and in A.D. 503[17] Clovis adopted Catholicism. The decision was dramatic, for Clovis thereby became the only Catholic ruler in the west, the other barbarian kings being Arians. By this strategem, Clovis insured for himself the loyalty of all Catholics in the west, not only in those areas ruled by the Franks, but also in lands ruled by the Visigoths and Ostrogoths

17. J.M. Wallace-Hadrill, *The Barbarian West* (New York: Harper Torchbooks, 1962), p. 71.

who were Arians. We have already seen that in the seige of Arles the Catholic bishop, Caesarius, was more than willing to help the Franks against the Arian Visigoths and it is not improbable that Clovis was in fact depending on such forms of support.

Moreover, the Church in Gaul was grateful to Clovis for his decision and because he had adopted Catholicism not out of any condition of weakness as had the Visigoths, the Frankish kings never felt obliged to the Catholic clergy nor did they feel compelled to make concessions to the Church that were not deemed to be in their best interests or in the interests of their subjects. This latter point is rather important where the Jews are concerned for the Church was never able to influence the kings against the Jews in Gaul as it did in Visigothic Spain. Consequently, we find that under the early Merovingians, relations between the Jews and the Gallic inhabitants remained cordial. After the Frankish conquest, they were allowed to live according to the precepts of their religion and they were allowed full expression of all those rights that were guaranteed them by the Roman laws that still continued in effect.

However, the situation was somewhat different in the kingdom of Burgundy where the king, Sigismund, embraced the Catholic faith (A.D. 516) at a time of grave danger to the security of his territories. A short time later (A.D. 534) the Franks attacked him and his kingdom was incorporated into Gaul. Perhaps Sigismund hoped to secure his kingdom internally by uniting his own Catholic populace behind him rather than allowing them to choose between the Burgundians and the Catholic Franks. Whatever his reason, the Jews became the target of his piety. In an attempt to show his devotion to his new faith and his disdain for the recalcitrant sect (and thereby his sincere devotion to the Church), the king passed a law that actually forbid the Jews to protect themselves if attacked by a Christian, no matter what the cause! The law plainly stated that no Jew, whatever justification he might have, was permitted to lift a hand against a Christian. The penalty was to be loss of the guilty hand; if the Jew wished to redeem his way-ward member, he could do so by paying a substantial fine. But should a Jew presume to raise a hand against a priest, there was to be no redemption; the penalty was death.[18]

When Clovis died in A.D. 511 his newly founded empire was partitioned and each of his four sons received a section and in each section, a separate capital was established. Childebert ruled from Paris, Chlodomir from Orleans, Chlotar from Soissons, and Theodoric from Rheims. Despite the division of empire, the initial understanding among the brothers was that each would come to the aid of the other if one were threatened. Luckily for the Franks, the two most formidible powers in the west—the Ostrogoths and the Visigoths were having their own problems at this time and no danger presented itself.

Although Burgundy was conquered in A.D. 534, for the most part, the period of Frankish conquest was at an end. In A.D. 558 Gaul was temporarily reunited under Chlotar, a fortunate turn of affairs for it was only through a united effort that the Franks were able to check the expansion of warlike tribes who began to impinge on Gaul's borders. However, unification was only temporary for in A.D. 561 Chlotar died and the empire was again cut into four parts, each having the same capital as before. Under Chlotar II, the empire was once more brought together under a single king—this time for sixteen years. But the monarchy had little strength left and the aristocracy slowly availed itself of the vestiges of regal power. The last king to maintain the throne in its previous image of authority was Dagobert (A.D. 629-639), Chlotar II's son, who ruled from the province of Austrasia. Following his death, the aristocracy along with the Church took over the control of the Frankish states in all but name.

In A.D. 711, the Moors invaded Spain and after putting an end to the Visigothic kingdom they turned to Gaul, but fortu-

---

18. *Burgundian Code,* 102. Trans. by K. Fischer (Phila.: Univ. of Penn. Press, 1949).

nately for that country, another dynamic personality emerged during this era in the guise of Charles "Martel," who established a new dynasty to succeed the moribund Merovingians.

The Merovingian State

During the Merovingian era, Gaul was ruled as the private domain of the king like a vast country estate owned by a wealthy and omnipotent landowner.[19] Initially there was no authority hierarchy: all power rested in the king's hands and his decisions, arbitrary or well thought out, became the law of the land, with no opportunity for challenge. But though he retained outright control over every matter, expedience in local affairs demanded an appointed official as the king's representative. This individual was usually a "Count" and his office required the administration in all its details of the areas to which he was appointed. Under the Merovingians, the Count was not hired, but instead he paid for the right to receive a portion of the products from the estates that he supervised, along with one-third of the legal fines that were to be sent to the king.[20]

All property, public and private, in theory belonged to the king and taxes were remitted to him for his own use. The previous system of Roman taxation, customs duties, etc. was also maintained in full rigor and no doubt these burdens resulted in bitterness and hostility on the part of the people. On some occasions the king was compelled to use force in order to quell rebellious undercurrents from the dissatisfied native population. Especially was this the case when the king instituted the collection of the personal head tax that the inhabitants regarded as a sign of social inferiority.[21] To the Franks, the natural way to increase the treasury was to plunder foreign powers; taxation was simply not contemplated.

19. F. Lot, *The End Of The Ancient World and the Beginnings Of The Middle Ages.* (New York: Harper Torchbooks, 1961), p. 346.
20. *Ibid.*, p. 350.
21. *Ibid.*, p. 351.

Class distinctions that had been very noticeable during the early Merovingian period slowly disappeared as the pure ancient Gallo-Roman families dwindled, mainly as a result of either mixed marriages with Franks or through celibate service to the Church. Apparently one could pass easily from the political nobility of the Gallo-Romans to the ecclesiastic hierarchy of the Catholic Church in Gaul.[22] This had been the case with Sidonius Apollinaris, who initially began his career as a Gallo-Roman potentate and then, feeling the call of the clergy (or failing in the tradition of his ancestors), had himself consecrated to the Church. Politically, however, there was not much of a change; the Church and the nobility both wielded a considerable amount of power since each was entrusted with the machinery of the civil laws. However, under the last kings of the dynasty, the aristocracy regained some of its lost prestige and they were able to secure permanent possession of lands previously granted them only temporarily, and they were also able to exempt themselves from various land and toll taxes. These gains are readily understandable in light of the declining power of the Merovingians for had the kings been able to prevent these changes, it is a surety that they would have done so.

As regards the position of the Church in Merovingian Gaul, there is no evidence of anything like the aggressive policy followed by the Spanish episcopate. Probably, this resulted from the fact that Arianism and other heretical movements offered no threat to Catholicism in Gaul. The bishops, recruited mainly from the Gallo-Roman aristocracy, were even able to secure a kind of quasi-independence from the monarchy due to their religious status, and their own concomitant wealth and social prestige. The bishops were, in fact, demi-kings in their own dioceses. They were the chief administrators and protectors of the people living under their direction, and they often won the loyalty of these people not only through their devotion

22. See Parkes, p. 319.

to their religious duties, but also through their efforts to inter-
vene on behalf of their subjects in the tax system imposed by
the king. In this latter endeavor, some of the bishops met with
a fair amount of success in securing exemption for their dioceses. At the same time, some of them even wrested possession of royal lands from the monarchy, thereby expanding their
own jurisdiction.[23]

Legal powers involving civil cases also passed into their
hands as the Church gained more and more prerogatives from
the Merovingians. However, this does not mean that the kings
were the dupes of the bishops; it was just that the kings
realized that the Church constituted a potent force in control-
ling a potentially rebellious rabble that was not completely disposed to the monarchy. Furthermore, while the bishops did
rule almost as independent lords, their appointment was still
subject to the king's final approval[24] so that the king was able
to retain some control over the Church. It was not until the
seventh century A.D. that the bishops attempted to usurp the
king's authority in Gaul.

The Church and the Jews

The slow pace with which the Church progressed to its position as a secular lawmaker is documented in its councils
wherein the clergy initially only concerned itself with matters
of Church discipline and practices. As in most countries taken
over by barbarian tribes, one finds that before the Church attained any importance, relations between the Jews and the native inhabitants was often friendly. When bishop Hilary of
Arles died (mid-fifth century A.D.) we are told that the Jews of
Arles wept alongside the other citizens and they could even be
heard chanting psalms in his honor.[25] Had he died about one

23. Lot, p. 386.
24. *Ibid.,* 387.
25. *Patrologia Latina,* 50, 1243.

hundred years later this would not have been possible, for in A.D. 589 the Council of Narbonne passed a canon that prohibited the Jews from singing psalms even in their own processions.[26] On the other hand, the biographer of Hilary of Poitiers, who died in the late fourth century, relates that this bishop not only refused to eat with the Jews, he even refused to acknowledge their greeting when they passed him in the street,[27] though why the Jews would want to eat or communicate with anyone with his attitude is difficult to understand.

Regulations restricting interaction with the Jews were begun by the Council of Vannes (A.D. 465), which forbid clergymen to share any meals with Jews. This interdiction was extended to the lay society as well by the Third Council of Orleans (A.D. 538)[28] and was repeated by the First Council of Macon A.D. 581),[29] indicating that it was not obeyed to any great extent. As previously noted, restriction on conviviality had its origin at the Council of Elviar (ca. A.D. 300). The frequent and repeated references prohibiting such interaction testifies to the cordiality existing between Jews and Christians despite the Church's fear that a sense of Christian inferiority was being created (see below). Most likely these gatherings were held mainly in the rural areas where the Church's restrictive pronouncements did not penetrate until late in the Merovingian era due to the paucity of clergymen in these communities.

Ferreolus, bishop of Uzès (A.D. 553-581), was also known to have had amiciable relations with the Jews, but his motives appear to have been other than friendship since his uppermost desire was to convert them. We are told that he invited the Jews to share his food, but it is more likely that instead, he shared their meals since one of the causes for the numerous canons against eating with Jews was that they would not eat at Christian tables, hence the feeling of inferiority. Because of

26. Council of Narbonne, canon 9.
27. *Patrologia Latina*, 9, 187.
28. III Orleans, canon 13.
29. I Macon, canon 15.
30. Council of Elvira, canon 50.

his friendship with the Jews, the bishop was later accused of plotting with them and their Moorish allies against the throne, and he was banished to Paris.[31]

Gregory of Tours relates that Cautinus, the bishop of Clermont (A.D. 550-570) was also on familiar terms with the Jews only his motives were pecuniary rather than religious. According to Gregory, the bishop met with the Jews because he wanted to buy precious objects that Gregory maintained they sold at a higher price than they were worth.[32]

Next to communality, the danger of mixed marriages occupied much of the Church's attention. The Second Council of Orleans (A.D. 533) resolved that all such unions be dissolved on the penalty of excommunication[33] and this demand was repeated five years later at the Third Council.[34] The unusual practice of Jews seeking wives outside of their own community probably resulted from the fact that the feminine Jewish population was rather limited. Evidently the Church was unable to discourage Christian women from marrying Jews since the edict had to be issued twice.

By far the most often discussed matter at the councils had to do with Jewish ownership of slaves. The Third Council of Orleans passed a canon warning Jewish slave owners to make sure that they did not interfere with Christian servants who wanted to follow their religion.[35] In A.D. 581 the First Council of Mâcon expressly forbad Jews the right to own Christian slaves[36] but the canon was not observed, for in A.D. 630 the Council of Reims passed a canon forbidding the sale of Christians to Jews.[37] But no matter what the Church demanded, the economic conditions of these times determined the outcome of the slavery issue and as long as there was an economic advan-

---

31. *Gallia Christiana,* vol. 6, (1939): p. 613.
32. Gregory of Tours, *History of the Franks,* 4.8.12.
33. II Orleans, canon 14.
34. III Orleans, canon 13.
35. III Orleans, canon 13.
36. I Mâcon, canon 16.
37. Council of Reims, canon 11.

tage to be had by Christians in allowing Jews to have a part in the slave markets, the practice would continue to flourish.

One of the more unusual canons issued during this era concerned the presence of Jews among Christians during the observance of Easter. The Third Council of Orleans actually forbade Jews to be seen in the company of Christians from Maundy Thursday until four days later[38] and this injunction was followed by the First Council of Mâcon's decree that Jews were not to appear on the streets or in any public places during the Easter observances.[39] This latter canon even had secular backing since king Childebert passed a law similar to this canon several years earlier.[40] Apparently, celebration of the Easter holiday involved drunkenness, loud singing, and sundry disgraceful acts that the Jews could not fail to observe. Occasionally, when Christians and Jews hurled insults at each other, the Jews would throw back contemptuous accusations based upon what they observed at the Easter celebrations. It was to prevent the reoccurrence of such insults that the Church had these laws passed.

Although Jews were forbidden to hold public office by Roman law, the councils found it necessary to reissue the restriction. The First Council of Clermont (A.D. 535) forbade Jews to serve as judges over Christians[41] and this was repeated at Mâcon with the addendum that they were also not to be tax collectors.[42] However, Jews must have remained at these posts since in A.D. 613 the Council of Paris resolved that no Jew should be allowed to exercise military [?] or official authority over Christians. Those that did so, had to be baptised along with their families.[43] Seventeen years later this interdiction was again issued at Reims.[44]

---

38. III Orleans, canon 30.
39. I Mâcon, canon 14.
40. *Ibid.*
41. I Clermont, canon 8.
42. I Mâcon, canon 2.
43. Council of Paris, canon 17.
44. Council of Reims, canon 11.

It is noteworthy that almost the entire run of Church proscriptions dealing with the Jews were redundant since they were all included in the Theodosian Code, which had been adopted by the Franks. Since the Jews were regarded as Roman citizens, they were liable to each article of that law code. The fact that there was repetition, often excessive, merely illustrates the weakness of unpopular legislation. But it is also noteworthy that these Frankish councils had little to say regarding Jewish political rights. Mainly they directed themselves to religious and social questions and unlike their counterparts in Spain, no reference was ever made to the forced conversion of Jews.

However, this form of fanaticism did not completely bypass the Merovingian era. We have already mentioned that bishop Ferreolus was accused of treason because of his affiliation with the Jews. When the aforementioned bishop finally arrived to defend himself before king Childebert, he found it difficult to prove that he had not conspired to overthrow the monarchy and the king had him banished to Paris, where he remained for three years until he was finally able to disprove the accusation or else assure the king that it was unfounded. Filled with bitterness, the bishop made his way back to his diocese and immediately prepared to show all that he had in truth, been wrongly accused. A local synod was quickly summoned and Ferreolus disclosed a plan to force all the Jews of the district to receive the holy rites—those who resisted were to be driven from the diocese. Thereafter, no Jews were to be permitted to live in Uzès.[45] Such devotion to his religion could not but assure his accusers that he was a loyal subject.

Another incident occured in A.D. 576. Avitus, the bishop of Clermont, had been trying to persuade the Jews that Christianity was superior to Judaism and he was finally able to convince one of the Jews of that city. As the convert was marching with some other catechumens in a procession, one of the local Jews, to show his disgust, poured rancid oil over the

45. *Gallia Christiana*, vol. VI (1739): p. 613.

parading convert. The Christian gathering that witnessed the insult immediately sought to stone the perfidious Jew. The bishop supposedly tried to persuade them to hold their anger back, but the mob could not be appeased, and it turned on the local synagogue and obliterated it. For the time, justice had been done. The following day the bishop began to feel that one Jewish convert was not much to show for all his efforts, and since it was his duty to increase the Christian fold, he issued an ultimatum to the Jews: baptism or banishment. According to Gregory of Tours, five hundred Jews submitted to baptism "with tears of joy" and the bishop "united them in the bosom of our mother church." The Jews who preferred banishment left the city for Marseilles.[46] However, this turned out to be an unfortunate choice for relocation since a short time after their arrival the leading clerics of Marseilles gave them the same alternative.[47]

The number of converts cited by Gregory is most likely a gross exaggeration. It is doubtful that there were that many Jews in Clermont to be baptised. Even if there were, the conversions were only perfunctory since in A.D. 583 they were compelled to accept baptism once more. This time it was the king, Chilperic, who offered them the compromise. Again many Jews came forth to accept the rites, but it was not long before they reverted to their former religion; Gregory adds that these Jews only submitted in the first place to avoid punishment,[48] as if there were a possibility that they could have been motivated by some other factor.

In still another incident, Gregory indicates that the synagogue in Orleans was burned and that the Jews expected that king Guntram would make the guilty parties indemnify the Jews for their loss. Perhaps they believed Guntram to be another Theodoric. If so, their belief was quite unrealistic. As the king was passing through Orleans on his way to Paris, the

46. Gregory of Tours, *Hist.*, 5.6.11.
47. (Pope) Gregory, Letters, 1,45.
48. Gregory of Tours, *Hist.*, 6.16.17.

entire city turned out to meet him, including the Jews, who could be heard singing praises to the king. The king interpreted the gesture merely as an attempt to flatter him into ordering the Christians to rebuild the synagogue: "Woe to the race of Jews, ever evil and faithless and crafty of heart. They acclaimed me this day with praise and flattery. . . .simply in the hope that I might order the rebuilding at public cost, of their synagogue, which the Christians some time ago destroyed. The Lord forbiddeth any such deed, and I will never do it."[49]

In A.D. 613 anti-Jewish sentiment in Visigothic Spain culminated in the persecution sponsored by king Sisebut. The entire Jewish population was given the alternative of conversion or expulsion. Those who chose the latter naturally came to Gaul, the country nearest Spain. But the Jewish population explosion in Gaul was short-lived. Eleven years later all the Jews of Gaul were likewise given the same choice by Dagobert, the last Merovingian to rule in Gaul.

Like the motives of his counterpart in Spain, Dagobert's reasons are difficult to explain. Graetz's[50] improbable evaluation was that this "most anti-Jewish monarch in the whole history of the world" was actually embarrassed that Sisebut, the Visigothic king, had shown himself to be possessed of a deeper religious devotion *à propos* his fiat of exile and Dagobert was simply not going to permit such one-upsmanship.[51] The patristic account maintains that Dagobert was acting on the request of the Byzantine emperor, Heraclius. Apparently the latter had seen some sign in the stars suggesting that his empire would be laid waste by a circumcised people. Taking this to mean the Jews, he decreed that all Jews living in all the Roman provinces were to be either bap-

49. *Ibid.*, 8.1.
50. *Hist. of the Jews*, vol. III, p. 40.
51. In this, as in many of the claims made by Graetz, one must appreciate the utterly Jewish viewpoint taken by the historian. Graetz typically accounts for any and all anti-Jewish actions through an exposition of the personalities of those responsible. Rarely does he stop to consider social, political, religious, or economic motives underlying anti-Jewish actions.

tised or driven from the empire and he wrote to Dagobert that he should see that the same thing be done in Gaul.[52] Dagobert did so[53] but probably for other reasons.[54]

Contemporary with this event was the baptismal order issued by bishop Sulpicius, who resorted to coercion after all his attempts at gentle persuasion failed.[55] Katz[56] places the date of Dagobert's decree at A.D. 633 and presumes that Sulpicius' order was issued at the same time. Parkes,[57] on the other hand, places Dagobert's decree around A.D. 624, and maintains that Sulpicius' was somewhat later. Both agree that Sulpicius did not preceed Dagobert and therefore he would only have been carrying out the law of the land. Possibly when the bishop's biographer was chronicling the event, he decided that the bishop ought to be given credit for his zealous work in bringing new converts to the Church and he made it appear that Sulpicius was acting on his own initiative.

There are a number of other patristic notices of the Jews that ought to be mentioned. One which is worthy of attention comes from the pen of Venantius Fortunatus, who, at the request of Gregory of Tours, wrote a poem to commemorate Avitus' baptism of the Jews. Notably, it is the first work of its kind suggesting that Jews smelled differently than Christians, for the poet writes that the moment the Jews were cleansed with the baptismal water their bitter odor was washed away and a sweet smell filled the air.[58] [59]

There are two stories about the bishop of Paris, St. Germanus, and the Jews, whose purpose is the glorification of the bishop's Christian power. The first legend relates that during

52. Ps. Fredegarius, Chron. 4.65 in *P.L.* 71, 646.
53. Gesta Dagoberti in *P.L.* 96, 1405.
54. The Jews may have been suspected of plotting with the Moors who shortly thereafter conquered Spain.
55. Vita Sulpicii in *P.L.* 80, 579.
56. Katz, p. 26.
57. Parkes, p. 335.
58. *Carmina* in MGH AA 4,1, 110.
59. Cf. II *Corinthians*, 15: "For we are unto God a sweet savour of Christ, in them that are saved. . . ."

one of his journeys the bishop met a young man who told him that he was being led into slavery by the Jews because he refused to abide by Jewish laws. Immediately after hearing this outrage the priest made the sign of the cross over the man's chains and they fell off.[60] Katz[61] presumes the imaginary chained man was a baptised Jew while Parkes[62] contends he was a Christian. In the second legend Germanus miraculously heals a Jewish woman suffering from a respiratory disease by placing his hand on her forehead. Immediately a scintillating fire was seen emerging from the woman's nose as the devil fled her newly blessed body. As a result of the dramatic cure the woman and a large number of Jews who witnessed the event voluntarily accepted baptism.[63]

Gregory of Tours relates a story with a transparent moral concerning those who appeal to the Jews for help. Leunast, archdeacon of Bourges, had lost his sight because of a cataract. After consulting many doctors, he finally came to the Church of St. Martin and by fasting and praying, he was able to regain his sight. However, the archdeacon wanted to make sure that he would permanently have his sight and for insurance he consulted a Jewish doctor! The result was inevitable by patristic standards: his blindness returned and further appeal through the holy shrine was useless.[64] Trachtenberg[65] states that stories of this genre were circulated to keep Christians from visiting Jewish doctors because patients who were often cured would believe that the Jews had greater power over evil than did Christians.

A final anecdote, reminiscent of the early Jewish-Christian debates, concerns a Jew named Priscus, Gregory of Tours, and Chilperic the king. According to this fable, Priscus happened to come to the royal court while the king was in Nogent pre-

60. *Vita St. Germani* in MGH AA 4,2,24.
61. Katz, p. 24.
62. Parkes, p. 336.
63. *Vita St. Germani*. MGH AA 4,2,22.
64. Gregory of Tours, *Hist.*, 5.6.
65. Trachtenberg, ch. 6.

paring for a journey to Paris. Chilperic had been accustomed to treating Priscus was a fair amount of familiarity since the Jew had helped him purchase some precious goods, and while they were talking, the king playfully seized the Jew by the hair and called to the bishop to "lay thy hands on him." Priscus resisted, and the king accused him of having a hard heart and a false knowledge of the Scriptures; the challenge turned into a debate between Gregory and Priscus. Texts were cited all over the place but the bishop could not convince the "wretch." Finally the king became bored and interrupted, asking Gregory for his blessing before he set out on his journey.[66]

Apparently the debate had some effect on the king for in A.D. 582 he ordered the baptism of the Jews living in and around Paris. Again, Priscus resisted and for his obstinacy was jailed. But on account of his friendship with the king, plus an attractive bribe, Priscus obtained his freedom. After his release, he happened to meet a baptised Jew and an argument ensued that so enraged the converted Jew that shortly thereafter he slew Priscus while the latter was walking to a clandestine synagogue. Revenge was not long in coming, and the assassin himself was assassinated by Priscus' relatives.[68]

Dagobert's decree ordering the forced baptism of the Jews in A.D. 633 is the last recorded mention we have of the Jews in Gaul for approximately one hundred and fifty years. From the silence, it seems that the Jews were in fact exiled from the Frankish empire. But this is extremely unlikely; the paucity of references to them is more likely to have been due to a lack of eventful occurrences between the Jews and the native population. We have seen that despite similar orders for their total exile in Spain, the Jews were never completely driven from the empire and those that did apostasize, only did so temporarily. That this was the case in Gaul also, is offered by the discovery of an inscription in Latin from the tombstone of three children.

66. Greg. of Tours, *Hist.*, 6.5.
67. Greg. of Tours, *Hist.*, 6.17.

The epitaph, (written in A.D. 688) although mainly in Latin, is notable because it contains one sentence in Hebrew: "Peace be unto Israel."[68]

68. See Katz, p. 148.

13

Conclusion

IN THE preceding pages one can discern two definitive aspects of anti-Semitism in the ancient world. The first is pre-Christian and involves the reaction of the Greeks and Romans toward the Jews. The second involves Judaism's confrontation with its religious rival, Christianity.

As far as the former period is concerned, one is faced with a dichotomy in the attitude of the Greeks and Romans toward Judaism. On the one hand, there were those who were attracted to Judaism's message of morality, its antiquity, and its ceremony. At the same time, there were those who expressed disgust, not with the religion qua religion, but with the attitude and behavior of its practitioners. For one thing, the Jews had a haughty conception of their religion and customs. To them Judaism and the Jews were superior to other religions and other peoples. For another, the Jews attempted to extract guarantees from those in authority so that these customs would be respected by the inhabitants of the countries in which the Jews were living.

In essence, however, the confrontation was restricted to social criticism during the Greco-Roman period.[1] When the Ro-

---

1. See R.L. Wilken's review, "Judaism In Roman And Christian Society," *Journal of Religion* 47 (1967): 313-30.

mans became masters of the world, there were short outbreaks of persecution in Alexandria and in Asia Minor, but these were sporadic and short-lived. Generally, the Roman authorities safeguarded Jewish privileges and likewise extended to the Jews the essence of the *pax Romana*.

The Christian era, however, saw the beginning of persecution on the basis of religious disagreement. In the first two centuries of the current era, Christianity was locked in a theological battle with Judaism and a social battle with the Empire. This placed Christian writers in the unhappy position of having to defend their faith on two fronts instead of one. Consequently, two different kinds of treatises appeared: polemics directed at Judaism and apologies directed at the Roman government. With regard to the former, Judaism was characterized as an obtuse, decadent, and hostile enemy. Its opposition to Christianity was emphasized and this attitude became an integral part of the Christian's feeling about Judaism.

When the Roman world finally adopted Christianity as its cult religion, it also adopted the Church's attitudes toward its enemies and, consequently, the legislation that was enacted by the emperors in the fifth and sixth centuries reflected the polemical aspects of Christianity's denigration of its rival. As a result, the Jew became a despicable citizen who had to be isolated so that he might not contaminate the rest of society—a development that has continued until well up into the nineteenth century. This political-legal side of anti-Semitism no longer exists in our present-day society. However, as pointed out by Glock and Stark,[2] its religious etiology is still very much a part of life in the twentieth century.

---

2. C.Y. Glock and R. Stark, *Christian Beliefs and Anti-Semitism* (New York: Harper and Row, 1966).

Bibliography

Abel, E.L. "The Myth of Jewish Slavery in Ptolemaic Egypt." *Revue des études Juives* 127 (1968): 253-58.

————. "Were the Jews Banished from Rome in 19 A.D.?" *Revue des études Juives* 127 (1968): 275-79.

————. "Jesus And The Cause of Jewish National Independence." *Revue des études Juives* 128 (1969): 247-52.

————. "The Psychology of Memory and Rumor Transmission and Their Bearing on Theories of Oral Transmission in Early Christianity." *Journal of Religion* 51 (1971): 270-81.

————. "Who Wrote Matthew?" *New Testament Studies* 17 (1972): 138-52.

Acta Sanctorum. Paris and Rome: V. Palmé, Various dates.

Akerman, J.Y. *Numismatic Illustrations Of Narrative Portions Of The New Testament.* Chicago: Argonaut Press, 1966.

Ante-Nicene Fathers. Grand Rapids, Michigan: Wm. B. Eerdmans Company, 1951, 10 vols.

Baron, S.W. *The Social and Religious History of the Jews.* New York: Columbia University Press, 1952.

Baum, G. *Is The New Testament Anti-Semitic?* New Jersey: Deus Books, 1965.

Bell, H.I. *Jews and Christians in Egypt.* London: Oxford University Press, 1924.

————. "Antisemitism in Alexandria." *Journal of Roman Studies* 31 (1941): 1-18.

————. *Egypt From Alexander The Great To The Arab Conquest.* Oxford: Oxford Clarendon Press, 1948.

Bevan, E.R. *History of Egypt under the Ptolemaic Dynasty.* London: Methuen Co., 1927.

Bickerman, E.J. "The Colophon Of The Greek Book of Esther." *Journal of Biblical Literature* 63 (1944): 356-62.

Blinzler, J. *The Trial of Jesus.* Westminster, Maryland: Newman Press, 1959.

Blumenkranz, B. *Juives et Chrétiens Dans La Monde Occidentale.* Paris: Mouton, 1960.

Bottéro, J. *Le Probléme des Habiru.* Paris: Imprimé Nationale, 1954.

Branton, R. "Resurrection In The Early Church." In *Early Christian Origins.* Ed. by A. Wikgren. Chicago: Univ. of Chicago Press, 1961.

Brown, J. "Christian Teaching And Antisemitism." *Commentary* 24 (1957): 494-501.

Büchler, A. "The Priestly Dues and the Roman Taxes in the Edicts of Caesar." In *Studies in Jewish History.* Ed. by I. Brodies and J. Rabinowitz. London: Oxford University Press, 1956.

Bultmann, R. *History of the Synoptic Tradition.* New York: Harper and Row, 1968.

Carmichael, J. *The Death of Jesus*. New York: Macmillan Co., 1962.

Carrington, P. *The Early Christian Church*. Cambridge: Cambridge Univ. Press, 1957.

Chrysostom, St. J. *Oeuvres completes*. Paris: L. Vives, 1867, 10 vols.

Cicero. *Pro Flaccus*. Cambridge: Harvard University Press (Loeb Lib.), 1937.

Cochrane, C.N. *Christianity and Classical Culture*. Oxford: Oxford Clarendon Press, 1940.

Codex Theodosius. Princeton: Princeton University Press, 1952.

Cowley, A.E. *Aramaic Papyri of the Fifth Century B.C*. Oxford: Oxford Clarendon Press, 1923.

Cullmann, O. *The State in the New Testament*. New York: Charles Scribner's Sons, 1956.

Cumont, F. "Les mysteres De Sabazius et le Judaisme." *Comptes-Rendues Acadamie des Inscriptions et Belles-Lettres* 115 (1906): 63-79.

————. *The Oriental Religions in Roman Paganism*. New York: Dover Publications, 1956.

Davis, S. *Race Relations in Ancient Egypt*. London: Methuen Co., 1951.

Dio Cassius. *Roman History*. Cambridge: Harvard University Press, (Loeb Lib.), 1954.

Diodorus Siculus. *Histories*. Cambridge: Harvard University Press (Loeb Lib.), 1950.

Dopsch, A. *The Economic and Social Foundations of European Civilization*. London: K. Paul, Trench, Trubner and Co., 1937.

Downey, G. *History of Antioch in Syria*. Princeton: Princeton University Press, 1961.

Edgar, C.C. *Zenon papyri*. Ann Arbor, Mich.: University of Michigan Press, 1931.

Ehrenberg, V. *The Greek State*. New York: W.W. Norton, 1964.

Emmet, C.W. "The Third Book of Maccabees." In *Apocrypha and Pseudipigrapha of the Old Testament*. Ed. by R. H. Charles. Oxford: Oxford Clarendon Press, 1913.

Ewald, H. *History of the Jews*. London: Longmans, Green and Co., 1878-1886, 8 vols.

Festinger, L., Riecken, H.W., and Schacter, S. *When Prophecy Fails*. New York: Harper and Row, 1964.

Fischer, K. *Burgundian Code*. Philadelphia: University of Pennsylvania Press, 1949.

Flannery, E.H. *The Anguish of the Jews*. New York: Macmillan Co., 1964.

Frend, W.H.C. *Martyrdom And Persecution In The Early Church*. Oxford: B. Blackwell, 1965.

Fuks, A. "Aspects of the Jewish Revolt in A.D. 115-117." *Journal of Roman Studies* 51 (1961): 98-104.

Gallia Christiana. Paris: various dates, 16 vols.

Giles, Wm. *Heathen Records to the Jewish Scripture History*. London: Cornish, 1856.

Ginsburg, M.S. "Fiscus Judaicus." *Jewish Quarterly Review* 21 (1930): 281-91.

Glock, C.Y. and Stark, R. *Christian Beliefs and Anti-Semitism.* New York: Harper and Row, 1966.

Goodenough, E.R. *Jewish Symbols in the Graeco-Roman Period.* Toronto: McClelland and Stewart Ltd., 1953.

Graetz, H.H. *History of the Jews.* Philadelphia: Jewish Publication Society, 1946.

Greenberg, M. *The Hab/piru.* New Haven: American Oriental Society, 1955.

Gregory of Tours, *History of the Franks.* Oxford: Oxford Clarendon Press, 1927.

Gressman, H. "Jewish Life in Ancient Rome." In *Jewish Studies in Memory of Israel Abrahams.* New York: Jewish Institute of Religion, 1927.

Guterman, S. *Religious Toleration and Persecution in Ancient Rome.* London: Aiglon Press, 1951.

Haddad, G. *Aspects of Social Life in Antioch in the Hellenistic Roman Period.* London: Hofner, 1949.

Hadas, M. *Aristeas to Philocrates.* New York: Harper Brothers, 1951.

Hay, M. *Europe And The Jews.* Boston: Beacon Press, 1961.

Heath R. *Anabaptism.* London: Alexander and Shepherd, 1895.

Hefele, C.J. *A History Of The Christian Councils.* Edinburgh: T. and T. Clark, 1871, 5 vols.

Heinemann, I. "The Attitude of the Ancient World Towards Judaism." *Review of Religion* 4 (1939-1940): 385-400.

Hodgkin, T. *The Letters of Cassiodorus.* London: H. Frowde, 1886.

Homes-Dudden, F.H. *Gregory the Great.* London: Longmans, Green, and Co., 1905.

Huidekoper, F. *Judaism at Rome.* New York: David G. Francis, 1891.

Interpreter's Bible. Nashville: Abingdon Press, 1954.

Isaac, I. *The Teaching of Contempt.* Toronto: McGraw-Hill, 1965.

Jerome. *Contra Rufinium.* Washington, D.C.: Catholic University Press, 1965.

Jones, A.H.M. *The Greek City From Alexander To Justinian.* Oxford: Clarendon Press, 1967.

Jones, H.S. "Claudius And The Jewish Question At Alexandria." *Journal of Roman Studies* 16 (1926): 17-35.

Josephus. *Works.* Philadelphia: John C. Winston Co., 1957.

Julian. "To The Community of the Jews." In Adler, M. "The Emperor Julian and the Jews." *Jewish Quarterly Review* 5 (1893): 622-24.

Juster, J. *La condition légale des Juives sous les Rois Visigoths.* Paris: Girard, 1912.

―――. *Les Juives dans l'Empire Romain.* Paris: P. Geuthner, 1914, 2 vols.

Justin Martyr. *Dialogue With Trypho.* New York: Macmillan Co., 1930.

Katz, S. "Pope Gregory the Great and the Jews." *Jewish Quarterly Review* 24 (1933): 113-36.

―――. *Jews in the Visigothic and Frankish Kingdoms of Spain and Gaul.* Cambridge: Mediaeval Academy of America, 1937.

Kilpatrick, G.D. *The Origins of the Gospel According to St. Matthew*. Oxford: Oxford Clarendon Press, 1946.

Klausner, J. *Jesus of Nazareth*. London: George Allen and Unwin Ltd., 1947.

————. *From Jesus to Paul*. Boston: Beacon Press. 1961.

Kraeling, K. *The Jewish Community at Antioch*. New Haven: Yale University Press, 1932.

Krauss, S. "The Jews in the Works of the Church Fathers." *Jewish Quarterly Review* 5 (1893): 122-57; 6 (1894): 225-61.

Lear, F.S. "The Public Law of the Visigothic Code." *Speculum* 26 (1951): 1-23.

Leon, H.I. *The Jews of Ancient Rome*. Philadelphia: Jewish Publication Society, 1960.

Levi, I. "Saint Cesare et les Juives d'Arles." *Revue des études Juives* 30 (1895): 295-98.

Lex Romana Visigothorum. Ed. by S.P. Scott. Boston: Boston Book Co., 1910.

Lieberman, S. "Palestine In The Third And Fourth Centuries." *Jewish Quarterly Review* 36 (1946): 329-70.

Livy. *A History of Rome*. Cambridge: Harvard University Press (Loeb Lib.), 1960.

Loeb, I. "Notes sur l'histoire et les antiquities Juives en Espagne." *Revue des études Juives* 2 (1881): 137-38.

Loisy, A. *The Birth of the Christian Religion*. New York: Univ. Books, 1962.

Lot, F. *The End of the Ancient World*. New York: Harper Torchbooks, 1961.

Malalas, J. *Chronicles*. Chicago: University of Chicago Press, 1940.

Meek, T.J. *Hebrew Origins*. New York: Harper Brothers, 1936.

Milne, J.G. *History of Egypt under Roman Rule*. London: Methuen and Co., 1912.

————. "The Ruin Of Egypt By Roman Mismanagement." *Journal of Roman Studies* 17 (1927): 1-13.

Momigliano, A. *Claudius, the Emperor and his Achievement*. New York: Barnes and Noble, 1962.

Monumenta Germaniae Historica. Ed. by G.H. Pertz. Hanover: 1874, 25 vols.

Moore, G.F. *Judaism in the First Three Centuries of the Christian Era*. Cambridge: Harvard University Press, 1927.

Neubauer, A. "The Early Settlement of the Jews in Southern Italy." *Jewish Quarterly Review* 4 (o.s. 1892): 606-25.

Newman, L.I. *Jewish Influence on Christian Reform Movements*. New York: Columbia University Press, 1925.

Nicene and Post Nicene Fathers. New York: Christian Library Co., 1890, 10 vols.

Noth, M. *The History of Israel*. London: Adam and Charles Black, 1960.

Oesterley, W.O.E. and Robinson, T.H. *A History of Israel*. Oxford: Oxford Clarendon Press, 1934.

————. "The Cult of Sabazius." In *The Labyrinth*. Ed. by S.H. Hooke. New York: Macmillan Co., 1935.

Parkes, J. *The Conflict of the Church and the Synagogue*. Cleveland: World Publishing Co., 1961.

Patrologia Graeca. Ed. by J.P. Migne. Various dates. 161 vols.

Patrologia Latina. Ed. by J.P. Migne. Various dates. 221 vols.

Peake, A.S. *A Commentary on the Bible.* London: T.C. and E.C. Jack Ltd., 1929.

Petronius, *Satyricon.* New York: Century Co., 1929.

Philo. *Legatio ad Gaium.* Leiden: E.J. Brill Co., 1961.

Polybius. *The Histories.* New York: G.P. Putnam's Sons, 1927.

Procopius. *History of the Wars.* New York: Washington Square Press, 1967.

Radin, M. *The Jews among the Greeks and Romans.* Philadelphia: Jewish Publication Society, 1915.

Raisin, J.S. *Gentile Reactions to Jewish Ideals.* New York: Philosophical Library, 1953.

Reinach, Th. *Textes d'auteurs Grecs et Romains relatifs au Judaisme.* Paris: E. Leroux, 1895.

Robinson, J.A.T. "The Destination and Purpose of St. John's Gospel." *New Testament Studies* 6 (1960): 117-31.

Rostovtzeff, M. "Roman Exploitation of Egypt in the First Century A.D." *Journal of Economic and Business History* 1 (1929): 337-64.

Rostovtzeff, M.I. *Social and Economic History of the Hellenistic World.* Oxford: Oxford Clarendon Press, 1941.

Roth, C. *The Jews of Italy.* Philadelphia: Jewish Publication Society, 1946.

Runes, D.D. *The Jew and the Cross.* New York: Citadel Press, 1966.

258 THE ROOTS OF ANTI-SEMITISM

Schizas, P.M. *Offences Against the State in Roman Law.* London: University of London Press, 1926.

Schoenfeld, J.J. *The Passover Plot.* New York: Bantam, 1967.

Schoeps, J.J. *The Jewish-Christian Argument.* New York: Holt, Rinehart, and Winston, 1963.

Schürer, E. *A History of the Jewish People in the Time of Jesus.* New York: Schocken Books, 1961.

Schweizer, E. *Jesus.* London: A.C. Black, 1971.

Scott, E.F. *The Nature of the Early Church.* New York: Longmans, Green and Co.,1941.

Scullard, H.H. *From the Gracchi to Nero.* London: Methuen Co., 1965.

Segré, A. "The Status Of The Jews In Ptolemaic And Roman Egypt." *Jewish Social Studies* 6 (1944): 375-400.

————. "Antisemites in Hellenistic Alexandria." *Jewish Social Studies* 8 (1946): 127-36.

Sidonius. *Letters.* Ed. by O.M. Dalton. *Oxford: Oxford Clarendon Press, 1915, 2 vols.*

Sikes, W.W. "The Anti-Semitism of the Fourth Gospel." *Journal of Religion* 21 (1941): 23-30.

Stauffer, E. *Jesus and His Story.* New York: A. Knoff, 1960.

Suetonius, T.C. *Twelve Caesars.* New York: Macmillan Co., 1914.

Talmud (Babylonian). London: Soncino Press, 1938, 13 vols.

Tacitus. *The Annals.* Cambridge: Harvard University Press (Loeb Lib.), 1951.

———. *The Histories.* Cambridge: Harvard University Press (Loeb Lib.), 1951.

Tarn, W.W. *Hellenistic Civilization.* Cleveland: Cleveland World Pub. Co., 1961.

Taubenschlag, R. *The Law of Graeco-Roman Egypt In The Light of The Papyri.* New York: Herald Square Press, 1944.

Tcherikower, V. "Palestine under the Ptolemies." *Mizraim* 4-5 (1937): 9-25.

———. "Syntaxis and Laographia." *Journal of Juristic Papyrology* 4 (1950): 179-207.

———. *Hellenistic Civilization and the Jews.* Philadelphia: Jewish Publication Society, 1959.

———. "The Third Book Of Maccabees As A History Source of Augustus' Time." *Scripta Hierosolymitana* 3 (1961): 1-26.

———. and Fuks, A. *Corpus Papyrorum Judaecorum.* Cambridge: Harvard University Press, 1960, 3 vols.

Trachtenberg, J. *The Devil and the Jews.* New Haven: Yale University Press, 1943.

Vogelstein, H. *Jews in Rome.* Philadelphia: Jewish Publication Society, 1940.

Wallace, S.L. *Taxation in Egypt from Augustus to Diocletian.* Princeton: Princeton University Press, 1938.

Wallace-Hadrill, J.M. *The Barbarian West.* New York: Harper Torchbooks, 1962.

Weiss, J. *Earliest Christianity.* New York: Harper Torchbooks, 1959.

Westerman, W.L., Keyes, C.W., and Liebesny, H. *Zenon Papyri.* New York: Columbia University Press, 1934-1940.

William, A.L. *Adversus Judaeos.* Cambridge: Cambridge University Press, 1935.

Zeitlin, S. "The Tobias Family and the Hasmoneans." *Proceedings of the American Academy for Jewish Research* 4 (1933): 169-223.

————. *The Rise and Fall of the Judean State.* Philadelphia: Jewish Publication Society, 1962.

Ziegler, A.K. *Church and State in Visigothic Spain.* Washington, D.C.: Catholic University Press, 1930.

Index

261